Annals of Music in America

A CHRONOLOGICAL RECORD OF SIGNIFICANT MUSICAL EVENTS, FROM 1640 TO THE PRESENT DAY, WITH COMMENTS ON THE VARIOUS PERIODS INTO WHICH THE WORK IS DIVIDED

BY
HENRY C. LAHEE

BOSTON
MARSHALL JONES COMPANY
MDCCCCXXII

COPYRIGHT, 1922
BY MARSHALL JONES COMPANY
PRINTED OCTOBER, 1922

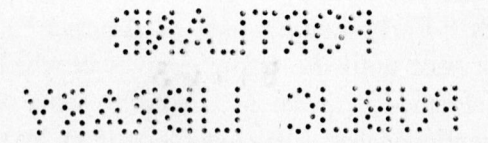

THE PLIMPTON PRESS · NORWOOD · MASSACHUSETTS
PRINTED IN THE UNITED STATES OF AMERICA

PREFACE

THE object of this book is to give as complete a record as possible of the beginning and progress of music in the United States of America.

The first things recorded are regarded as important. Hence such items as the printing of the first book on music, the importation of the first pipe organs, the establishment of the early musical societies are recorded, while similar events of a more recent date are of no special importance.

The first performance of significant works — operas, oratorios, symphonies and other choral and orchestral works — are chronicled as carefully as possible; also the first appearance in America of noted musicians.

It has been practically impossible to find accurate data about the works of the older composers, — Haydn, Mozart and others, for while there are many programs in which their names are mentioned the work played is seldom specified (see Mr. O. G. Sonneck's " Early Concert-Life in America "), and one must wait until the period arrives in which the work performed is specified. Probably some of the works mentioned had earlier performances by small organizations but the performances recorded here are in all probability the first adequate ones.

Among the items recorded are some which cannot be regarded as marking the musical progress of the country, and yet are items of musical interest; — the first performance of "The Star-Spangled Banner" and of "America" do not mark any progress and yet are historic events.

The establishment of Gilmore's Band and Sousa's Band are items of interest rather than of educational progress.

In compiling this work such newspapers as are available have been consulted, also the programs of the leading choral and orchestral societies. Valuable help has been gained from the excellent works of Mr. Oscar G. Sonneck, Mr. E. H. Krehbiel, Mr. Philip Goepp, Mr. George P. Upton, Allston Brown and other writers on the American stage, and above all from the admirable notes of Mr. Philip Hale in the programs of the Boston Symphony Orchestra. It would be ungracious to close this preface without acknowledging with gratitude the valuable assistance of Miss Barbara Duncan of the Boston Public Library.

HENRY C. LAHEE

CONTENTS

CHAPTER		PAGE
	Preface	v
I.	1640–1750	1
II.	1750–1800	5
III.	1800–1825	14
IV.	1825–1850	20
V.	1850–1875	36
VI.	1875–1890	64
VII.	1890–1900	95
VIII.	1900–1921	117
	Index of Compositions	193
	Miscellaneous Items	280

ANNALS OF MUSIC IN AMERICA

Annals of Music in America

Chapter I

1640 – 1750

THE Annals of Music in America during the first hundred years contain very little that would seem to be of any importance to the musicians of today. Nevertheless it is as interesting to note the beginnings of music in this newly settled country as to watch the appearance of the baby's first tooth.

The first settlement at Plymouth took place in 1620, and we find that in 1640 the colonists were already busy with the printing press in Cambridge, Mass., and the second book which came from the press was a reprint of an English Psalm book, printed under the title of the Bay Psalm Book. This was not an original work, but its production shows that music was already a living problem, and was even then part of the life of the colonists.

Practically nothing more of note happened until the importation of the first pipe organ, in 1700. This was quickly followed by other similar instruments in different parts of the country, and even by the building of organs by Americans, the first being by John Clemm in New York, which contained three manuals and twenty-six stops, and the next by Edward Bromfield in Boston. Bromfield's organ had two manuals and 1200 pipes, but was not completed when he died in 1746.

The early history of music in New England, as handed down to us by writers on the subject, seems to have consisted chiefly of church singing, concerning which there were many controversies. The early composers of New England were mainly occupied in composing psalm tunes, and in teaching singing schools.

The accounts of secular music come chiefly from Charleston, S. C., at which place many musicians entered this continent after visiting the West Indies. In fact, the first song recital on record in America took place at Charleston in 1733, while Boston had a concert in 1731 and Charleston had one in 1732. Charleston also claims the first performance of ballad opera on record in America (1735).

It must not, however, be supposed that New England had no secular music. The concert above mentioned goes to show the contrary. Also there is a record of small wind instruments, such as oboes and flageolets, being brought to Boston for the purposes of trade — possibly with the idea that New England shepherds might play to their sheep, as shepherds in other countries are supposed to do.

We know that every farm had its spinning wheel

and that clothes were made of the homespun woollens, but neither historian nor poet has ever pictured a New England shepherd with the shepherd's pipe. Imagination has not so far run riot.

Music was in a very elementary stage during the first hundred years. The country was sparsely populated, and music depends on the existence of a community. Even in 1750 the cows, according to tradition, were still occupied, during their daily peregrinations, in laying out the streets of the future city of Boston, — a city which was destined to be one of the leaders in matters musical.

NOTE. *When a work is mentioned as " given " or " played " or " presented," it means the first performance in America. When " produced " or " production " or " première " is used the first public performance anywhere is indicated.*

1640. The " Bay Psalm Book " published, first American book of sacred music. The second book printed in America.
1700. The first pipe organ to reach America from Europe was placed in the Episcopal Church at Port Royal, Va. About 1860 it was removed to Hancock, and later to Shepherdstown, W. Va.
1712. First practical instruction book on singing in New England, published by John Tufts of Newbury, Mass.
1713. First pipe organ brought into New England presented to King's Chapel, Boston, by Thomas Brattle. (Now in St. John's Chapel, Portsmouth, N. H.)
1720. First singing societies established in New England.
1716. First mention of the importation of flageolets, hautbois and other instruments, by Edward Enstone, of Boston.
1722. A playhouse existed near the market place, Williamsburg, Va. The first theatre known to exist in America.
1728. A pipe organ placed in Christ Church, Philadelphia.

1731. Dec. First concert recorded in Boston, given at the rooms of Mr. Pelham, near the Sun Tavern.

1732. April. A concert given for the benefit of Mr. Salter, at the Council Chamber, Charleston, S. C.

1733. A pipe organ placed in Trinity Church, Newport, R. I., being the second organ in New England.

1733. Feb. 26. First song recital recorded in America, given at the playhouse in Queen St., Charleston, S. C.

1735. Feb. 8. First performance of ballad opera on record in America — "Flora, or Hob in the Well" — given at the Courtroom, Charleston, S. C.

1735. July 1.–1794. Dec. 25. James Lyon, psalmodist. Probably the second American composer.

1736. Jan. 12. The first concert recorded in New York City, given for the benefit of Mr. Pachelbel. (Probably not the first concert given in that city.)

1737. First Pipe Organ completed in America, built by John Clemm, and placed in Trinity Church, New York City. Three manuals, twenty-six stops.

1737. Sept. 21–1791. May 9. Francis Hopkinson. The first American poet-composer.

1741. Moravian settlement established in Bethlehem, Pa. Became noted in musical matters.

1742. June. First Fingstude held at Bethlehem, Pa. Eighty people present.

1743. Records of this date show that two organs existed in the Moravian Church, Broad St., Philadelphia, Pa., and that stringed instruments were used in the services, also that instruments (violin, viola da braccio, viola da gamba, flutes and French horns) were played for the first time in the Moravian Church, Bethlehem, Pa.

1745–6. The first pipe organ built in New England, in Boston, by Edward Bromfield. Two manuals and twelve hundred pipes. Bromfield died in 1746 before completing the instrument.

1746. Oct. 7. William Billings. First New England composer, organizer of singing societies, etc. Billings died Sept. 29, 1800.

CHAPTER II

1750 – 1800

THE first item of especial interest in this period is the performance of the " Beggar's Opera " at the " Theatre in Nassau Street," New York. This theatre was a rather tumbledown affair and was not built for the purpose. It had a platform and rough benches. The chandelier was a barrel hoop through which several nails were driven, and on these nails were impaled candles, which provided all the light, and from which the tallow was likely to drip on the heads of such of the audience as had the best seats.

But three years later (in 1753) Lewis Hallam, who had been giving performances with his company in the more southern States, got permission to build a theatre on the site of this old place, and the house was opened in September with a play, " The Conscious Lovers," followed by a ballad farce, " Damon and Phillida."

In 1759 we find the first avowedly musical organization in America, " The Orpheus Club," was in existence in Philadelphia, and concerts were becoming more frequent. We also find a St. Cecilia Society founded in Charleston, S. C., an organization which lasted for a hundred and fifty years.

Other societies followed at short intervals and in widely scattered localities; the "Handel Society" of Dartmouth College, about 1780, the "Stoughton (Mass.) Musical Society," 1786, and "The Musical Society" of New York City, all tend to show that social centres were developing, and the people were finding expression in music.

An indication of what had been growing by degrees is found in the reports of concerts. Mention of instruments such as violins, French horns, oboes, trombones, etc., was made here and there, and especially in connection with the Moravian settlements in Bethlehem, Pa., where was established the first music school.

We find the first mention of an orchestra made in connection with a performance of "The Beggar's Opera" at Upper Marlboro, Md., in 1752, and a few years later (1788) a great concert was given in Philadelphia with an orchestra of fifty and a chorus of two hundred performers.

There is also a record of a concert given in Charleston, S. C., in 1796, when an orchestra of thirty instruments was employed in a performance of Gluck's overture to "Iphegénie en Aulide," and Haydn's "Stabat Mater."

It is quite possible that orchestras were used more or less in other concerts. Mr. Sonneck shows, in his "Early Concert-Life in America," many programs in which orchestral works are mentioned. And it is well to state here that it is almost impossible to locate the first performance in America of many of the works of the older composers, including Haydn and Mozart, because no opus number is mentioned, nor anything to indicate the identity of the work. Pleyel, Gluck and Clementi were much in vogue.

The American composer was beginning to be heard from during this period. Francis Hopkinson, who is generally regarded as the first American composer, wrote, in 1759, a song with the title "My Days Have Been So Wondrous Free." Some time later, in 1788, a small volume of songs was published under the title "Seven Songs," by the same composer.

Francis Hopkinson was a well-educated man, a signer of the Declaration of Independence, a member of the Convention of 1787 which formulated the Constitution of the United States, first Judge of the Admiralty Court in Pennsylvania, and author of many pamphlets and poems.

A man of entirely different calibre was William Billings, who was considered the first composer in New England. His compositions were chiefly "fuguing tunes," and he published several psalm books.

Billings was a tanner by trade, but a great musical enthusiast and organizer. The Stoughton (Mass.) Musical Society, which is the oldest musical society still in existence, was organized by Billings. Lack of education was no bar to his activities, and he accomplished much with very limited means.

It is said that Billings introduced the bass viol into the services of the Church, and thus began to break down the ancient Puritanical prejudices against musical instruments. He was also the first to use the pitch-pipe in order to ensure some degree of certainty in " striking up the tune " in church.

Again, we find the first American ballad operas during this period. Benjamin Carr, an Englishman who had been in America a couple of years, produced in 1796 a ballad opera, " The Archers of Switzerland," and, shortly afterwards, in the same year, with Pellesier (a Frenchman of recent arrival) as librettist, another ballad opera, " Edwin and Angelina," was staged in New York City. Though these works could hardly be called distinctively American, they were the first composed and produced in this country.

During the last decade of the 18th century some French actors and singers invaded the country and made New Orleans their headquarters. From that time on, for many years, New Orleans was prominent in the production of French operas and plays.

Theatres were built in several of the larger cities, and noted singers began to appear from abroad. The first of these appears to have been Miss Broadhurst, who appeared in Philadelphia in 1793, at the Chestnut Street Theatre. She was closely followed by Mrs. Oldmixon.

ANNALS OF MUSIC IN AMERICA

1750. April 30. "The Mock Doctor," and Dec. 3, "The Beggar's Opera," given at the "Theatre in Nassau St.," New York City. The first performances of ballad opera on record in that city.

1750. A Collegium Musicum was established about this time at Bethlehem, Pa.

1752. Sept. 14. First record of an orchestra being employed, at a performance of "The Beggar's Opera" at Upper Marlborough, Md.

1753. Sept. 13. The first theatre (built for the purpose) in New York City, erected in August and opened in September with "The Conscious Lovers" followed by the ballad farce, "Damon and Phillida," given by Lewis Hallam's company.

1754. First concert hall in Boston opened by Gilbert Deblois, at the corner of Hanover and Courts Sts.

1756. Mar. 16. New organ built by Gilbert Ash, dedicated at the City Hall, New York City, when an organ-concerto by G. A. Hasse was played.

In the same year a new organ was placed in King's Chapel, Boston, replacing the Brattle organ.

1756. The first mention of French horns in America made by Benjamin Franklin, writing of the fine music in the church at Bethlehem, Pa., where flutes, oboes, French horns, and trumpets were accompanied by the organ.

1757. Dr. Arne's "Masque of Alfred" given in Philadelphia by the students of the College of Philadelphia.

1759. The first known American song, "My Days Have Been so Wondrous Free," composed by Francis Hopkinson.

1759. The first avowedly musical organization in America, "The Orpheus Club," existed in Philadelphia, and was probably founded about this time.

1761. Feb. 3. Concert given by Mr. Dipper, organist of King's Chapel, Boston, in which two French horns were used. First mention of this instrument in New England.

1761. "Urania, or a Choice Collection of Psalm Tunes, Anthems, and Hymns, from the most approved Authors," published in Philadelphia, by James Lyon, A.B.

1762. A St. Cecilia Society (which lasted for one hundred and fifty years) formed in Charleston, S. C.

1765. A concert of "Musical Glasses" given in Philadelphia.

1765. June 3. The New York *Mercury* announced a series of summer concerts (open air) to be given at Ranelagh Gardens. These concerts were continued for four years.

1769. First American spinet made by John Harris, in Boston.

1770. Jan. 9. Handel's "Messiah" performed in part (sixteen numbers) at Trinity Church, New York City.

1770. Milton's "Masque of Comus" given by the Hallam Company, in Philadelphia.

1770. "The New England Psalm Singer" published in Boston, by William Billings.

1770. The pipe organ said to have been used for the first time in a Congregational church in America (Philadelphia).

1774. John Behrent, of Philadelphia, said to have made the first American piano.

1780. (c) The Handel Society of Dartmouth College organized at Hanover, N. H.

1784. A "Harmonic Society" formed about this time at Fredericksburg, Va.

1786. Stoughton (Mass.) Musical Society formed by William Billings, with Squire Elijah Dunbar of Canton as President; probably oldest singing society now in existence in America.

1786. Nov. 9. A society formed in New York City, at Mr. Hulett's rooms, for promoting vocal music.

1787. "Uranian Society" formed in Philadelphia for the improvement of church music. Continued till 1800.

1787. First pipe organ west of the Alleghanies set up in Cookstown (now Fayette City), Pa. Built by Joseph Downer, who was born in Brookline, Mass., 1767 (Jan. 28) and trekked to Pennsylvania with his family. The organ is preserved at the Carnegie Institute, Pittsburgh.

1788. May 4. A great concert given with an orchestra of fifty and a chorus of two hundred, in the Reformed German Church in Philadelphia, Pa.

1788. "The Musical Society" of New York City established.

1788. Publication of a book entitled "Seven Songs" by F.

ANNALS OF MUSIC IN AMERICA

Hopkinson (1737–1791), the first publication in America of songs by a native composer.

1789. May. 15. Concert given at Salem, Mass., by Gottlieb Graupner in which first mention is made of the use of the oboe (hautbois) in New England.

1790. June 4. A company of French comedians gave a performance, in French, of the opera "The Mistress and Maid" at Baltimore, Md.

1790. Oct. 7. First performance in America of Audinet-Gossec's "Le Tonnelier" given at the City Tavern, New York City.

1790–1800. During this period the following musical works were known and performed in New Orleans, Charleston, S. C., Baltimore, Philadelphia and New York City: Rousseau's "Pygmalion" and "Devin du Village"; Dalayrac's "Nina" and "L'Amant Statue"; Monsigny's "Déserteur"; Grétry's "Zémire et Azor," "La Fausse Magie" and "Richard Coeur de Lion," by a company of French comedians.

1791. A "Cecilia Society" formed in New York City. Lasted but a short time. An "Apollo Society" was also in existence.

1792. Oliver Holden, composer of "Coronation" and other well known hymn tunes, published his "American Harmony," and in 1793, "The Union Harmony."

1792–1872. Lowell Mason. Composer, educator in music. First teacher of singing in the public schools. President of the Handel and Haydn Society, Boston.

1793. "Uranian Society" of New York City, organized for sacred vocal music.

1793. Miss Broadhurst, a noted singer, made her American début in Philadelphia.

1793. Jacob Kimball (1761–1826, born Topsfield, Mass.,) published his "Rural Harmony."

1793. A company of French players reached America from San Domingo, remaining three years. They played in Norfolk, Va., in 1793, Charleston, S. C., 1794, Richmond, Va., 1795, Boston, Jan. 1796, and Philadelphia, Dec. 1796.

1793. A "Cecilia Society" was in existence at this time in Newport, R. I.

1794. Paisiello's opera "The Barber of Seville" (English version) was played in Baltimore, Philadelphia, New York City and elsewhere.

1794. Mrs. Oldmixon, a noted singer, made her first appearance in America at the Chestnut St. Theatre, Philadelphia, in "Robin Hood."

1796. April 18. "The Archers of Switzerland," an opera by B. Carr, produced in New York City. It is claimed by some authorities that this was the first American opera.

1796. July. Gluck's overture to "Iphegénie en Aulide," and Haydn's "Stabat Mater," given in Charleston, S. C., with an orchestra of about thirty instruments. Mrs. Pownall, J. H. Harris and Mr. Bergman, soloists.

1796. Dec. 19. Production in New York City of "Edwin and Angelina," music by Pellesier. Also said to be the first opera of American composition. (Carr was English, Pellesier French.)

1797. Anniversary meeting of the Concord (N. H.) Musical Society.

1797. Jan. 25. First recorded performance in America of Grétry's opera, "Richard Coeur de Lion," given at the Federal St. Theatre, Boston.

1798. Columbia Garden Summer Concerts established in New York. Lasted till 1800.

1798. Concerts are on record as having been given at Albany, N. Y., April 18; New Brunswick, N. J., Dec. 11; Trenton, N. J., Dec. 18; also an interesting group in Salem, Mass., by Gottlieb Graupner.

1798. Jan. 29. Park Theatre opened in New York City with a performance of a musical piece entitled "The Purse, — or American Tar." This theatre was, for twenty years, important in local musical history.

1798. April 25. First public performance of "Hail Columbia" by Gilbert Fox in Philadelphia. The words were written by Joseph Hopkinson Smith (1770–1842) and sung to the tune of "The President's March." First sung under the

title of "Federal Song" but changed a few days later to "Hail Columbia."
1799. A "Musical Society" existed in Baltimore.
1799. "Euterpean Society" formed in New York City.
1799. "The Vintage," an American opera by Pellisier and Dunlap, produced in New York City.

CHAPTER III

1800 – 1825

IN 1800 we find the first mention of the use of the bassoon. This was in Bethlehem, Pa., and it seems to complete the list of instruments for the average orchestra. Notwithstanding the record of the importation of oboes, many years earlier, and the fact that Graupner, one of the leading musicians in Boston about this time, was, or had been an oboeist, some historian has stated that even well into the nineteenth century there was only one oboe player in the United States, and he lived in Baltimore. Surely this must be an error.

In December 1800 we find the first annual concert of the Philharmonic Society in New York City. This society died in a few years, and in 1820 another Philharmonic Society was formed. This society also dwindled, though it did not die, for in 1840 it was reorganized, and has ever since taken a leading part in the musical life of New York.

Many musical societies made a beginning. Few lived long. But of those which lived perhaps the most noted is the Handel and Haydn Society of Boston, formed in 1815. This society gave what was claimed to be the first complete performance of Handel's "Messiah," but it is also claimed that this was done in 1801 in the hall of the University of Pennsylvania.

The Handel and Haydn Society also gave what was called the first complete performance of Haydn's "Creation," an honor which is also ascribed to King's Chapel in 1816, while portions had been performed in 1811 at Bethlehem, Pa. Thus it is difficult to fix definitely the first performances of many of the large works. In later days, especially in the case of Wagner's operas, portions were given at concerts long before complete stage performances were essayed.

Another musical society which is in existence at the present day, and which undoubtedly has had much influence on the musical life of America, was the Pierian Sodality of Harvard University, established in 1808 by the undergraduates.

In Philadelphia we find the establishment of the Musical Fund Society, which, for a number of years, did much to promote good music in that city. At its first concert, on April 24, 1821, Beethoven's First Symphony was played for the first time in America. Mr. Goepp gives us a full account of this and tells us that the whole symphony was too severe a task for an audience of that period, so the performance was broken and diversified by vocal and other solos between the movements.

New England possessed several musical societies in 1821, by which performances of oratorio were given. The Sacred Music Society was formed in New York City in 1823 and lasted till 1849. So it may easily be seen that, as the population increased, musical societies were soon established.

Theatres, while not strictly part of the musical life of the country, can hardly be separated from it because they were the home of ballad operas, and all musical stage representations. They were already in existence in New York, Boston, and Philadelphia before the beginning of the nineteenth century, but we find in 1807, the opening of "Le Théâtre St. Philippe" in New Orleans with Méhul's one-act opera, "Une Folie." This theatre being burned in 1817, a new one, "Le Théâtre d'Orléans," was built and opened in the following year. This theatre was the finest in the country at that time and was the home of opera for a number of years. The record of opera in New Orleans is incomplete, but it is well known that New Orleans was the home of French opera in America long before it became popular in other parts of the country.

But America was gradually edging up to the time of grand opera. Singers were arriving from abroad and brought with them their ambitions. We find that an English version of Rossini's opera, "Il Barbiere," was given at the Park Theatre, New York City, in 1819, with Miss Leesugg as Rosina, and in 1823 an English version of Mozart's "Le Nozze di Figaro" was presented. Again in the early part of 1825, Weber's opera "Der Freyschütz" was presented, in English, at the Park Theatre, with Miss Kelly and Mrs. de Luce in the leading parts. Similar performances followed in other cities, and the country was thus gradually prepared for the real thing, — grand opera, — in its native language.

While the record of items during the period 1800 to 1825 is not very long it still shows considerable progress. The people grew up in a country where there was little musical cultivation, where there were small communities, and where the struggle for existence had been the first consideration. They responded warmly to the efforts of the country singing teacher, the choral society promoter, and later to the producer of opera, and if history shows many failures, it may be pointed out that these failures could not have taken place if no effort had been made. Perhaps efforts in many cases were premature. Also there was much to learn in the management of masses of people. The virtues of a true democracy are nowhere more necessary than in a choral society.

1800. Bassoon used in Bethlehem, Pa.
1800. Dec. 23. First Annual Concert of the Philharmonic Society given at Tontine Hall, Broadway, New York City.
1801. Handel's "Messiah" given in the hall of the University of Pennsylvania, Philadelphia.
1802. "Harmonic Society" founded in Philadelphia.
1803. Benjamin Crehore of Milton, Mass., made the first pianoforte in New England.
1807. Massachusetts Musical Society formed in Boston for improving the mode of performing sacred music. Ceased to exist in 1810.

1807. "Le Théâtre St. Philippe" opened in New Orleans with a one-act opera by Méhul, — "Une Folie."
1808. The Pierian Sodality, half musical, half social club organized by the undergraduates of Harvard University.
1809. Haydn Society formed in Philadelphia.
1811. John Davis, from San Domingo, opened the "Théâtre d'Orléans" in New Orleans.
1811. Haydn's "Creation" and "The Seasons" performed in part at Bethlehem, Pa.
1813–1893. John S. Dwight, editor, critic, member of Brook Farm community, and founder in 1852 of "Dwight's Journal of Music," the first publication of its kind in America.
1814. Sept. 14. The words of "The Star-Spangled Banner" written by Francis Scott Key during the bombardment of Fort Henry. They were published next day as a "Broadside" and on the 20th appeared in the "Baltimore Patriot." The tune of "Anacreon in Heaven" was adapted by the author.
1815. April 20. Handel and Haydn Society, Boston, organized with Thomas S. Webb as President. At the first concert the chorus consisted of about one hundred, of whom ten were women. Orchestra a dozen instruments, and organ.
1816. First complete performance of Haydn's "Creation" given at King's Chapel, Boston.
1817. Charles B. Incledon, noted English tenor singer, visited America.
1818. New Théâtre d'Orléans, the finest in the United States, opened in New Orleans. The old theatre was burned in 1817. The new theatre was the home of opera for some years.
1818. Dec. 25. The Handel and Haydn Society of Boston gave what is called the first complete performance of Handel's "Messiah" in America. (Philip Goepp states that the "Messiah" was given in 1801, in the hall of the University of Pennsylvania.)
1819. "Haydn Society" formed in Cincinnati, O.
1819. Feb. 16. First complete performance of Haydn's

"Creation" given by the Handel and Haydn Society, Boston. (This was claimed also in 1816 for a performance at King's Chapel.)

1819. An English version of Rossini's "Barber of Seville" given in New York City, with Miss Leesugg as *Rosina*, at the Park Theatre.

1820. Philharmonic Society organized in Bethlehem, Pa. (Originally the Collegium Musicum of 1750.)

1820. Two musical societies formed in New York City, viz, — the Philharmonic, and the Euterpean.

The Philharmonic used to engage prominent artists. It gradually dwindled but was reorganized in 1840.

The Euterpean gave concerts which were usually followed by a supper and a ball. It ceased to exist about 1845.

1820. Aug. 30. George F. Root, noted American song-writer. Died Aug. 6, 1895.

1820. The Philadelphia Musical Fund Society established. Gave its first concert April 24, 1821, when Beethoven's First Symphony was played for the first time in America. (Between the movements vocal and other solos were given by sundry artists.)

1821. New England musical matters on record of this year are: An oratorio given by the Psallion Society of Providence, R. I.;

A performance of music by the New Hampshire Musical Society at Hanover, N. H.;

The existence of a Beethoven Society in Portland, Me.

1823. Production in New York City of "Clari, the Maid of the Mill," ballad opera by Sir Henry Bishop and J. Howard Payne. This opera contains the song, "Home, Sweet Home." Was presented in London on May 23.

1823. May 23. Mozart's opera, "The Marriage of Figaro" (Bishop's English version), presented in New York City at the Park Theatre.

1823. The pianoforte manufacturing house of Jonas Chickering established in Boston.

1823–1849. Sacred Music Society, New York City.

1824. St. Cecilia Society formed in Philadelphia.

CHAPTER IV

1825 – 1850

DURING these twenty-five years the list of items on record is far greater than during any preceding period of similar time. Possibly this may be accounted for by the greater facilities for travel both by sea and land. Railroads were gradually spreading out through the country, and helping to develop distant trading stations into towns and cities. Steamships were making the voyage from Europe a more feasible adventure. We shall see this as we proceed.

In what we may call the domestic side of music we find the establishment of more singing societies in all the eastern cities. There was practically no "west" in 1825, but Chicago shows up in 1834 with "The Old Settlers' Harmonic Society." The story of Chicago's early musical days may be read in Mr. George P. Upton's book of reminiscences. The remarkable part of it seems to be that Chicago grew phenomenally, and today stands as a rival to New York in all matters musical, although in 1825 Chicago was merely a trading post and New York was already a city of some size.

The musical convention came into being. The

first is said to have been held at Concord, N. H., in September 1829. There is also a claim that the first musical convention was held in Montpelier, Vt., in 1839 but this is not quite correct. It may have been the first convention in Vermont. Musical conventions became popular and frequent and are so even to the present day, though the methods and matter have changed with the times.

Another item which may come under the head of domestic music is the beginning of music teaching in the public schools. This was effected by Lowell Mason, as an experiment, in 1838. At the present day chorus singing in the public schools has become an important matter, and is almost universal.

In 1838 we find a Philharmonic Society in St. Louis, showing that St. Louis was not far behind Chicago in getting into the musical world.

In Boston an Academy of Music was established by Lowell Mason in 1833. It had a large number of pupils, and there was an orchestra in connection with it, which gave several concerts. But the Harvard Musical Association, which was founded in 1837, seems to have been the chief propelling power to orchestral music in Boston, until the formation of the Boston Symphony Orchestra. In New York the Philharmonic Society was reorganized and was, as it has been ever since, the most prominent orchestral organization of that city.

In 1848 two complete orchestras came to America, Gungl's, which gave a number of concerts, chiefly of light music, and the Germania, which consisted of a number of refugees from the German government. These men gave concerts of a finer type than had yet been given in America. Their career as an organization was not long, and it ended in disaster, but many of the members became prominent in musical matters in various cities, and in this way the Germania orchestra had a beneficial and lasting effect upon music in this country.

In the forties began the stream of violin and piano virtuosi which has continued in ever-increasing volume to the present day. Ole Bull, violinist, in 1843, Vieuxtemps and Artôt, violinists, and Leopold von Meyer, pianist, in 1844, were the first.

Perhaps the development of opera may be considered of greater interest than other musical items. In 1825 Manuel Garcia arrived in New York, and gave the first performances of Italian opera. In his company were his daughter Maria, who married one Malibran and remained in New York for about two years. At the end of this time she left her husband and returned to Europe, where she had a short but very brilliant career. Young Garcia, the son, who also sang, afterwards became one of the greatest singing teachers in Europe, and invented the laryngoscope. Pauline, who became Madame Viardot, and lived to a great age, was too young to participate in Garcia's performances in New York. For many years she was one of the great singing teachers in Paris.

Garcia did not stay very long in New York, but he began the efforts to present Italian opera, which were continued by many others from time to time, usually with disaster. Nevertheless, the history of the period from 1825 to 1850 is full of first performances of Italian opera. In 1848 the Havana Company visited the United States, and was considered the finest company that had been heard until that time.

In the same year Max Maretzek appeared in New York and at once entered the operatic field, with which he was prominently occupied during the next period.

Before finishing the review of this period we must not forget the production William Henry Fry's opera, "Leonora." This was the first grand opera written and produced by an American. It had several representations, but does not seem to have lived long. The same, however, may be said of many of the Italian operas which were presented during this and later periods. A careful perusal of the list will show the names of operas long since defunct, so far as the American public is concerned. Yet there are many, which were first presented to the American public in this period, and which are as popular today as ever, — in fact no good opera company can afford to be without them. Opera was well started by 1850.

1825. Mar. 12. Weber's opera "Der Freyschütz" presented in English at the Park Theatre, New York City, with Miss Kelly and Mrs. de Luce in the leading parts.

1825. Nov. 26. First season of Italian grand opera in America opened in New York city with a performance of Rossini's "Il Barbiere," by Manuel Garcia's company.

This company included Manuel Garcia, his son Manuel (later a renowned vocal teacher, and inventor of the laryngoscope), his daughter, Maria Félicité (the great Malibran), his daughter Pauline (later Madame Viardot, one of the great vocal teachers of Paris) and others of less note.

The other operas presented during this season were:

1825. Dec. 31. "Tancredi," Rossini.
1826. April 25. "Semiramide," Rossini.
1826. May 23. "Don Giovanni," Mozart.
1826. Dec. 27. "L'Amante Astuto," Garcia.

Also (dates uncertain):

"La Figlia del Aria," Garcia.
"Il Turco in Italia," Rossini.
"La Cenerentola," Rossini.

1826–1864. Stephen Foster. Noted song writer.

1827. July 13. The French Opera Company from New Orleans, which visited Philadelphia, and several other cities, opened a season at the Park Theatre, New York City, with Rossini's "La Cenerentola." They also presented "Jean de Paris," "La Dame Blanche," "Joconde," "Les Visilandines," etc.

1827. Sept. 28. Boieldieu's opera "Jean de Paris" presented in New York City, with Malibran. Later in the season the same composer's "Caliph of Bagdad" was given.

1827. Oct. 9. Weber's opera "Oberon" presented in Philadelphia.

1827. Oct. 9. Farewell of Madame Malibran (Maria Félicité Garcia) at the Bowery Theatre, after two years' residence in New York City.

1828. An English version of "Il Barbiere di Seviglia," and "Der Freyschütz" given in Boston with Miss George, Mrs. Papanti, Mr. Comer, and Mr. Horn as leading singers.

1829. Sept. First musical convention held under the auspices of the Central Musical Society of Concord, N. H.
1829. May 8.–1869. Dec. 18. Louis Moreau Gottschalk, brilliant pianist. Born in New Orleans.
1829. Jan. 24.–1908. July 14. William Mason, noted American pianist and teacher.
1831. Sept. 6. American début of Miss Hughes at the Park Theatre, New York City, in "The Marriage of Figaro."
1832. Mar. 17. Mozart's opera "Die Zauberflöte" presented in Philadelphia.
1832. July 4. The National Hymn "America" first sung in public at a children's celebration of Independence Day, at the Park St. Church, Boston. The words were written in February by the Rev. Samuel F. Smith, and were sung to the tune of "God Save the King."
1832. Sept. 25. First appearance, in concert, of an Italian opera company organized by Lorenzo da Ponte, Italian poet and librettist, at Niblo's Garden, New York City. The leading singers were Signora Pedrotti and Signori Fornisari and Montrésor. The opera performances were given at the Bowery Theatre. Sig. Rapetti, conductor.
1832. Oct. 19. Mercadante's opera "Elisa e Claudio" presented in New York City with Pedrotti (début) and Salvione (début).
1832. Nov. 5. Rossini's opera "L'Italiana in Algeri" given in New York City with Verducci, Fanetti, Fornisari, etc.
1832. Dec. 5. Bellini's opera "Il Pirata" by same company.
1832. Dec. 22. Rossini's sacred opera "Mosè in Egitto" by same company.
1833. Mar. 13–20. Rossini's opera "Othello" presented twice during this week, in New York City, by same company.
1833. June 20. Auber's opera "Fra Diavolo" presented at the Park Theatre, New York City.
1833. Sept. 4. American début of Mr. and Mrs. Wood in "Cinderella" at the Park Theatre, New York City.
1833. Nov. 18. Verdi's opera "La Gazza Ladra" given in New York City, at the Bowery Theatre, by the Italian Opera Company.

1833. Academy of Music founded in Boston by Lowell Mason. Enrolled twenty-two hundred pupils the first year.

1834. Mar. 21. Rossini's opera "La Donna del Lago" given at the Bowery Theatre, New York City, with Clotilde and Rosina Fanti, Marozo, Raviglia and Sapignoli.

1834. Mar. 22. Salvione's opera "La Casa dei Venderi."

1834. Mar. 24. Rossini's "Matilda de Shabran" with Fanti.

1834. April 7. Meyerbeer's opera "Roberto il Diavolo," presented in English at the Park Theatre, New York City, by Mr. and Mrs. Wood.

1834. July 9. First music school in Chicago opened by Miss Wyeth.

1834. July 12. Pacini's opera "Gli Arabi nelli Gallie" given at the Bowery Theatre, New York City, with C. Fanti, R. Fanti, Bordogni, Raviglia, Sapignoli.

1834. Nov. 10. Bellini's opera "La Straniera" given in New York City, with C. and R. Fanti, Porto, Montrésor, Sapignoli.

1834. Nov. 25. Rossini's opera "Edoardo e Cristina" given in New York City, with Fanti, Fabj, Porto, Sapignoli.

1834. Dec. 12. Rossini's opera "L'Inganno Felice" given in New York City by the Italian Opera Company.

1834. Dec. 11. "Old Settlers' Harmonic Society" organized in Chicago.

1834–1901. Charles R. Adams, noted tenor and vocal teacher. One of the first American singers to make a career in Europe.

1834–1891. Eben Tourjée, noted organizer of musical affairs. Began class-system of pianoforte-teaching in America at Providence, R. I., in 1851. Founded a Musical Institute at East Greenwich, R. I., in 1859, and the New England Conservatory of Music in Boston, 1867. Was one of the chief organizers of the Peace Jubilee, and one of the founders of the Music Teachers' National Association.

1835. Feb. 6. Rossini's opera "L'Assedio di Corinto" given in New York City with Fanti, Julia Wheatley, Ravaglia. During this season Rossini's "Turco in Italia" and Cimarosa's "Il Matrimonio Segreto" are said to have been presented by this Italian company.

1835. April 8. Charlotte Cushman, noted actress, made her first public appearance as a singer in a performance of "The Marriage of Figaro" in Boston, with Mr. and Mrs. Wood.

1835. Nov. 13. Bellini's opera "La Sonnambula" given in English with Mr. and Mrs. Wood in the leading parts, in New York City.

1835. German Maennerchor of Philadelphia (the oldest German singing society in America) founded by Philip Wolsifer.

1835. Oliver Ditson began publishing music in his own name in Boston, but the firm of O. Ditson and Company can be traced back to 1783, when E. Batelle opened the Boston Book Store at 8 State Street.

1835–1905. Theodore Thomas, noted musician and conductor of:
  1862–1891 Brooklyn Philharmonic Society.
  1864–1878 New York Symphony Society.
  1865–1891 New York Summer Garden Concerts.
  1873–1894 Cincinnati Festivals.
  1877–1890 Chicago Summer Night Concerts.
  1877–1891 Philharmonic Society, New York.
  1882–1891 Philadelphia Symphony Orchestra.
  1891–1905 Chicago Symphony Orchestra.

1837. Harvard Musical Association organized in Boston.

1837. The pianoforte manufacturing house of Knabe established in Baltimore.

1837. Oct. 30. American début of Madame Caradori-Allan, noted soprano, in Rossini's opera "Il Barbiere di Seviglia" at the Park Theatre, New York City.

1837. An orchestra organized by the Academy of Music in Boston. It remained in existence until 1847.

1838. Philharmonic Society formed in St. Louis.

1838. The Sacred Music Society of New York City, gave a performance of Mendelssohn's oratorio "St. Paul," two years after it had been produced at Dusseldorf.

1838. June. 18. Donizetti's opera "L'Elisir d'Amore" presented at the Park Theatre, New York City, with Madame Caradori-Allan, Placide, Morley, Macklin and Jones.

1838. Mr. and Mrs. Seguin, noted singers, arrived in New York City and organized an English Opera Company, which traveled extensively till 1847.

1838. Music first taught in the public schools in Boston by Lowell Mason.

1839. April 29. Meyerbeer's opera "Les Huguenots" presented in New Orleans.

1839. The first Musical Convention held in Montpelier, Vt., under the direction of G. S. Prouty and Moses E. Cheney.

1839. Sept. 9. Beethoven's opera "Fidelio" presented in English at the Park Theatre, New York City, with Miss Poole, Giubelei, Manvers and Martyn.

1839–1906. John Knowles Paine. American composer. First professor of music at Harvard University. Appointed in 1876 (instructor 1872).

1839–1909. Dudley Buck. Noted musician. First American composer to gain general recognition.

1840. Mar. 20. Hérold's opera "Zampa" presented in New York City.

1840. Mar. 30. Adam's opera "Le Postillon de Longjumeau" presented in New York City.

1840. Mendelssohn's oratorio "Elijah" sung by the Handel and Haydn Society, Boston.

1840. Beethoven's Fifth Symphony given by the Musical Fund Society in Philadelphia.

1840. John Braham, noted English tenor, visited America.

1841. The Hutchinson family — camp-meeting singers, known all over the United States for many years — began their career.

1841. Jan. 11. Bellini's opera "Norma" presented by the Woods at the Chestnut St. Theatre, Philadelphia.

1841. Mar. 31. Schumann's First Symphony given by the Musical Fund Society (G. Suk, conductor) in Boston.

1841. Dec. 28. Donizetti's opera "Lucia di Lammermoor" given in New Orleans.

1842. The Chicago Sacred Music Society formed. It was short-lived.

1842. Jan. 15. Beethoven's Sixth (Pastoral) Symphony given

ANNALS OF MUSIC IN AMERICA

in Boston, at a concert of the Academy of Music. Also Cherubini's overture to " Les deux Journées."

1842. Feb. 26. C. M. von Weber's " Jubilee " overture given at a concert of the Academy of Music, Boston.

1842. Mar. 20. Spohr's oratorio " The Last Judgment " given in Boston by the Handel and Haydn Society.

1842. Oct. 31. Handel's oratorio " Israel in Egypt " (music by Handel and Rossini) given by the Seguin Opera Company at the Park Theatre, New York City.

1842. Nov. 12. Beethoven's Second Symphony (D) given at the Academy of Music, Boston.

1842. Nov. 22. Handel's oratorio " Acis and Galatea " given by the Seguin Company at the Park Theatre, New York City.

1842. Dec. 7. First concert of the New York Philharmonic Society, given at the Apollo rooms, New York City.
Program:
Beethoven Symphony No. 5 (conducted by U. C. Hill).
Weber, Scene from " Oberon " (Mme. Otto).
Hummel, Quintet for piano and strings.
Weber, Overture to " Oberon " (conducted by Mr. Etienne).
Rossini, Duet from " Armida " (Mme. Otto and C. E. Horn).
Beethoven, Scene from " Fidelio " (C. E. Horn).
Mozart, Aria from " Belmont and Constance " (Mme. Otto).
Kalliwoda, New Overture in D (Conducted by Mr. Timm).
Beethoven's " Eroica " was played at the second concert, Feb. 18, 1843. There were only three concerts in the first season.

1842. Dec. 13. Rossini's opera " Guillaume Tell " presented by the French Company in New Orleans.

1843. Jan. 7. Haydn's " Military " Symphony (G. major) played at the Academy of Music, Boston.

1843. Feb. 9. Donizetti's opera " La Favorita " presented by the French Company in New Orleans.

1843. Feb. 18. Beethoven's Third Symphony, " Eroica," given by the Philharmonic Society, at the Apollo rooms, New

York City. (This work was played as a Septet by the Musical Fund Society in New York City, in 1828.)

1843. Feb. 26. Rossini's "Stabat Mater" given by the Handel and Haydn Society, Boston.

1843. Mar. 6. Donizetti's opera "La Fille du Régiment" presented by the French Company in New Orleans.

1843. May 25. Auber's opera "L'Ambassadrice,"

1843. June 17. Auber's opera "Le Domino Noir," and

1843. July 3. Auber's opera "Pré aux Clerc" presented in New York City, at Niblo's Gardens, by the French Company from New Orleans.

1843. Oct. 3. Donizetti's opera "Gemma di Vergi" presented at Niblo's Gardens, New York City, with Majocchi, prima donna, and Perozzi.

1843. Nov. 25. Ole Bull, noted Norwegian violinist, made his American début at the Park Theatre, New York City.

1843. Dec. 15. Donizetti's opera "Marino Faliero" presented at the Park Theatre, New York City.

1843–1863. Philharmonic Concerts, Boston.

1844. Jan. 15. Mozart's "Jupiter" Symphony (Fourth, in C) given by the Philharmonic Society, New York City.

1844. Feb. 2. Bellini's opera "I Puritani" presented at Palmo's Opera House, New York City, with Signora Borghese.

1844. Mar. 16. Spohr's First Symphony (D minor) given by the Philharmonic Society, New York City.

1844. Mar. 18. Bellini's opera "Beatrice di Tenda" presented at Palmo's Opera House, New York City, with Majocchi, prima donna.

1844. April 27. Donizetti's opera "Lucrezia Borgia" presented in New Orleans.

1844. May 6. Donizetti's opera "Anne Boleyn" presented in English by the Seguin Company at the Park Theatre, New York City.

1844. Nov. 16. Ricci's opera "Chiara de Rosenburgh" presented at Palmo's Opera House, New York City, with Borghese, Antignone, Valtellina, and Sanquirico.

1844. Nov. 16. Beethoven's "Egmont" overture given at the Academy of Music, Boston.

ANNALS OF MUSIC IN AMERICA

1844. Nov. 16. Mendelssohn's "Hebrides" overture and Beethoven's Eighth Symphony (F major) given by the Philharmonic Society, New York City, G. Loder conducting.

1844. Nov. 25. Balfe's opera "The Bohemian Girl" given by the Seguin Company in New York City.

1844. Nov. 28. Donizetti's opera "Belisario" presented at Palmo's Opera House, New York City, with Borghese, Pico, Perozzi and Tomaso.

1844. Dec. 14. Beethoven's "Battle of Waterloo" (Wellington) Symphony given at the Tabernacle, Broadway, New York City, by a "powerful and sufficient orchestra" under U. B. Hill, in aid of a fund for the French Free School.

1844. Dec. 15. Henri Vieuxtemps, noted Belgian violinist, made his American début at a concert at the Park Theatre, New York City.

1844. Alexandre Artot, French violinist, and Leopold von Meyer, German pianist, made their first American tour.

1844. New York Musical Institute established. It was merged into the Harmonic Society in 1849.

1845. Jan. 11. Spohr's overture to "Jessonda" given by the Philharmonic Society, New York City.

1845. Jan. 26. Handel's oratorio "Samson" performed by the Handel and Haydn Society, Boston.

1845. Mar. 1. W. Sterndale Bennett's overture to "Die Najaden" given by the Philharmonic Society, New York City.

1845. April 19. Mendelssohn's "Zum Märchen von der Schönen Melusine" given by the Philharmonic Society, New York City.

1845. June 4. Production, in English, of William H. Fry's grand opera "Leonora" at the Chestnut St. Theatre, Philadelphia, — the first grand opera written by an American. The Italian version was given at the Academy of Music, New York City, in March, 1858. The cast at Philadelphia was P. Richings, Ed. Seguin, Brunton, Frazer, Mrs. Seguin and Miss Ince. In the New York production Sig. Rocco, Gassier, Barratini, Tiberini, Madame de la Grange, Madame d'Angri and Madame Morra.

1845. Nov. 22. Mendelssohn's "Scotch Symphony" given by the Philharmonic Society, New York City, G. Loder conducting.

1845. Dec. 21. Handel's oratorio "Moses in Egypt" given by the Handel and Haydn Society, Boston.

1846. Jan. 17. Mendelssohn's Pianoforte Concerto in G Minor given by the Philharmonic Society, New York City, with H. C. Timm as soloist.

1846. Feb. 14. Spohr's overture to "Faust" given at the Philharmonic Concerts, Boston.

1846. Mar. 7. Kalliwoda's First Symphony (D minor) given by the Philharmonic Society, New York City.

1846. Mar. 9. Donizetti's opera "Don Pasquale" presented in English at the Park Theatre, New York City.

1846. May 20. Beethoven's Ninth Symphony (D minor) given by the Philharmonic Society of New York at Castle Garden, New York City.

1846. Steyermark's Orchestra of twenty men visited America and made their first appearance in New York City.

1846. Oct. 12. Camille Sivori, noted Italian violinist, made his American début in a concert at the Broadway Tabernacle, New York City.

1846. Nov. 21. Berlioz's overture to "King Lear" given by the Philharmonic Society of New York City. A. Boucher, conductor.

1847. Jan. 4. Donizetti's opera "Linda di Chamounix" presented at Palmo's Opera House, New York City, with a company including Clotilde Barili, Mlle. Pico, Benedetti, Sanquirico and Barili. Rapetti, conductor.

1847. Jan. 9. Deutscher Liederkranz organized in New York City, with Dr. Ludwig as conductor.

1847. Jan. 9. Mendelssohn Festival held at the Castle Garden, New York City, under U. C. Hill.

1847. Jan. 9. The Havana Opera Company arrived in America with Luigi Arditi as conductor. The company included Fortunata Tedesco, prima donna, Perelli, tenor, Cesar Badiale, bass, also Bottesini, the noted double-bass virtuoso.

1847. Jan. 3. Coppola's opera "Nina Pazza per Amore" presented by the Havana Company at the Park Theatre, New York City.

1847. Mar. 3. Verdi's opera "I Lombardi" presented at Palmo's Opera House, New York City, with Narili, Patti, Beneventano.

1847. April 15. Verdi's opera "Ernani" presented at the Park Theatre, New York City, by the Havana Company, with Tedesco, Perelli and Novelli. Arditi conducting.

1847. April 23. First season of Italian opera in Boston, begun with "Ernani" at the Howard Athenaeum, given by the Havana Opera Company.

1847. May 13. Musical Fund Society organized in Boston. Lasted till 1856.

1847. June 12. Pacini's opera "Saffo" presented at the Park Theatre, New York City, by the Havana Opera Company.

1847. Aug. 4. Madame Anna Bishop, noted English singer, made her American début at the Park Theatre, New York City.

1847. Nov. 14. Mozart's Third Symphony (E flat major) and Bristow's Concert Overture (Opus 3) given by the Philharmonic Society of New York City.

1847. American début of Teresa Truffi, soprano, in "Ernani" at the Astor Place Opera House, New York City, which was opened in this month under the management of Patti, Sanquirico and Pogliano. The company included Clotilde and Antonio Barili, Benedetti and Sanquirico.

1847. Dec. 5. Handel's oratorio "Judas Maccabeus" given by the Handel and Haydn Society in Boston.

1847. Mozart Society organized in Chicago, under the direction of Frank Lumbard.

1848. Jan. 8. Beethoven's Seventh Symphony (in F, — "Pastoral") given by the Musical Fund Society, Boston.

1848. Feb. 1. Bellini's opera "I Capuletti e Montecchi" presented at the Astor Place Opera House, New York City, for the début of Caterina Barili Patti, as *Romeo*.

1848. Feb. 14. Mercadante's opera "Il Guiramento" presented at the Astor Place Opera House, New York City, with Truffi, Benedetti, Rossi and Beneventano.

1848. April 4. Verdi's opera "Nabucco" presented at the Astor Place Opera House, New York City, with Truffi, Amalia Patti.

1848. April 11. Schumann's secular cantata, "Paradise and the Peri," given in New York City, by the Musical Institute, Henry C. Timm conducting.

1848. April 29. Spohr's Symphony in E flat, given by the Philharmonic Society, New York City.

1848. May 4. Wallace's opera "Maritana" given by the Seguin Company in Philadelphia.

1848. May 14. Mendelssohn's "Midsummer Night's Dream," music given by the Germania Orchestra in New York City.

1848. Oct. 2. American début of Maurice Strakosch, noted conductor and impresario, at the First Grand Musical Festival of the season, at the Broadway Tabernacle, New York City, given by the "Italian Opera Company of the United States."

1848. Oct. 5. The Germania Orchestra, consisting of German revolutionary refugees, organized and gave their first concert in America at Niblo's Garden, New York City.

1848. Nov. 16. Gungl's Orchestra of twenty-five players gave their first concert in New York City, at the Broadway Tabernacle, after which they made a tour of the United States, playing chiefly dance-music.

1848. Dec. 2. W. Sterndale Bennett's overture to "Die Waldnymphe" given by the Philharmonic Society, New York City.

1848. Edouard Remenyi, noted Hungarian violinist, made first American tour, and Richard Hoffman was the first noted pianist to visit Chicago.

1848. Musical Convention held in Chicago for the first time.

1848. During this season the Havana Opera Company again visited America bringing Steffanone, Bosio, Tedesco (soprani); Vietto (contralto); Salvi, Bettini and Lorini (tenori); Badiali, Setti, Marini, and Coletti (bassi) — the best company heard in America up to that time.

Also Max Maretzek arrived in New York and began his career as impresario. His company included Madame

Laborde, and Truffi (soprani); Amalia Patti (contralto); Benedetti and Arnoldi (tenori); Giubeli, Rossi and Salvatore Patti (bassi). Also, later, Teresa Parodi. His first public appearance was on Oct. 5, at the Chestnut Street Theatre, Philadelphia, conducting " Norma."

1849. Nov. 24. Beethoven's Fourth Symphony (B flat major) given by the Philharmonic Society, New York City, also Mendelssohn's Violin Concerto (E minor) with Joseph Burke as soloist.

1849. Dec. 10. Donizetti's opera " Marie de Rohan " presented in New York City, on which occasion Giuletta Perrini, Italian soprano, made her American début supported by Patti, Forti, Giubelei and Beneventano.

1849. Dec. 16. Donizetti's opera " Il Poliuto " performed as an oratorio (The Martyrs) by the Handel and Haydn Society, Boston.

1849. Saengerfest held in Cincinnati, O.

1849. Musikverein founded in Milwaukee, Wis.

1849. The Artists' Union Opera Company formed in New York City, including Bosio, De Vries, Bettini, Lorini, Badiali, and Coletti. They gave what they claimed was the first performance in America of Meyerbeer's opera " Roberto il Diavolo. (See April 7, 1834).

1849–1874. Sacred Harmonic Society, New York City.

CHAPTER V

1850 – 1875

DURING this period musical events moved forward quite rapidly, and though there was a pause during the years of the Civil War — from 1861 to 1865 — after that time increasing energy was in evidence.

Possibly one of the most significant events was the establishment of "Dwight's Journal of Music," in Boston, the first journal in America devoted entirely to musical matters. It was published every two weeks, and while the greater part of the space was devoted to musical affairs in Europe, yet there were letters and reports from various centres in this country, which make the Journal something of a history in itself. Moreover, John S. Dwight helped very materially in bringing to the American people something in the way of musical criticism, which was sadly needed. Indeed, anyone who takes the trouble to look over the reports of concerts and operas in the daily papers of these times will be surprised at the absurdity of the comments on the performances of the noted musicians. Ritter, for instance, quotes a criticism of a pianoforte recital where the critic was much pleased by a "double run on the chromatic scale, in which the semitones were distinctly heard." With singers the chief point was whether the singer of this season could sing louder than the singer of last season. John S. Dwight was the pioneer of musical criticism in America, — an intellectual man, one of the noted band of idealists who were in the "Brook Farm" movement. "Dwight's Journal of Music" went out of existence in 1881. Musical criticism has since become a specialized art.

Musical societies were multiplying, — Cincinnati and Milwaukee had them, and in Chicago the "Philharmonic Society" was organized. In 1850 also the Worcester (Mass.) "Festivals" began, and in 1858 the Peabody Institute concerts, in Baltimore.

In 1858 the "Mendelssohn Quintet" was formed, and for many years toured the country giving concerts of a high standard, and doing much to raise the level of musical taste. This organization had its beginning in Boston, but it traveled so widely that it may be said to have belonged to the nation.

Towards the end of this period the "Apollo Club" was organized in Chicago, and it is today one of the most excellent clubs in America. The following year the "Cecilia Society," in Boston, was organized and likewise still exists and flourishes. But these are only a few.

The American composer was beginning to show himself — perhaps not yet very brilliantly in comparison to the great men of Europe — but he was beginning to be heard from. William H. Frye, besides his two operas, composed several symphonies, which were played by Jullien's Band in 1853. Also a " Grand Symphony " in 1855 and " The Pilgrims' Cantata " by C. C. Perkins, were performed in Boston, and we have record of an oratorio, " The Cities of the Plains," by Dawley, in 1855. Apart from these efforts the American composer seems to have been inconspicuous. In fact there were no facilities for the study of music or for the hearing of music which could be compared, as a training school for composers, with the musical centres of Europe, so that the efforts of these earlier composers may be considered, in some respects, premature, and prompted by energy and ambition rather than by scientific preparation.

The story of grand opera of this period is one of perpetual striving for the unattainable. In Chicago the first performance of grand opera was given in 1850. Chicago is now a rival of New York in matters of opera.

San Francisco heard its first opera in 1853. The gold fever of 1849 drew people of all kinds to California, and among them were musicians. Henri Herz, the French pianist, reached California in 1849 when the excitement was at its highest, and he gives an interesting account of his adventures. It may also be well to mention here Signora Biscaccianti, who went to San Francisco in 1852, and was there more or less till 1864. Signora Biscaccianti was one of the first American singers to achieve a measure of success in Europe. She was the daughter of a musician named Ostinelli, was born in Boston, where she met with some success as a singer, went to New York and thence to Europe. Another American who was, perhaps, better known in her own country was Miss Isabella Hinkley who appeared in 1861, but another who appeared in New York in the same year, became still better known and was prominent for many years, Clara Louise Kellogg. Eighteen hundred and fifty-nine was the year of Adelina Patti's début.

The list of great singers who were imported during this period is long. We can but touch on it, — there was Jenny Lind in 1850, then came Marietta Alboni in 1851. Two years later Sontag, and the next year Grisi and Mario. In 1865 came Parepa Rosa, and in 1870 Christine Nilsson. In 1873, Maurel and Campanini. In 1855 Brignoli appeared, and was for many years a great popular favorite.

We find efforts in New York to promote German opera. Operas by Germans — "Fidelio" for instance — had been heard together with operas by Italians, and others, but now Wagner came above the horizon, and German opera began to mean Wagner. So we find "Tannhäuser" and "Lohengrin" in New York in 1859, — quite inadequate performances according to the opinion handed down to posterity, — but yet, performances. They were followed in 1862 by "Der Fliegende Holländer," all worthy but inadequate efforts. Maretzek and Strakosch were the chief figures in grand opera during this period, but there were spasmodic efforts by others which need not be recorded.

Pianists were not so numerous as later. Alfred Jaell had apppeared and, in 1854, Dr. William Mason returned from Europe and established himself in New York, but was not known as one of the traveling virtuosi. He had a great influence in musical education, for many years. Anna Mehlig visited America in 1869.

In 1862 Louis M. Gottschalk, a native of New Orleans, returned to America after a brilliant career in Europe, and he appears to have been the first American to have made a career as a piano virtuoso.

Violinists were few in comparison to singers,— Miska Hauser, Pablo Sarasate, in 1850, and Camilla Urso in 1852. Then a space of twenty years without any great virtuoso.

An important matter in the musical life of America was the establishment of conservatories. There had already been the Academy of Music in Boston, which enrolled twenty-two hundred pupils the first year, but the conservatory idea appears to have developed just after the Civil War, for we find in 1865 a conservatory of music established with Oberlin College, in 1871 Illinois College at Jacksonville followed suit, and in 1873 Northwestern

University. In the meantime, in 1867, we find the Boston Conservatory, under Julius Eichberg, the New England Conservatory, under Eben Tourjée, the Cincinnati Conservatory, and the Chicago Academy of Music, which became the Chicago Musical College, — and in 1877, a couple of years after this period, Syracuse University added a conservatory.

1850. Jan. 12. Mendelssohn's "Meerstille und Glückliche Fahrt" and "Capriccio Brillante," with William Scharfenberg as soloist, given by the Philharmonic Society, New York City.

1850. Jan. 19. Beethoven's Third Pianoforte Concerto given by the Musical Fund Society, Boston, with G. F. Hayter, soloist.

1850. Mar. 9. Handel's oratorio "Jephtha" given by the Musical Education Society, Boston, under G. J. Webb and Lowell Mason.

1850. Mar. 11. American début of Signora Steffanone in "Norma" at Niblo's Garden, New York City, with the Havana Company.

1850. Mar. 18. American début of Angiolina Bosio, soprano, at Niblo's Garden, New York City, in "Lucrezia Borgia" with the Havana company.

1850. Mar. 23. C. C. Perkins's "Grand Symphony" given by the Musical Fund Society, Boston.

1850. April 1. Meyerbeer's opera "L'Etoile du Nord" presented at the Opera House, New Orleans, La.

1850. April 2. Meyerbeer's opera "Il Profeta" presented at the Opera House, New Orleans, La.

1850. April 16. Verdi's opera "Attila" presented at Niblo's Garden, New York City, by the Havana Company with Fortunata Tedesco, Corradi-Setti, Marini and Lorini.

1850. April 24. Verdi's opera "Macbeth" presented at Niblo's Garden, New York City, with Bosio and Badiali in the leading parts.

1850. June 24. Meyerbeer's opera "Les Huguenots" presented in New York City, by the Havana Company. (See New Orleans April 29, 1839.)

1850. Sept. 11. American début of Jenny Lind (in concert) at the Castle Garden, New York City. Her first selection was "Casta Diva" from "Norma."

1850. Oct. 24. First concert of the Chicago Philharmonic Orchestra, organized by Julius Dyhrenfurth. (On Feb. 2, 1853, the Legislature of Illinois incorporated the Society by an act entitled "An Act to Encourage the Science of Fiddling.")

1850. Nov. 4. American début of Teresa Parodi at the Astor Place Opera House, New York City, as *Norma*, under Maretzek.

1850. Nov. 22. Donizetti's opera "Parisina" presented at the Astor Place Opera House, New York City, by Maretzek, with Truffi, Forti, Rossi and Beneventano.

1850. Dec. 7. Beethoven's "Leonora Overture" No. 3, given at a concert of the Musical Fund Society, Boston. G. J. Webb conducting.

1850. Dec. 21. Mozart's Symphony in G minor given by the Musical Fund Society, Boston, at Tremont Temple, from a manuscript presented by C. C. Perkins.

1850. First performance of grand opera in Chicago given during this season, — "La Sonnambula," with Elisa Brienti, Manvers and Giubelei in the leading parts.

1850. Miska Hauser and Pablo Sarasate, noted violinists, made their first American tours.

1850. Worcester (Mass.) Festival Association organized. Reorganized in 1866, and chartered in 1872.

1851. Jan. 3. Production of Maurice Strakosch's opera "Giovanni di Napoli" at the Astor Place Opera House, New York City.

1851. Jan. 11. Schubert's Symphony in C major given by the Philharmonic Society, New York City. Th. Eisfeld conducting.

1851. Sept. 23. American début of Catherine Hayes, noted singer, at a concert in Tripler Hall, New York City.

ANNALS OF MUSIC IN AMERICA

1851. Nov. 15. Mendelssohn's "Italian Symphony" given at a concert of the Musical Fund Society in Tremont Temple, Boston. G. J. Webb conducting.

1851. Dec. 7. American operatic début of Marietta Alboni, great contralto, in "La Cenerentola," with Sangiovanni, Barili and Rovere at the Astor Place Opera House, New York City. She had appeared in concert at Tripler Hall, June 23.

1852. April 17. Mendelssohn's Pianoforte Concerto in D minor, given by the Philharmonic Society, New York City, with W. Scharfenberg as soloist.

1852. Oct. 15. American début of Alfred Jaell, noted pianist, at Tripler Hall, New York City.

1852. Oct. 27. Verdi's opera "Luisa Miller" presented at the Chestnut St. Theatre, Philadelphia, with Caroline Richings and Madame Bishop in the leading parts.

1852. Oct. 29. Camilla Urso, noted violinist, made her American début at a concert in Tripler Hall, New York City.

1852. Nov. 1. Flotow's opera "Martha" given in New York City, with Madame Anna Bishop in the title-rôle, under direction of Bochsa.

1852. Nov. 13. Gade's "Ossian Overture" given by the Philharmonic Society, New York City.

1852. Nov. 20. Music Hall, Boston, dedicated with a concert given by the Handel and Haydn Society and the Musical Fund Society combined.

1852. Dec. 12. Gade's First Symphony (E minor) given by the Germania Orchestra in Boston.

1852–1859. Chicago Männergesang-Verein.

1852–1881. Dwight's Journal of Music, Boston. The first American Musical Journal.

1853. Jan. 1. Haydn's Eighth Symphony given by the Musical Fund Society, Boston. F. Suck conducting.

1853. Jan. 10. American début of Henrietta Sontag, noted soprano, in "La Figlia del Reggimento" supported by Badiali and Pozzolini, at Niblo's Garden, New York City.

1853. Jan. 12. American début of Signor Rocco, famous buffo.

1853. June. First performance of a symphony in Chicago, — Beethoven's Second, given by the Germania Orchestra.

1853. Sept. 26. First concert given by Louis A. Jullien, in New York City, beginning an American tour. During the visit of Jullien and his band they produced the following works of William H. Frye: "Christmas, or Santa Claus," "The Breaking Heart," "Childe Harold," and "A Day in the Country."

1853. Nov. 19. Wagner's overture to "Rienzi" played, from MS. by the Germania Orchestra in Boston.

1853. Nov. 22. Beethoven's Violin Concerto (first movement only) played in Boston, with August Fries as soloist. (Complete work given in 1859 with Julius Eichberg, soloist.)

1853. Nov. 26. Spohr's ninth symphony, "The Seasons," given by the Philharmonic Society, New York City.

1853. The first performance of Italian opera in San Francisco, Cal., was given this season by Madame Thillon, — "Ernani."

1853. Louis Moreau Gottschalk, the first American pianist of international renown, returned to America and began concert touring. In three seasons he gave more than 1100 concerts.

1853. The pianoforte manufacturing house of Steinway and Sons established in New York City.

1854. Jan. 14. Schumann's Second Symphony (C major) given by the Philharmonic Society, New York City.

1854. Feb. 4. Beethoven's Fourth Pianoforte Concerto (B flat) given by the Germania Orchestra in Boston with Robert Heller as soloist.

1854. Mar. 4. Beethoven's Fifth Pianoforte Concerto (E flat) given by the Germania Orchestra in Boston, with Robert Heller as soloist.

1854. April 22. F. Schneider's Twentieth Symphony given by the Philharmonic Society, New York City.

1854. Oct. 2. Opening of the Academy of Music, New York City. A performance of "Norma," with Grisi and Mario in the leading rôles. They had previously made their American débuts in "Lucrezia Borgia" at Castle Garden under Hackett's management. (The Academy of Music was the home of opera until 1866, and was frequently used for this purpose until 1896.)

1854. Oct. 9. Louisa Pyne, noted English singer, made her American début as *Amina* in "La Sonnambula," at the Broadway Theatre, New York City.

1854–1910. William H. Sherwood, noted American pianist and teacher.

1855. Feb. 13. American début of Madame F. Vestvali, as *Arsace* at the Metropolitan Theatre, New York City, with Grisi and Mario.

1855. Feb. 17. Haydn's Fifth Symphony given by the Musical Fund Society, Boston, and together with the Handel and Haydn Society, C. C. Perkins's "The Pilgrims' Cantata."

1855. Mar. 12. American début of Luigi Brignoli, Italian operatic tenor, as *Edgardo* in "Lucia di Lammermoor" supported by Vestvali, Amodio and Rocco, — in New York City.

1855. April 30. Verdi's opera "Il Trovatore" presented in New York City, with Vestvali, Steffanone, Brignoli and Amodio, at the Academy of Music.

1855. May 8. American début of Madame Anna de la Grange in "Il Barbiere" at the Academy of Music, New York City.

1855. Sept. 27. Production of George Bristow's opera "Rip van Winkle" at Niblo's Garden, New York City, by the Pyne and Harrison Opera Company.

1855. Oct. 1. American début of Madame Nantier-Didiér as *Arsace* in "Semiramide" at the Academy of Music, New York City.

1855. Oct. 6. The first attempt at German opera made in New York City, at Niblo's Garden, under Julius Ungher. "Der Freyschütz," "Martha," "Masaniello," and "Czar und Zimmerman" were presented by a company including Carolina Lehman, Madame d'Ormy, Madame Seidenberg, Schraubstadter, Quint and Vineke.

1855. Oct. 30. Rossini's opera "Semiramide" presented by Maretzek at the Academy of Music, New York City.

1855. Nov. 18. Handel's oratorio "Solomon" given by the Handel and Haydn Society, Boston.

1855. Dec. 8. An American oratorio "The Cities of the

Plain," by F. T. S. Darley, produced by the Harmonia Sacred Music Society in Philadelphia.

1855–1863. Philharmonic Society, Boston, Carl Zerrahn, conductor.

1855–6. Sigismund Thalberg, noted pianist, and Henri Vieuxtemps, great violinist, made a concert-tour in America.

1856. Mar. 17. Adelaide Phillips, noted contralto, made her operatic (American) début as *Azucena* in "Il Trovatore," in New York City.

1856. Oct. Flotow's opera "Stradella" presented at Niblo's Garden, New York City.

1856. Dec. 3. Verdi's opera "La Traviata" presented at the Academy of Music, New York City, with Madame de la Grange, Brignoli and Amodio.

1856. Dec. 29. Beethoven's opera "Fidelio" presented in German at the Broadway Theatre, New York City, when Mademoiselle Johansen made her American début in the title rôle. (Ritter states that this opera was given in English by the Seguin Company on Sept. 9, 1856 — the first representation in America.)

1856. The Academy of Music in Philadelphia opened.

1856. The Cecilia Society and Harmonic Society organized in Cincinnati, O.

1856–7. During this season an orchestra, under Carl Bergmann, giving concerts at the City Assembly rooms, New York City, is said to have performed for the first time in America:
Beethoven's Seventh Symphony — in A.
Mozart's Symphony in D major.
Haydn's Symphony in G major (see 1843, Jan. 7).
Beethoven's Pianoforte Concertos in E flat and G.

1857. Jan. 3. Wagner's "Faust Overture" given by the Philharmonic Society, Boston, Carl Zerrahn, conductor.

1857. Jan. 18. Mozart's "Requiem" given by the Handel and Haydn Society in Boston.

1857. Jan. 21. Strakosch appointed manager of the Academy of Music, New York City.

1857. Jan. 24. Berlioz's "Roman Carnival" overture given by the Philharmonic Society, New York City.

1857. Feb. 7. Schumann's Symphony in D given by the Philharmonic Society, New York City.

1857. Feb. 23. American début of Marietta Gazzaniga as *Leonora* in "Il Trovatore" at the Academy of Music, Philadelphia. She appeared in New York City as *Violetta* in "La Traviata" on April 13.

1857. Nov. 2. Début of Madame d'Angri as *Arsace* in "Semiramide" at Castle Garden, New York City.

1857. Nov. 19. Wagner's overture to "Lohengrin" given by the Philharmonic Society, New York City.

1857. Nov. 21. Schumann's "Manfred Overture" given by the Philharmonic Society, New York City.

1857. Nov. 30. American début of Carl Formes, noted German basso, as *Bertram* in "Roberto," at the Academy of Music, New York City.

1857. Dec. 30. American début of Madame Anna Caradori, as *Fidelio*, at the Academy of Music, New York City.

1857–65. Chicago Musical Union. C. M. Cady, conductor.

1857. An orchestra was established in Brooklyn, N. Y., with Theodore Eisfeld as conductor. It is claimed that this orchestra introduced to America Beethoven's Third and Seventh Symphonies, and Mendelssohn's Fourth.

1858. Jan. 9. Nicolai's overture to "The Merry Wives of Windsor" given by the Philharmonic Society, New York City.

1858. Mar. 6. Hiller's Symphony in F, given by the Philharmonic Society, New York City.

1858. April 24. Schumann's Overture, Scherzo and Finale given by the Philharmonic Society, New York City.

1858. Oct. 20. American début of Maria Piccolomini, noted soprano, as *Violetta*, in "La Traviata" at the Academy of Music, New York City.

1858. Nov. 1. During a season of opera begun on this date and ended Jan. 30, 1859, the following operas were presented in New Orleans, La., probably for the first time in America:
Ambroise Thomas' "Le Caid."
Donizetti's "La Favorita."
Halévy's "Jaquarita l'Indienne."

Grisar's "Les Amours du Diable."
Adam's "Châlet" and "Si J'Etais Roy."
Halévy's "La Juive."
Auber's "Les Diamans de Couronne."
Halévy's "Reine de Chypre."

1858. Nov. 23. Mozart's opera "Nozze di Figaro" presented in Italian at the Academy of Music, New York City, with Carl Formes as *Figaro*, supported by Madame von Berkel, Ghioni, Piccolomini, etc.

1858. The Mendelssohn Quintet organized in Boston — August Fries, first violin, Francis Riha, second violin, Edward Lehman, viola and flute, Thomas Ryan, viola and clarinet, Wulf Fries, violoncello. This was a pioneer organization in Chamber Music, and traveled extensively for many years.

1858. The French Opera Company from New Orleans appeared in Chicago.

1859. Feb. 26. Mozart's Pianoforte Concerto in E flat major given at the Philharmonic concerts, Boston, with B. J. Lang as soloist.

1859. Mar. 26. Schumann's Pianoforte Concerto in A minor (Op. 54) given by the Philharmonic Society, New York City, with S. B. Mills as soloist.

1859. Mar. 26. Beethoven's music to Goethe's drama "Egmont" given entire at the Philharmonic Concerts, Boston, with readings from the drama by Mrs. Barrow.

1859. April 4. Wagner's opera "Tannhäuser" presented at the Stadt Theatre, New York City, under Carl Bergmann, with Madame Seidenburg as *Elizabeth*, Pickaneser as *Tannhäuser*, Lehmann as *Wolfram*, and the Arion Society as chorus.

1859. April 30. Liszt's symphonic poem "Les Préludes" given by the Philharmonic Society, New York City.

1859. May 25. Donizetti's opera "Il Poliuto" presented at the Academy of Music, New York City, with Piccolomini, Brignoli, Barili.

1859. Aug. 27. Wagner's opera "Lohengrin" presented at the Stadt Theatre, New York City, under Carl Bergmann, with Seidenberg, Pickaneser and Lehmann.

ANNALS OF MUSIC IN AMERICA

1859. Nov. 7. Verdi's opera "I Vespri Sicilienne" presented at the Academy of Music, New York City, with Brignoli and Colson.

1859. Nov. 24. Operatic début of Adelina Patti at the Academy of Music, New York City, as *Lucia*, supported by Brignoli.

1859. New French Opera House built in New Orleans, La.

1859. Patrick Sarsfield Gilmore organized his noted band in Boston, Mass.

1860. Jan. 14. Spohr's Double Symphony, for two orchestras, given in Boston.

1860. Jan. 27. Rossini's opera "Otello" presented in New Orleans, La.

1860. Feb. 11. Lachner's "Festival Overture" given by the Philharmonic Society, New York City.

1860. Mar. 3. Mendelssohn's overture "Die Weihe des Hauses" given by the Philharmonic Society in Boston, Carl Zerrahn conducting.

1860. Mar. 3. Liszt's seventh symphonic poem, "Fest-Klänge," given by the Philharmonic Society, New York City.

1860. Mar. 19. Verdi's opera "Rigoletto" presented in New Orleans, La.

1860. Mar. 24. Liszt's symphonic poem "Tasso" given by the Philharmonic Society, New York City.

1860. May 31. Verdi's opera "I Masnadieri" presented by Maretzek at the Academy of Music, New York City, with Oliviera, Guerra and Luisia.

1860. Sept. 19. American début of Pauline Colson in "I Vespri Sicilienne" at the Academy of Music, New York City.

1860. Sept. 27. Pacini's opera "Medea" presented at Niblo's Garden, New York City.

1860–1868. Chicago Philharmonic Society (reorganized) under Hans Balatka.

1860. An Oratorio Society organized by R. Herold in San Francisco, Cal.

1860–1861. The Briggs House Concerts given in Chicago — the first Chamber Music Concerts in that city. Henri de Clerque, first violin; Buderbach, violoncello; Paul Becker, piano.

1861. Jan. 9. Liszt's symphonic poem "Ce qu'on entend sur le Montagne" given by the Philharmonic Society in New York City.

1861. Jan. 23. American début of Isabella Hinkley as *Lucia* at the Academy of Music, New York City, supported by Steffani, Coletti.

1861. Feb. 3. Schumann's Third Symphony (E flat major) given by the Philharmonic Society, New York City.

1861. Feb. 11. Verdi's opera "Un Ballo in Maschera" given at the Academy of Music, New York City, with Colson, Adelaide Phillips, Hinckley, Brignoli, Ferri.

1861. Feb. 27. American début of Clara Louise Kellogg as *Gilda* in "Rigoletto" at the Academy of Music, New York City, under Grau and de Vivo.

1861. Mar. 16. Mozart's Eighth Pianoforte Concerto (in D) given by the Philharmonic Society, New York City, with Richard Hoffman, as soloist.

1861. April 20. Mendelssohn's "First Walpurgis Night" given by the Philharmonic Society, New York City.

1861. Masse's opera "Les Nôces de Jeanette" with Kellogg, Elena, Mancini, Debreuil, given at the Academy of Music, Philadelphia, Pa., also Donizetti's "Betley," with Miss Hinkley, Brignoli, Lusini.

1861. Nov. 9. Chopin's Second Pianoforte Concerto given by the Philharmonic Society, New York City, with S. B. Mills as soloist.

1861–1908. Edward MacDowell. Noted American pianist, composer and teacher.

1862. Jan. 30. Mendelssohn's "Hymn of Praise" given in the Old South Church, Boston, under the direction of B. J. Lang.

1862. Mar. 8. Schubert's "Grand Fantasia" given by William Mason at a concert of the Philharmonic Society, Boston.

1862. May 13. Music of Wagner's opera "Der Fliegende Holländer" given at Irving Hall, New York City, under the direction of Theodore Thomas.

1862. Sept. 18. Auber's "Grand Inauguration March" given at a concert in New York City, by Theodore Thomas.

ANNALS OF MUSIC IN AMERICA

1862. Sept. 22. Operatic début of Carlotta Patti as *Amina* in "La Sonnambula," supported by Miss Stockton, Sbriglia and Susini, in New York City.

1862. Oct. 10. Mozart's opera "Entführung aus dem Serail" presented in New York City, at Wallack's Theatre, under the direction of Carl Anschutz.

1862. Nov. 24. Meyerbeer's opera "Dinorah" presented in New York City.

1862. Teresa Carreño, great Venezuelan pianist, first appeared in New York City, as a child pianist.

1862–1901. Ethelbert Nevin. Song composer.

1863. Mar. 7. Berlioz's "Corsair Overture" given in New York City, by Theodore Thomas.

1863. April 6. Petrella's opera "Ione" presented at the Academy of Music, New York City, with Medori, Sulzer, Mazzolini, and Bellini, under Maretzek.

1863. April 15. Verdi's opera "I duo Foscari" presented at the Academy of Music, New York City, with Medori, Mazzolini, Bellini and Coletti, under Maretzek.

1863. April. William H. Fry's opera "Notre Dame de Paris" produced at the Academy of Music, Philadelphia.

1863. May 4. Verdi's opera "Aroldo" presented at the Academy of Music, New York City, under Maretzek, with Mazzolini, Bellini and Coletti.

1863. Nov. 2. Inauguration of the great organ in Music Hall, Boston, when Charlotte Cushman, Lyman Wheeler, and Mrs. J. F. Houston took leading parts in the ceremonies.

1863. Nov. 7. Ferdinand Hiller's Second Pianoforte Concerto (in A) given by the Philharmonic Society, New York City.

1863. Nov. 11. Peri's opera "Judith" presented at the Academy of Music, New York City, by Maretzek, with Medori, Mazzolini, Bellini and Biachi.

1863. Weber's opera "Euryanthe" said to have been presented at Wallack's Theatre, New York, by Carl Anschutz.

1863. Nov. 18. Gounod's opera "Faust" presented at the Academy of Music, Philadelphia, by the German Opera Company. Was given in New York, Nov. 26.

1863–1872. The Mendelssohn Society, New York City.

1864. Jan. 30. Liszt's "Faust Symphony" (F minor) given by the Philharmonic Society, New York City, assisted by the Arion Society.

1864. The first complete performance of Haydn's oratorio, "The Seasons" given in Boston, under the direction of B. J. Lang.

1864. Nov. 4. American début of Jennie van Zandt, as *Gilda* in "Rigoletto" at the Academy of Music, New York City.

1864. Nov. 25. Donizetti's opera "Don Sebastian" presented at the Academy of Music, New York City.

1864. Dec. 3. Lachner's Suite in D minor given by Theodore Thomas, in New York City, also the second part of Berlioz' dramatic symphony "Romeo et Juliette."

1864. Great Band Festival in New Orleans, La., under P. S. Gilmore.

1865. Jan. 13. Bach's Toccata in F given in New York City by Theodore Thomas.

1865. Feb. 18. Raff's symphony "An das Vaterland," and Beethoven's Triple Concerto, for piano, violin and cello, given in New York City by Theodore Thomas.

1865. Feb. 18. Beethoven's Second Pianoforte Concerto (B flat) given by the Brooklyn Philharmonic Society.

1865. Feb. 24. Verdi's opera "La Forza del Destino" presented in New York City, with Carozzi-Zucchi, Massimiliani and Bellini.

1865. Mar. 4. Hohnstock's overture, "Hail Columbia," given by Theodore Thomas in Brooklyn, N. Y.

1865. Mar. 11. Haydn's First Symphony (E flat) given by the Philharmonic Society, New York City.

1865. April 8. Mozart's Symphony Concertante for violin and viola, — Bach's Passacaglia, — and Schumann's overture to "Die Braut von Messina" given in New York City by Theodore Thomas.

1865. April 20. Crosby Opera House in Chicago, dedicated. Performances were given there by a company brought by Jacob Grau and including Clara Louise Kellogg and Zucchi, sopranos; Morensi, Fischer and Zapucci, contraltos; Massimiliani, Mazzolini and Lotti, tenors; Bellini, Orlan-

ANNALS OF MUSIC IN AMERICA

dini, Lorini and Debreuil, baritones; Susini, Colletti, Muller, Perni and Ximenes, basses, and Carl Bergmann, conductor.

1865. Sept. 11. First appearance in America (in concert) of Madame Parepa-Rosa, at Steinway Hall, New York City.

1865. Nov. 11. Liszt's symphonic poem "Mazeppa" given by Theodore Thomas, in New York City.

1865. Dec. 1. Meyerbeer's opera "L'Africaine" given at the Academy of Music, New York City, with Carozzi-Zuecchi as *Selika* and Mazzoni as *Vasco da Gama*. Carl Bergmann, conductor.

1865. Dec. 2. Liszt's Pianoforte Concerto in E flat given in New York City, under Theodore Thomas.

1865. Dec. 28. The first concert of the Harvard Musical Association in Boston. Mozart's Symphony in G minor was performed.

1865. Germania Männerchor organized in Chicago, Ill.

1865. Peabody Institute Concerts established in Baltimore, Md.

1865. Conservatory of Music opened in connection with Oberlin College (Ohio) which was founded in 1834.

1865. Opera given in San Francisco, Cal., by a company including Morelli, Barilli, Sbriglia and Adelaide Phillips. Twenty-four operas were presented.

1866. Jan. 13. Beethoven's Choral Fantasia, and Bargiel's Symphony in C, given in New York City, by Theodore Thomas.

1866. Jan. 27. Berlioz' "Fantastic Symphony" given by the Philharmonic Society, New York City.

1866. Feb. 10. Mozart's Concerto in E flat, for two pianos, and Weber's "Invitation to the Dance" given by Theodore Thomas, in New York City.

1866. Feb. 28. Cherubini's overture to "Anacreon" given in Boston, by the Harvard Musical Association.

1866. Mar. 1. Schumann's overture to "Genoveva" given in Boston, by the Harvard Musical Association.

1866. Mar. 10. Introduction to Wagner's opera "Tristan und Isolde" given by the Philharmonic Society, New York City.

1866. Mar. 22. Schubert's overture to "Fierabras" given by the Harvard Musical Association, in Boston.

1866. Aug. 29. Mozart's Andante, Variations, and Minuetto, and his "Turkish March" given by Theodore Thomas, in New York City.

1866. Oct. 13. Minnie Hauck, noted American soprano, made her début in "L'Etoile du Nord" at the Academy of Music, New York City, before going to Europe.

1866. Oct. 20. Vorspiel to Wagner's opera "Die Meistersinger" given by Theodore Thomas, in New York City.

1866. Oct. 27. J. J. Abert's First Symphony, and Schubert's "Reiter March" given by Theodore Thomas, in Brooklyn, N. Y.

1866. Nov. 17. Liszt's "Nachtlicher Zug," from "Faust," given by the Philharmonic Society, New York City, and "Bristow's "Columbus Overture" produced at the same concert.

1866. Dec. 2. Beethoven's Overture in C (Opus III), and Grimm's Suite in Canon Form given in New York City, by Theodore Thomas.

1866. Dec. 8. Liszt's "Mephisto Waltz" given in Brooklyn, N. Y., by Theodore Thomas.

1866. The Summer Night Concerts at Terrace Gardens, New York City, were inaugurated this year, by Theodore Thomas.

1867. Jan. 12. Raff's Suite in C (Opus 101) given in New York City, by Theodore Thomas.

1867. Jan. 19. Berlioz's "Romeo et Juliette" overture given by the Brooklyn Philharmonic Society, under Theodore Thomas.

1867. Feb. 7. Handel's oratorio "Jephtha" given by the Handel and Haydn Society, in Boston.

1867. Mar. 13. Entr'acte from Schubert's "Rosamunde" given in New York City, by Theodore Thomas.

1867. Mar. 18. American operatic début of Euphrosyne Parepa-Rosa, great soprano, in "Il Trovatore" at the Academy of Music, New York City.

1867. April 3. Petrella's opera "Il Carnival di Venezia" presented at the Academy of Music, New York City.

1867. April 3. Molique's Concerto for Violoncello given by the Philharmonic Society, Brooklyn, N. Y., under Theodore Thomas.

ANNALS OF MUSIC IN AMERICA

1867. July 1. J. Strauss's "Blue Danube" waltz, and the ballet music from Gounod's opera "The Queen of Sheba," given by Theodore Thomas, in New York City.

1867. July 5. Liszt's march "Vom Fels zum Meer" given by Theodore Thomas, and on the 7th Strauss's waltz "From the Mountains," and the overture to Schubert's "Rosamunde," in New York City.

1867. July 14. J. Strauss's "Bürgesin" and polka mazurka "Lob der Frauen" given in New York City, by Theodore Thomas.

1867. Aug. 13. Schumann's "Träumerei" given for the first time in America by Theodore Thomas, in New York City.

1867. Oct. 7. Bach's Third Suite, in D, given by Theodore Thomas, in New York City.

1867. Oct. 26. Schubert's "Unfinished Symphony" given in New York City, by Theodore Thomas.

1867. Nov. 9. Mendelssohn's "Trumpet Overture"; Haydn's theme and variations on "Kaiser Franz Hymn"; and Berlioz's overture to "Benvenuto Cellini" given by the Brooklyn Philharmonic Society, Theodore Thomas conducting.

1867. Nov. 21. Cherubini's overture to "Medea" given in Boston, by the Harvard Musical Association.

1867. Dec. 14. Gounod's opera "Romeo et Juliette" presented at the Academy of Music, New York City, by Maretzek, with Minne Hauck as *Juliette*.

1867. Dec. 14. Vieuxtemps's Violin Concerto in D given by the Brooklyn Philharmonic Society, with Camilla Urso as soloist.

1867. Dec. 15. Beethoven's "Prometheus" music given by Theodore Thomas, in New York City.

1867. Dec. 21. Ritter's overture to "Othello" given in New York City, by the Philharmonic Society.

1867. French Opera Bouffe introduced to New York City, by F. L. Bateman, at the French Theatre, where Offenbach's "La Grande Duchesse" ran for 180 nights.

1867. In this year the following Conservatories of Music were established:

The Boston Conservatory, Julius Eichberg, director, Boston, Mass.

The New England Conservatory, Eben Tourjée, director, Boston, Mass.

The Cincinnati Conservatory, Clara Bauer, director, Cincinnati, O.

The Chicago Academy of Music, Dr. F. Ziegfeld, director, Chicago, Ill. (Later known as the Chicago Musical College.)

1868. Jan. 11. Liszt's symphonic poem "Die Ideale" given by Theodore Thomas, in New York City.

1868. Jan. 25. C. C. Converse's "Festival Overture" produced by the Brooklyn Philharmonic Society.

1868. April 13. Gade's cantata "The Crusaders" given by the Parker Club, in Boston, J. C. D. Parker, conductor.

1868. April 18. Liszt's symphonic poem "Héroïde Funébre" given in New York City.

1868. May. 24. Reinecke's overture "King Manfred" given in New York City, by Theodore Thomas.

1868. Oct. 21. Handel's "Royal Fireworks" music given in New York City, by Theodore Thomas.

1868. Nov. 11. Salem (Mass.) Oratorio Society founded. Carl Zerrahn was elected as conductor at a later meeting.

1868. Nov. 28. Gade's overture "Hamlet" given by the Philharmonic Society, New York City.

1868. Dec. 4. Haydn's Symphony in B flat given in Boston, by the Harvard Musical Association.

1868. Dec. 10. Joachim's "Hungarian Concerto" for violin given by the Harvard Musical Association, in Boston, with B. Listemann as soloist.

1868. Dec. 12. Schubert's Twenty-third Psalm, also Mozart's First, Second, and Third Motets given in New York City, by Theodore Thomas.

1868. Bruch's First Violin Concerto (G minor) given at a concert of a New York Conservatory, with Richard Arnold as soloist.

1868. Theodore Thomas established his Symphony Orchestra in New York City.

ANNALS OF MUSIC IN AMERICA

1869. Jan. 9. Catel's overture to "Semiramide" given by the Philharmonic Society, New York City.

1869. Jan. 16. Rubinstein's musical portrait "Faust," and Gade's "Spring Fantasia" given in New York City, by Theodore Thomas.

1869. Feb. 6. Mendelssohn's "Reformation" Symphony, and Schubert's Symphony in B minor, given by the Philharmonic Society, in New York City.

1869. Feb. 11. Barnett's cantata "The Ancient Mariner" given under Mr. Sharland, at the Mt. Pleasant Congregational Church, Roxbury, Mass.

1869. Feb. 18. Gade's Second Symphony (in E) given by the Harvard Musical Association, in Boston.

1869. Mar. 13. Max Bruch's Symphony in E flat given by Theodore Thomas, in New York City.

1869. April 3. Singer's Fantasia for Pianoforte and Orchestra; Volkmann's "Festival Overture," and Liszt's symphonic poem "Prometheus" given by Theodore Thomas, in New York City.

1869. May 8. Schumann's "Manfred" music given by the Philharmonic Society, New York City, with Edwin Booth as reader.

1869. May. 12. Schubert's "Italian Overture" given by Theodore Thomas, in New York City.

1869. June 15. First concert of the Peace Jubilee in Boston.

1869. July 20. Strauss's waltz "Wein, Weib, und Gesang" given in New York City, by Theodore Thomas.

1869. Dec. 2. Anna Mehlig, noted pianist, visited America and played at Miss Porter's School, Farmington, Conn. She appeared on Dec. 18, at the Brooklyn Academy of Music.

1869. Dec. 15. A season of six nights of Russian opera begun at the Théâtre Française, New York City, under Leon Jasievitch, with Levitzkaya as leading soprano, and Dimitri d'Agreneff, tenor. The opera "Askold's Tomb" was given.

1869. Dec. 30. Haydn's Fifth Symphony (in D) given by the Harvard Musical Association, in Boston.

1869. First of twenty-two annual tours made this season by the Theodore Thomas Orchestra.

1869–1874. Church Music Association, New York City. The first performance in America of Beethoven's Mass in D was given by this Association.

1870. Jan. 8. Raff's Second Symphony (in C) given by the Philharmonic Society, New York City.

1870. Jan. 22. A Russian Male Choir of nine voices, under Dimitri Agreneff Slaviansky, visited America.

1870. Feb. 17. Mozart's Second Pianoforte Concerto (D minor) given by the Harvard Musical Association in Boston.

1870. Feb. 28. Mendelssohn's overture to "Ruy Blas" given in Boston.

1870. May 7. Selections from Wagner's "Die Meistersinger" played by the Philharmonic Society, New York City.

1870. May. 9. Liszt's "Goethe March" given in New York City, by Theodore Thomas.

1870. May 26. Dargomysky's "Cosatchague" given by Theodore Thomas, at the Central Park Garden, New York City. (Selections from opera.)

1870. July 14. Glinka's "Jota Aragonese" given by Theodore Thomas, at Central Park Garden, New York City, and

1870. Aug. 25. Glinka's "Kamarinskaja."

1870. Sept. 19. American début of Christine Nilsson, noted soprano, at a concert in Steinway Hall, New York City. Her operatic début took place Oct. 25, 1871, at the Academy of Music, as *Lucia*, under Carl Rosa.

1870. Nov. 12. Mozart's opera "Der Schauspieldirektor" given in New York City.

1870. Marie Krebs, noted German pianist, visited America.

1871. Jan. 5. Karl Goldmark's overture to "Sakuntala" given by the Harvard Musical Association, in Boston.

1871. Jan. 7. Rubinstein's "Ocean Symphony" given by the Philharmonic Society, New York City.

1871. Feb. 23. Gade's Third Symphony (A minor) given by the Harvard Musical Association, Boston.

1871. May 3. Rossini's "Messe Solennelle" given in Boston, under the direction of George W. Whiting.

1871. May. 7. Mozart's overture to "Idomeneo" given by the Philharmonic Society, New York City.

1871. June 13. Reinecke's "Festival Overture,"
1871. June 22. Wagner's "Kaiser March," and
1871. June 27. Joachim's First March (in C) given by Theodore Thomas, in New York City.
1871. July 19. Rubinstein's overture to "Dimitri Donskoi,"
1871. July 21. Joachim's Second March (in D) given by Theodore Thomas, in New York City.
1871. Aug. 10. Rheinberger's "Wallenstein's Camp,"
1871. Aug. 17. Schubert's March in B minor,
1871. Sept. 8. Wagner's "Hildegung's March," given by Theodore Thomas, in New York City.
1871. Sept. 18. American début of the noted German tenor, Theodore Wachtel, at the Stadt Theatre, New York City, in "Le Postillon de Longjumeau."
1871. Nov. 9. Schubert's overture to "Alfonso and Estrella" given by the Harvard Musical Association, in Boston.
1871. Nov. 22. Ambroise Thomas's opera "Mignon" given at the Academy of Music, New York City, with Christine Nilsson in the title-rôle.
1871. Nov. 23. Mozart's Symphony in C given by the Harvard Musical Association; also Handel's Concerto for oboe, with A. Kugler as soloist, in Boston.
1871. Dec. 2. Rubinstein's Pianoforte Concerto in D minor given in Boston, by Theodore Thomas Orchestra, with Marie Krebs as soloist.
1871. Dec. 6. Introduction and final scene from Wagner's opera "Tristan und Isolde"; also Raff's Symphony in F, given by Theodore Thomas in Boston.
1871. Dec. 7. Haydn's Third Symphony (E flat) given by the Harvard Musical Association, in Boston.
1871. The Illinois College Conservatory of Music, Jacksonville, Ill., established, with I. B. Posnawski as director.
1871. The Apollo Club (male voices) established in Boston with B. J. Lang as conductor.
1872. Jan. 6. Reinecke's Pianoforte Concerto in F sharp minor (Op. 72) given by the Philharmonic Society, New York City, with S. B. Mills as soloist.
1872. Jan. 20. Cherubini's opera "Les Deux Journées" (The

Water Carriers) presented in Boston, by Madame Parepa-Rosa and her company. First New York performance was Feb. 10.

1872. Jan. 20. Liszt's symphonic poem "Orpheus" given in New York City, by Theodore Thomas.

1872. Feb. 1. Haydn's "Oxford Symphony" (in G) given by the Harvard Musical Association, in Boston.

1872. Feb. 14. American début of Charles Santley, noted English baritone, in "Zampa" at New York City.

1872. Feb. 23. Gade's Third Concert Overture given in Boston, by the Harvard Musical Association.

1872. Mar. 7. Taubert's "Arabian Nights" overture; and Mozart's Seventh Pianoforte Concerto (C minor) with Hugo Leonhard as soloist, given by the Harvard Musical Association, in Boston.

1872. Mar. 22. Ambroise Thomas's opera "Hamlet" presented in New York City, with Christine Nilsson as *Ophelia*, Annie Louise Cary as *The Queen*, Brignoli as *Laertes*, A. Barre as *Hamlet*, Coletti as *The Ghost*, Reichardt as *Horatio*, and Locatelli as *Polonius*.

1872. May 30. Rubinstein's humoresque "Don Quixote," given in New York City, by Theodore Thomas.

1872. Aug. 1. Raff's overture to "Dame Kobold," and

1872. Sept. 17. Wagner's "Ride of the Valkyries" given by Theodore Thomas, in New York City.

1872. Sept. 23. Anton Rubinstein, great Russian pianist, and Henri Wieniawski, noted violinist, made their American début at Steinway Hall, New York City, and then toured the country.

1872. Sept. 30. American début of Pauline Lucca, noted soprano, as *Selika* in "L'Africaine" at the Academy of Music, New York City, under Maretzek.

1872. Nov. 22. Ambroise Thomas's opera "Mignon" presented at the Academy of Music, New York City, with Christine Nilsson and Capoul in the leading parts.

1872. Dec. 3. Liszt's eleventh symphonic poem, "The Battle of the Huns" (Hunnenschlacht), given at a concert in Boston, by Theodore Thomas.

1872. Dec. 14. Raff's Fourth Symphony (in G) given by the Philharmonic Society, New York City.

1872. Second Peace Jubilee held in Boston.

1872. Orpheus Club (male chorus) formed in Philadelphia.

1872. Emil Sauret, noted French violinist, made his first concert tour in America.

1873. Jan. 9. Cherubini's overture to "Ali Baba" played in Boston.

1873. Jan. 18. Liszt's "Hirtengesang" from "Christus" given by the Philharmonic Society, New York City.

1873. Jan. 21. First concert of the Apollo Club of Chicago, given at Standard Hall. The club was organized Sept. 1872, with George P. Upton, president, and Silas Pratt, conductor.

1873. Feb. 15. Gade's Eighth Symphony (B minor) given by the Philharmonic Society, New York City.

1873. Mar. 13. Mozart's Pianoforte Concerto in A given by the Harvard Musical Association, in Boston.

1873. May 22. J. O. Grimm's Second Suite in Canon Form given by Theodore Thomas, in New York City.

1873. May 29. Brahm's Serenade in D given by Theodore Thomas, in New York City.

1873. June 3. Production of John K. Paine's oratorio "St. Peter" at Portland, Me., with Emma Thursby, Adelaide Phillips, George Osgood, and Rudolphson as soloists.

1873. June 12. Svensden's First Symphony (in D) given by Theodore Thomas, in New York City.

1873. Sept. 18. Svensden's symphonic overture "Sigurd Slembe" given by Theodore Thomas, in New York City, and Sept. 23, A. Hamerik's "Nordish Suite."

1873. Oct. 1. American début of Italo Campanini, great Italian tenor, as *Gennaro* in "Lucrezia Borgia," in New York City, at the Academy of Music.

1873. Oct. 3. American début of Victor Maurel, great French baritone, as *Valentine* in "Faust" at the Academy of Music, New York City.

1873. Oct. 7. American début of Ilma di Murska, noted Polish soprano, as *Amina* in "La Sonnambula" at the Grand Opera House, New York City, under Strakosch.

1873. Nov. 6. W. Sterndale Bennett's Pianoforte Concerto in E given by the Harvard Musical Association, in Boston, with E. Perabo as soloist.

1873. Nov. 15. Max Bruch's introduction to "Loreley" given by the Philharmonic Society, New York City.

1873. Nov. 26. Verdi's opera "Aida" presented at the Academy of Music, New York City, by M. Strakosch with Torriani as *Aida*, Annie Louise Cary as *Amneris*, Campanini as *Rhadames*, Victor Maurel as *Amonasro*, Manetti as *Ramfis*, and Scolara as *The King*.

1873. Dec. 3. Raff's "Lenore Symphony" (fifth — in E) given by Theodore Thomas, in Boston.

1873. Germania Orchestra organized in Pittsburgh, Pa.

1873. A Conservatory of Music established in connection with Northwestern University, Evanston, Ill.

1873. Madame Julie Rivé-King, noted American pianist, made her début in Cincinnati, O.

1874. Jan. 10. Volkmann's Serenade in D minor given by Theodore Thomas, in Brooklyn, N. Y.

1874. Jan. 24. Rubinstein's character sketch "Ivan IV" given in New York City, by Theodore Thomas, and

1874. Jan. 28. Meyerbeer's "Inauguration March."

1874. Feb. 14. George F. Bristow's "Arcadian Symphony" given by the Philharmonic Society, New York City, also Gade's overture to "Michael Angelo."

1874. May 8. Bach's Passion Music according to St. Matthew given, in part, by the Handel and Haydn Society in Boston. Selections had been given May 13, 1871, and the work was given complete, in two concerts in 1879.

1874. May 14. Hofmann's "Hungarian Suite"; the overture to Gounod's "Le Médecin Malgré Lui"; and C. M. von Weber's overture to "Abou Hassan" given by Theodore Thomas, in New York City.

1874. May 20. Gounod's overture to "Mireille" given in New York City, by Theodore Thomas.

1874. May 21. Hiller's "Dramatic Fantasia," and Saint-Saën's "Marche Héroïque" given by Theodore Thomas, in New York City.

ANNALS OF MUSIC IN AMERICA

- 1874. July 16. Sullivan's overture to "The Tempest"; July 29, Massenet's "Scènes Pittoresques"; and July 30, Ferdinand David's "Festival March," given in New York City, by Theodore Thomas.
- 1874. Aug. 13. Reineke's "In Memoriam"; and Aug. 21, Zellner's "Die Schoene Melusine" given by Theodore Thomas, in New York City.
- 1874. Sept. 17. Rubinstein's "Ouverture Triomphale" given by Theodore Thomas, in New York City.
- 1874. Oct. 28. Grieg's Pianoforte Concerto in A minor, given at a Theodore Thomas concert in Boston, with Boskowitz as soloist.
- 1874. Nov. 14. Raff's Pianoforte Concerto, Opus 185, given by the Philharmonic Society, New York City, with Lina Luckhardt as soloist.
- 1874. Nov. 27. Bach's Suite in B minor given by Theodore Thomas, in New York City.
- 1874. Dec. 12. Bach's "Ciaconna" in D minor, arranged for orchestra by Raff, given by the Philharmonic Society, New York City.
- 1874. Madame Emmy Fursch-Madi made her American début in New Orleans, La., with the French Opera Company. She was heard in New York in 1882, and became professor of singing at the National Conservatory, New York City. Début Nov. 7, 1883, as *Ortrud* in "Lohengrin."
- 1874. Clara Louise Kellogg made her American operatic début under Maurice Grau, in New York City. (She had appeared as *Gilda* in "Rigoletto" at the Academy of Music in 1871 (Feb. 27), before going to Europe, and had concertized in the United States for four years, 1868–1872.)
- 1874. The Cecilia Society of Boston organized with B. J. Lang as conductor.

CHAPTER VI

1875 – 1890

THE period of fifteen years from 1875 to 1890 was most certainly a period of progress. Not only was the country growing rapidly in population and wealth, but means of communication were much greater and more efficient than in the preceding years. The present writer well remembers a journey from San Francisco to St. Louis, and on to Boston in 1878, when there was one single track railroad between Oakland and Omaha. Cheyenne consisted of two rows of primitive looking wooden houses, behind which were "anchored" many emigrants' wagons, or "prairie schooners" as they were called. Only a few years later (in the early eighties) Colonel Mapleson visited Cheyenne with his opera company, which included Patti and Gerster, and wrote thus of the place: "Although Cheyenne is but a little town, consisting of about two streets, it possesses a most refined society, composed, it is true, of cow-boys; yet one might have imagined oneself at the London Opera when the curtain rose, — the ladies in brilliant toilettes and covered with diamonds; the gentlemen all in evening dress. The entire little town is lighted by electricity. The clubhouse is one of the pleasantest I have ever visited, and the people are most hospitable."

This account reminds the writer of a visit, not so many years ago, to Oklahoma City where the ladies resembled those of Cheyenne. There was, however, but one gentleman, within the writer's range of vision, in evening dress. And when Mapleson visited Cheyenne Oklahoma was an Indian reservation. Thus has civilization advanced.

In 1875 San Francisco was already a good-sized city, but almost the whole country between San Francisco and Chicago and St. Louis has been developed since 1875.

In San Francisco we find the establishment of the "Loring Club" in 1877. But good music was getting its roots in deeper in the East. In New York the "Symphony Society" was founded by Dr. Leopold Damrosch in 1878, and was followed in 1881 by the "Boston Symphony Orchestra," which was established through the liberality of Major Henry L. Higginson.

"The Music Teachers' National Association" was also formed in 1876, and while it is not in the public eye in the way that opera and concerts are, yet its influence throughout the land has been very marked, and has led to state associations, with their annual conferences, and exchanges of views among teachers.

In the concert world we find the names of several celebrities,— Rubinstein had visited America in 1872, and Hans von Bülow in 1875, Moritz Rosenthal in 1888, and Godowski in 1890. We find also among the noted pianists who were first known here in this period Arabella Goddard, Rafael Joseffy, Fanny Bloomfield-Zeisler and Josef Hofmann.

Some noted violinists also visited America, August Wilhelmj in 1878, Ovide Musin, Teresina Tua, and in 1888 Fritz Kreisler. But perhaps the most noteworthy event was the appearance of Maud Powell, an American woman, whose career placed her in the front rank of violinists, and has but recently ended with her death.

Of singers there were a great many, but most of them appeared in opera. Of the Americans who gained international reputation were Emma Abbott, Alwina Valleria (of Baltimore), Lillian Nordica (Norton), Emma Nevada (Wixom), and Charles R. Adams.

Among the European celebrities who visited America were Madame Rudersdorff, Etelka Gerster, Scalchi, Marcella Sembrich, Amalia Materna, and Lilli Lehmann, also Alberto Stagno, Max Alvary, Albert Niemann, Francesco Tamagno.

This leads us to a short review of opera, and as New York City was the headquarters from which numerous companies issued to charm the rest of the country, a review of New York is practically a review of opera for the whole country.

From 1850 to 1875 opera is said to have "flourished on failure" chiefly under Maretzek and Strakosch. Also, opera meant Italian opera, or at least opera in Italian. There were spasmodic efforts to promote German opera, chiefly by Adolf Neuendorff, who managed the German Theatre in New York City from 1872 to 1883. In 1876 a Wagner Festival was given in New York, and in 1878 there was a short and unsuccessful season given by the Pappenheim Opera Company, during which " Rienzi " was sung for the first time in America. Theodore Thomas did much to prepare the way by playing excerpts from the Wagner operas at his concerts, but Dr. Leopold Damrosch in 1884 set on foot a movement which, during the next few years, brought to America several of the greatest German singers, and gave to the public adequate representations of many of the Wagnerian operas. Dr. Damrosch died in 1885 and his work was taken up by Anton Seidl, who had been associated with Wagner in the production of the " Ring " at Beyreuth. Under Seidl " Die Meistersinger " had its first performance in America, in 1886; " Tristan und Isolde " and " Siegfried " in 1887; " Die Götterdämmerung," in 1888, and " Das Rheingold " in 1889. Thus German opera was well launched in this period.

To return to Italian opera, — Colonel Mapleson invaded the United States in 1878 bringing with him a good company of singers. He did not go farther west than St. Louis. Several tours followed in succeeding years. During his third tour he gave the first performance in America of Boito's " Mefistofele," with Campanini, Valleria, Cary and Novara. About this time he found a strong competitor in Henry E. Abbey, who secured Nilsson as a counter-attraction to Patti who was under Mapleson. This competition caused Mapleson to proceed farther west, so he led his company as far as San Francisco, where he appears to have taken the town by storm, and, if his account is correct, the march in "Aida" was performed by six hundred of the State militia and he had the assistance of a military band and an extra chorus of three hundred and fifty voices. But Mapleson's enterprises were beset with difficulties and finally ended in disaster, although not for some years. To many people, who can remember the rivalry between Abbey and Mapleson in the eighties, when Patti, Gerster, Sembrich, Scalchi, Nilsson, Annie Louise Cary, Campanini, Ravelli and del Puente were in their prime, these were the days of Italian opera in America. Probably much was lacking in the staging and scenery, but the singers have been unsurpassed.

Before closing the review of this period we come to that which is of immense importance in the development of music in America, viz. the appearance of a number of composers who have taken high rank among the composers of the world; — John K. Paine, whose first symphony was produced in 1875, was followed shortly by Arthur Bird, George W. Chadwick, Horatio Parker, Harry Rowe Shelley, Dudley Buck and Edward A. MacDowell.

Nothing speaks more eloquently of the progress of music in America than the work of these men, and of several others of smaller achievements.

1875. Jan. 6. "Wotan's Departure" and "The Magic Fire Scene" from Wagner's opera "Die Walküre" given by Theodore Thomas, in Philadelphia.

1875. Jan. 8. Gluck's overture to "Paris and Helen" and Raff's Sixth Symphony (D minor) given by Theodore Thomas, in New York City.

1875. Jan. 15. Seifert's "Festival March" given by Theodore Thomas, in New York City.

1875. Jan. 16. Brahms's "Hungarian Dances" given (from MS.) by the Brooklyn Philharmonic Society.

1875. Jan. 22. Haydn's Ninth Symphony (in C) given by the Philharmonic Society, New York City.

1875. Feb. 6. Hofmann's "Frithjof" symphony given in New York City, by Theodore Thomas.

1875. Feb. 20. Spohr's Third Symphony (in C minor) given by the Philharmonic Society, New York City.

1875. Feb. 22. Dr. Leopold Damrosch's oratorio "Ruth and Naomi" sung by the Oratorio Society, New York City.

1875. Mar. 4. Rubinstein's Fourth (Dramatic) Symphony given by Theodore Thomas, in New York City.

1875. April 24. W. Sterndale Bennett's "Paradise and the Peri" given by the Philharmonic Society, New York City.

1875. May 1. The music of Mendelssohn's comic opera "The Wedding of Camacho" given by Theodore Thomas, in Chicago.

1875. May 27. Liszt's "Rhapsodie Hongroise" (number 1); Schubert's "Impromptu" in C minor; and Schumann's "Bilder aus Osten"; and on the 28th, Schubert's "Teufel's Lustschloss" given by Theodore Thomas, in New York City.

1875. June 3. Saint-Saëns's symphonic poem "Le Rouet d'Omphale,"

1875. June 17. von Weber's "First Symphony" (in C),

1875. June 22. Lizst's "Rhapsodie Hongroise" (number 6).
1875. June 24. Raff's "Sinfonietta" for wind instruments, given by Theodore Thomas, in New York City.
1875. Aug. 5. Mozart's Intermezzo for Strings,
1875. Aug. 10. Schubert's Octet for Strings,
1875. Aug. 20. Schubert's Tenth Symphony (in C) given in New York City, by Theodore Thomas.
1875. Sept. 7. W. Sterndale Bennett's Symphony in G minor,
1875. Sept. 14. The "Introduction" and "Siegmund's Love Song" from Wagner's opera "Die Walküre" given by Theodore Thomas, in New York City.
1875. Oct. 4. American début of Arabella Goddard, noted English pianist, at Steinway Hall, New York City.
1875. Oct. 18. American début of Madame Eugenie Pappenheim, dramatic soprano, in "Les Huguenots" at the Academy of Music, New York City, with the Wachtel Grand Opera Company.
1875. Oct. 18. American début of Dr. Hans von Bülow, great pianist, in Boston.
1875. Oct. 21. Emma Albani (Lajeunnesse) made her début in opera, as *Amina* in "La Sonnambula" at the Academy of Music, New York City. She afterwards went to Europe, and returned to America a mature singer in 1883.
1875. Oct. 25. Chaikovsky's Pianoforte Concerto, in B flat minor, given in Boston Music Hall, with Hans von Bülow as soloist.
1875. Nov. 17. Verdi's "Requiem Mass" given by the Italian Opera Company, at the Academy of Music, New York City.
1875. Dec. 4. Schumann's "Concertstücke," Opus 92, given by Theodore Thomas, in New York City.
1875. Dec. 27. Schubert's Pianoforte Sonata for Four Hands (Opus 140) orchestrated by Joseph Joachim, given by the Harvard Musical Association, in Boston.
1875. Cecilia Club organized in Philadelphia.
1876. Jan. 6. Schubert's "Marche Héroique" given by the Harvard Musical Association, in Boston.
1876. Jan. 24. American operatic début of Therese Tietjens, noted dramatic soprano, as *Norma*, at the Academy of Music,

New York City, under Strakosch. She had appeared in concert Oct. 4, 1875, with Arabella Goddard.

1876. Jan. 26. J. K. Paine's First Symphony produced by Theodore Thomas, in Boston.

1876. Jan. 29. Saint-Saëns's "Danse Macabre" given by Theodore Thomas, in New York City.

1876. Feb. 3. Saint-Saëns's Second Pianoforte Concerto (G minor) given by the Harvard Musical Association, in Boston, with B. J. Lang as soloist. Carl Zerrahn conducting.

1876. Feb. 17. Saint-Saëns's Violoncello Concerto in A minor given at a concert of the Harvard Musical Association, in Boston, with Wulf Fries as soloist.

1876. Feb. 19. Cherubini's overture to "Faniska" given by the Philharmonic Society, New York City.

1876. Feb. 25. Teresa Carreño, great pianist, appeared as a singer in the part of *Anna* in "Don Giovanni," under Strakosch, at the Academy of Music, New York City.

1876. Feb. 26. Raff's "Suite in F" given by Theodore Thomas, in New York City.

1876. Feb. 28. The first part of Liszt's oratorio "Christus" given by the Oratorio Society, New York City. (The whole work was performed by the same society Mar. 2, 1887.)

1876. April 17. American début of Anna del Belocca, contralto, in "Il Barbiere" at the Academy of Music, New York City, under Strakosch.

1876. April 16. Handel's oratorio "Joshua" given by the Handel and Haydn Society, in Boston.

1876. April 22. Chaikovsky's overture to "Romeo et Juliette" given by the Philharmonic Society, New York City, with Carl Bergmann as conductor.

1876. May 11. Wagner's "Centennial March"; Dudley Buck's "Centennial Meditation of Columbia"; and J. K. Paine's "Centennial Hymn" produced at the Centennial Exposition, in Philadelphia, under Theodore Thomas.

1876. Oct. 9. Saint-Saëns's symphonic poem "Phaeton" given by Theodore Thomas, in New York City.

1876. Nov. 8. Wagner's opera "Il Vascello Fantasma" given in Philadelphia in Italian by Madame Pappenheim.

1876. Nov. 14. Madame Annette Essipoff, pianist, made her début at Steinway Hall, New York City.

1876. Nov. 25. Bach's Suite in C given by Theodore Thomas, in New York City.

1876. Dec. 26. Music Teachers' National Association organized at Delaware, Ohio, by Eben Tourjée, Theodore Presser, G. W. Cole, W. H. Dana, and others.

1876. Loring Club formed in San Francisco, Cal.

1877. Jan. 13. K. Goldmark's symphony "Ländliche Hochzeit" and Haydn's "The Tempest" given by the Philharmonic Society, New York City.

1877. Jan. 16. Gade's "Noveletten" played in New York City, by the Theodore Thomas Orchestra.

1877. Feb. 23. American début of Emma Abbott, noted American soprano, in "La Figlia del Reggimento" at the Academy of Music, New York City, under the management of de Vivo.

1877. Mar. 1. Saint-Saëns's "Third Pianoforte Concerto (in E flat) given by the Harvard Musical Association in Boston, with B. J. Lang as soloist.

1877. Mar. 15. Ballet music from Saint-Saëns's opera "Samson et Dalila" played in St. Louis, by the Theodore Thomas Orchestra.

1877. Mar. 15. Brahms's "German Requiem" performed by the New York Oratorio Society.

1877. Mar. 25–31. A Wagner Festival held in Boston in which Madame Pappenheim and Madame Canissa, Albert Niemann, G. Unger and Gustav Siehr took leading parts.

1877. April 2. Verdi's opera "Don Carlos" presented at the Academy of Music, New York City, by the Havana Opera Combination, under Maretzek. (Admission one dollar, Reserved seat 50c extra.)

1877. May 17. Production of J. C. D. Parker's "Redemption Hymn" by the Handel and Haydn Society, Boston.

1877. June 6. Sullivan's cantata "On Shore and Sea" given under Theodore Thomas, in Chicago.

1877. July 5. Méhul's overture to "Horatio Coclès,"

1877. July 12. Hofmann's "Pictures from the North,"

1877. July 20. Massenet's "Variations" and Rameau's "Romanesca,"

1877. July 24. Saint-Saëns's "Suite" (Opus 48), given by Theodore Thomas, in Chicago.

1877. Nov. 2. J. K. Paine's symphonic fantasia on Shakespeare's "Tempest" given at Steinway Hall, New York City, by the Theodore Thomas Orchestra.

1877. Nov. 14. Saint-Saëns's fourth symphonic poem, "La Jeunesse d'Hercule," played at a Theodore Thomas Concert, in Boston.

1877. Nov. 20. Raff's Suite for Pianoforte and Orchestra (Opus 200) given by Theodore Thomas in New York City.

1877. Dec. 17. Brahms's First Symphony given in New York City, by Dr. Leopold Damrosch. (Given a week later by Theodore Thomas, in New York City, and Jan. 3, 1878, by the Harvard Musical Association, Boston.)

1877. Dec. 23. Parts 1 and 2 of Bach's "Christmas Oratorio" given by the Handel and Haydn Society, Boston, with Emma Thursby, Annie Louise Cary, W. J. and F. W. Winch as soloists. C. Zerrahn conducting.

1877. Music department established at Syracuse (N. Y.) University, with Wm. Schultze as director.

1877. Theodore Thomas began Summer Night Concerts in New York City.

1877. Tivoli Opera House in San Francisco, Cal., opened.

1878. Feb. 11. Madame Hermine Rudersdorff, who had been heard at the Peace Jubilees in Boston in 1871 and 1872, made her American operatic début as *Ortrud* in "Lohengrin."

1878. Feb. 14. Saint-Saëns's Fourth Pianoforte Concerto (in C minor) given by the Harvard Musical Association in Boston, with J. A. Preston, as soloist.

1878. Feb. 16. Goldmark's "Wedding March and Variations" given by Theodore Thomas, in Brooklyn, N. Y.

1878. Feb. 28. Wagner's "Siegfried Idyll" given by Theodore Thomas, in New York City.

1878. Mar. 5. Wagner's opera "Rienzi" presented at the Academy of Music, New York City, with Madame Pappenheim as *Adriane*, Miss Hüman as *Irene*, Charles R. Adams as *Rienzi*, and Blum as *Orsini*.

1878. May 14. O. Singer's "Festival Ode" given at the Cincinnati (O.) May festival with Madame Eugenie Pappenheim, C. R. Adams, and M. W. Whitney as soloists. Theodore Thomas conducting.

1878. Sept. 26. American début of August Wilhelmj, noted violinist, at Steinway Hall, New York City.

1878. Oct. 3. Brahms's Second Symphony (D major) given in New York City, by Theodore Thomas.

1878. Oct. 23. Bizet's opera "Carmen" presented at the Academy of Music, New York City, with Minnie Hauck, Madame Sinico, Italo Campanini, and Del Puente.

1878. Nov. 11. American début of Etelka Gerster, brilliant soprano, at the Academy of Music, New York City, as *Amina*, in "La Sonnambula," supported by Campanini and Galassi.

1878. Nov. 23. Ernst's violin concerto "Pathétique" given by the Philharmonic Society, New York City, with Edouard Remenyi as soloist.

1878. Dec. 19. Mozart Pianoforte Concerto in A major, given by the Harvard Musical Association, in Boston, with H. G. Tucker as soloist.

1878. Symphony Society of New York City founded by Dr. Leopold Damrosch.

1878. Cincinnati College of Music established, and Theodore Thomas appointed director.

1878–9. Oct. 15 to April. Colonel Mapleson made his first operatic tour in America, with a company which included Etelka Gerster, Minnie Hauck, Trebelli, Alwina Valleria, Campanini, Frapolli, Galassi, del Puente and Foli, with Arditi as conductor. Presented opera in New York, Chicago, Boston, St. Louis, Cincinnati, Philadelphia, Baltimore and Washington.

1879. Feb. 8. Chaikovsky's Third Symphony (in D) given by the Philharmonic Society, New York City.

1879. Feb. 23. Sullivan's oratorio "The Prodigal Son" given in Boston by the Handel and Haydn Society.

ANNALS OF MUSIC IN AMERICA

1879. April 11. Bach's "Passion according to St. Matthew" given complete, in two concerts, by the Handel and Haydn Society, in Boston.

1879. April 15. F. Kiel's oratorio "Christus" given by the Oratorio Society, New York City.

1879. May 9. Hiller's oratorio "Saul" given by the New York Liederkranz Society at the Academy of Music, New York City.

1879. May 10. Production of Bristow's "Great Republic Overture" by the Brooklyn Philharmonic Society, Theodore Thomas conducting.

1879. Oct. 13. American début of Rafael Joseffy, noted Hungarian pianist, at Chickering Hall, New York City.

1879. Oct. 22. American début of Alwina Valleria (A. V. Lohmann of Baltimore) as *Marguerite* in "Faust" at the Academy of Music, New York City.

1879. Dec. 3. Goldmark's "Penthesilea Overture" given in Cincinnati, by Theodore Thomas.

1879. Dec. 3. American début of Marie Marimon, as *Amina* in "La Sonnambula," supported by Campanini and del Puente, at the Academy of Music, New York City.

1879. Dec. 5. Dvořák's "Slavonic Dances" No. 7 and No. 8, also the first movement of Guilmant's "First Symphony" for organ and orchestra given at a Philharmonic Concert, in Boston, with Charles H. Morse as soloist.

1879. Dec. 8. Dedication of the Central Music Hall, Chicago. Carlotta Patti sang.

1879. Dec. 11. Production of George W. Chadwick's overture to "Rip van Winkle" by the Harvard Musical Association, in Boston.

1879–1883. Philharmonic Society, Boston.

1880. Jan. 8. Herman Goetz's Symphony in F major given by the Harvard Musical Association, in Cambridge, Mass.

1880. Jan. 17. Chaikovsky's "Suite for Giant Orchestra" given by the Symphony Society, New York City.

1880. Jan. 19. American début of Castelmary (Count A. de Castan), noted French baritone, as *Ramfis* in "Aida" at Booth's Theatre, New York City.

1880. Jan. 27. Mendelssohn's "Lauda Zion" given by the New York Vocal Union, at Chickering Hall, New York City.

1880. Feb. 4. Dvořák's third "Slavische Rhapsodie" given in Cincinnati, by Theodore Thomas.

1880. Feb. 12. Berlioz's opera "La Damnation de Faust" given in concert form, by the Oratorio Society of New York City. Dr. Leopold Damrosch, conductor. (Stage performance in 1908.)

1880. Feb. 22. H. Hofmann's cantata "Cinderella" given by the German Liederkranz, New York City.

1880. Feb. 28. The music of Meyerbeer's "Struensee" given at concert at Chickering Hall, New York City, under Mr. Carlberg.

1880. Mar. 10. Production of J. K. Paine's "Spring Symphony," by the Harvard Musical Association, in Cambridge, Mass.

1880. Mar. 11. Dvořák's second "Slavische Rhapsodie" given by the Symphony Society of New York City, Dr. Leopold Damrosch, conductor.

1880. May 29. Production of Dudley Buck's prize symphonic cantata, "The Golden Legend," at the Cincinnati Festival.

1880. May 7. Saint-Saëns's oratorio "Le Déluge" given by the Handel and Haydn Society in Boston.

1880. May. 10. Production of E. C. Phelps' symphony "Hiawatha" by Theodore Thomas, in New York City.

1880. Oct. 4. American début of Georg Henschel at a concert of the Symphony Society, in New York City.

1880. Oct. 18. American début of Luigi Ravelli, Italian tenor, as *Edgardo* in "Lucia" at the Academy of Music, New York City, under Mapleson.

1880. Nov. 19. First part of Liszt's symphony after "la Divina Commedia" given at a Philharmonic Society's Concert, in Boston, Bernhard Listemann conducting.

1880. Nov. 24. Boito's opera "Mefistofele" presented at the Academy of Music, New York City, with Annie Louise Cary, Campanini and Novara, under Mapleson.

1880. Music of the third act of "Die Götterdämmerung" given in New York and Brooklyn, by the Philharmonic

Societies of those cities united under Theodore Thomas, with Campanini, Remmertz, and Steinbuch as soloists.

1880. Mapleson made his third American operatic tour with a company which included Gerster, Valleria, Cary, Ravelli, and Campanini.

1881. Jan. 2. Haydn's "Surprise Symphony" given by the Brooklyn Philharmonic Society, Theodore Thomas conducting.

1881. Jan. 6. Hans von Bronsart's "Spring Fantasie" given by the Symphony Society, of New York City.

1881. Feb. 17. F. L. Ritter's "Second Symphony" given by the Harvard Musical Association, in Boston.

1881. Feb. 25. Handel's "L'Allegro, Il Penseroso, et Il Moderato" given by the Oratorio Society, in New York City.

1881. Mar. 11. Rheinberger's oratorio "Demetrius" given in New York City, under Theodore Thomas.

1881. Mar. 11. Svendsen's fantasia "Roméo et Juliette" given by Theodore Thomas, in New York City.

1881. Mar. 22. Andante and finale from Mozart's "Serenade" (No. 12) given at a Philharmonic Concert in Boston, also Saint-Saëns's "Suite Algérienne."

1881. Mar. 28. Schumann's "Scenes from Faust" given by the Cecilia Society, in Boston.

1881. April 1. The Nocturno from Mozart's Serenade (Op. 8), given at a concert under Theodore Thomas, in New York City.

1881. April 2. The ballet music from Rubinstein's opera "The Demon" given at a concert of the Philharmonic Orchestra, in Boston, also Bizet's suite "Arlésienne."

1881. May. Rubinstein's sacred opera "The Tower of Babel" given in New York City, by Dr. Damrosch. Also Berlioz's "Requiem."

1881. July 16. The ballet music from Rubinstein's opera "Nero" given in New York City, by Theodore Thomas.

1881. Oct. 14. Brahms's "Academic Overture" given in Boston, by the Theodore Thomas Orchestra.

1881. Oct. 22. Boston Symphony Orchestra, organized by Major

Henry L. Higginson, gave its first concert, with Georg Henschel as conductor.

1881. Oct. 29. Brahms's "Tragic Overture" given by the Boston Symphony Orchestra.

1881. Nov. 26. First complete performance in America of Joachim's "Concerto for Violin" (Op. 11) given by the Boston Symphony Orchestra, with Bernhard Listemann as soloist.

1881. Dec. 1. Grieg's "Norwegian Melodies" for Orchestra given by the Symphony Society in New York City. Also Saint-Saëns's "Pianoforte Concerto," with Madame Madeline Schiller as soloist.

1881. Dec. 10. Rubinstein's Fifth Symphony given in New York City, by Theodore Thomas.

1881. New York Chorus Society organized with six hundred voices under the direction of Theodore Thomas.

1882. Jan. 29. Raff's "Die Tageszeiten" for chorus, pianoforte and orchestra, given by the German Liederkranz in New York City.

1882. Feb. 11. Brahms's Rhapsody for contralto, male chorus and orchestra (Opus 53) given by the Boston Symphony Orchestra.

1882. Feb. 11. Huber's "Tell Symphony" given in New York City, by Theodore Thomas.

1882. Feb. 18. The overture to Massenet's "Phèdre" given by the Boston Symphony Orchestra. Also Bizet's overture "La Patrie." G. Henschel conducting.

1882. Mar. 9. R. Fuch's "Serenade in D" given by the Harvard Musical Association, in Boston.

1882. April 6. Berlioz's "Requiem" given by the New York Oratorio Society.

1882. April 15. Goetz's Violin Concerto given by Theodore Thomas in New York City.

1882. April 20. Dr. Leopold Damrosch's "Sulamith" given by the Oratorio Society of New York City.

1882. May 6. Second act of H. Berlioz' "Les Troyens" (The Fall of Troy) given at a musical festival in the armory of the Seventh Regiment in New York City, under Theodore

ANNALS OF MUSIC IN AMERICA

Thomas, with Madame Materna, E. Aline Osgood, E. Winant, Campanini, Galassi, Remmertz and M. W. Whitney as soloists.

1882. July 12. Hofmann's "Overture to a Drama," and on the 18th Liszt's Second "Mephisto" Waltz given by Theodore Thomas, in Chicago, Ill.

1882. Oct. 16. Offenbach's opera "Les Contes d'Hoffman" performed under the management of Mauric Grau, at the Fifth Avenue Theatre, New York City.

1882. Nov. 3. The "Vorspiel" to Wagner's opera "Parsifal" given by Theodore Thomas, in New York City. Also F. Cowen's "Scandinavian Symphony."

1882. Nov. 29. Guilmant's First Symphony for organ and orchestra, given at a Philharmonic Concert in Music Hall, Boston, with F. Archer as soloist. (The first movement had been given by C. H. Morse, Dec. 5, 1879.)

1882. Dec. 6. Gounod's oratorio "The Redemption" given (from manuscript) by the New York Chorus Society, under Theodore Thomas.

1882. Dec. 6. Saint-Saëns's ode "La Lyre et La Harpe" sung by the Arion Society, Providence, R. I., under Jules Jordan.

1882. Dec. 9. Gernsheim's Symphony in E flat, given by the Boston Symphony Orchestra.

1882. Dec. 13. Brahms's Pianoforte Concerto in B flat given by the Philharmonic Society, New York City, with R. Joseffy, soloist.

1882. Dec. 15. Max Bruch's Third Symphony (dedicated to the Symphony Society) given by that Society in New York City, conducted by the composer. At the same concert Rubinstein's Morceau Symphonique, "La Russie" was performed.

1882. Dec. 20. American début of Sophia Scalchi, noted contralto, as *Arsace* in "Semiramide," with Adelina Patti as *The Queen*, at the Metropolitan Opera House, New York City.

1883. Jan. 6. Dvořák's First Symphony (in D) given by Theodore Thomas, in New York City, and on the 10th Reinhold's Concert Overture.

1883. Jan. 11. Professional début of Madame Fannie Bloomfield Zeisler at Central Music Hall, Chicago, when she played Henselt's F minor concerto, with orchestra. Her début as a child took place in Chicago, Feb. 25, 1875.

1883. Jan. 13. G. W. Chadwick's "Thalia," an overture to an imaginary comedy, produced by the Boston Symphony Orchestra, conducted by the composer.

1883. Jan. 20. Massenet's "Scènes Alsaciennes"; and on the 27th F. Cowen's First Symphony (C minor) given by the Boston Symphony Orchestra.

1883. Jan. 31 Rheinberger's Symphony in F given by the Philharmonic Society, Boston, Carl Zerrahn conducting.

1883. Feb. 1. Scharwenka's Pianoforte Concerto given by Theodore Thomas in New York City, with X. Scharwenka as soloist.

1883. Feb. 3. Grieg's "Two Melodies" for strings (Opus 34) given by the Boston Symphony Orchestra.

1883. Feb. 16. The music of the "Good Friday Spell" from Wagner's opera "Parsifal" given by the Symphony Society, New York City.

1883. Feb. 17. Henschel's "Serenade for Strings" given by the Boston Symphony Orchestra; and on the 24th Chaikovsky's "Marche Slave."

1883. Mar. 3. Mackenzie's Scotch rhapsody "Bobbie Burns" given by Theodore Thomas in Brooklyn, N. Y.

1883. Mar. 10. J. K. Paine's symphonic poem "The Tempest" produced by the Boston Symphony Orchestra.

1883. Mar. 12. American operatic début of Madame Emma Albani (Marie Louise Cecilia Emma Lajeunnesse), noted soprano, on her return from Europe, as *Marguerite* in Gounod's "Faust" at the Academy of Music, New York City, with Scalchi, Ravelli and Galassi in support.

1883. April 2. Part VI of Bach's "Christmas Oratorio" given by the Cecilia Society in Boston.

1883. April 4. Svendsen's Legende "Zorahayda" given in Boston.

1883. May 1. Rubinstein's sacred opera "The Tower of Babel" given in concert form by the Handel and Haydn Society in Boston.

1883. May 2. J. K. Paine's oratorio "The Nativity" produced by the Handel and Haydn Society in Boston. Also Cherubini's Mass in D minor; and on the 4th, Max Bruch's oratorio "Arminius."

1883. July 18. Rubinstein's "Bal Costumé" (first series) given in Chicago, by Theodore Thomas.

1883. Oct. 23. Opening of the Metropolitan Opera House, New York City.

1883. Oct. 24. American début of Marcella Sembrich, great lyric soprano, in "Lucia di Lammermoor" at the Metropolitan Opera House, New York City.

1883. Oct. 26. American début of Alberto Stagno, noted Italian tenor, as *Manrico* in "Il Trovatore" at the Metropolitan Opera House, New York City, under Henry E. Abbey.

1883. Oct. 27. Delibes's "Cortège de Bacchus" from the ballet "Sylvia" given by the Boston Symphony Orchestra, and on

1883. Nov. 3. Liszt's "Hungarian Rhapsodie" in D.

1883. Nov. 16. American début of Ovide Musin, noted Belgian violinist, with the New York Symphony Orchestra, under Dr. Leopold Damrosch.

1883. Nov. 17. B. Godard's "Concerto Romantique" for violin given by the Boston Symphony Orchestra, with C. M. Loeffler as soloist; and on Dec. 1, the first performance (from MS.) of K. Mueller-Berghaus's "Romance" for violoncello.

1883. Nov. 21. Cowen's cantata "St. Ursula" given by the Oratorio Society, New York City.

1883. Nov. 26. Operatic début of Lillian Norton (Nordica) as *Marguerite* in "Faust" at the Academy of Music, New York City, under Mapleson. She returned with the Italian Company in 1889-90 but appeared with the Metropolitan Opera Company, Oct. 26, 1893.

1883. Dec. 7. Chaikovsky's Second Symphony (in C) given by the New York Symphony Society.

1883. Dec. 8. American début of Madame Helen Hopekirk, noted Scotch pianist, with the Boston Symphony Orchestra.

1883. Dec. 20. Ponchielli's opera "La Gioconda" presented at the Academy of Music, New York City, with Nilsson, Scalchi, Fursch-Madi, del Puente, and Novara.

1883. Dec. 22. Volkmann's Second Symphony (in B flat), and Saint-Saëns' ballet music to "Henry VIII" given by the Boston Symphony Orchestra.

1883–4. Grand opera given in the United States by Henry E. Abbey with a company which included Christine Nilsson, Alwina Valleria, Madame Fursch-Madi, Sophia Scalchi, Trebelli-Bettini, Campanini, Stagno, Novara, Capoul, Del Puente, Corsini, Kaschmann, and Marcella Sembrich.

1884. Jan. 5. Svendsen's Second Symphony (in B flat) given by the Boston Symphony Orchestra.

1884. Jan. 12. Mozart's Concerto for flute and harp (in C) given by the Boston Symphony Orchestra.

1884. Jan. 14. American début of Marianna Brandt, noted Austrian contralto, in "Fidelio" at the Metropolitan Opera House, New York City.

1884. Jan. 19. Villiers Stanford's Serenade in G given by Theodore Thomas, in New York City.

1884. Jan. 26. Spontini's overture to his opera "Olympia" given by the Boston Symphony Orchestra.

1884. Feb. 9. Liszt's third suite "Roma" given by the Boston Symphony Orchestra.

1884. Feb. 23. J. O. Grimm's Symphony in D minor given by the Boston Symphony Orchestra. Also Liszt's Pianoforte Concerto in A major, with Carl Baermann as soloist.

1884. Mar. 7. Selections from Berlioz's sacred trilogy "The Childhood of Christ" given by the Symphony Society of New York City.

1884. Production of G. W. Chadwick's Scherzo in F, also the entr'acte and finale of Massenet's "Les Erinnyes" given by the Boston Symphony Orchestra.

1884. April. 4. Beethoven's "Grand Quatuor" (Opus 131) (scored for full orchestra by Carl Mueller-Berghaus) given by the Boston Symphony Orchestra.

1884. May 1. Hamerik's "Christian Trilogy" given by Theodore Thomas, in Baltimore, Md.

1884. Oct. 24. Brahms's Third Symphony (in F) given at a Novelty Concert, under F. van der Stucken in New York City. Also Dvořák's "Husitska" overture.

ANNALS OF MUSIC IN AMERICA

1884. Nov. 8. Dvořák's "Scherzo Capriccioso," given by Theodore Thomas, in Brooklyn, N. Y.

1884. Nov. 21. American début of Madame Schroeder-Hanfstaengl in "Les Huguenots" at the Metropolitan Opera House, New York City.

1884. Nov. 22. The Pastoral from Bach's "Christmas oratorio," and Schumann's "Pictures from the Orient," given by the Boston Symphony Orchestra.

1884. Nov. 24. American début of Emma Nevada, noted soprano, as *Amina* in "La Sonnambula," at the Academy of Music, in New York City.

1884. Nov. 27. American début of Frau Seidl-Krauss, as *Elizabeth*, and Anton Schott as *Tannhäuser*, in Tannhäuser" at the Metropolitan Opera House, New York City.

1884. Dec. 6. Sgambati's Symphony in D major; Gustav Hollaender's "Romance" for violin and orchestra; and E. Chabrier's rhapsodie "España" given at a Novelty Concert, by Frank van der Stucken, in New York City.

1884. Dec. 13. R. Strauss's Symphony in F minor given by Theodore Thomas, in New York City.

1884. Dec. 18. Gounod's opera "Mireille" presented at the Academy of Music, New York City, with Emma Nevada as prima donna. (New Orleans, La., Dec. 29.)

1884. Dec. 20. Lalo's "Rhapsodie Norvégienne" (in A), and the music of Rubinstein's ballet "La Vigne" given by the Boston Symphony Orchestra.

1884. A series of Wagner festival concerts given in New York City, under Theodore Thomas.

1884. The Chicago Conservatory of Music established, in Chicago, Ill.

1885. Jan. 5. American operatic début of Frau Amalie Materna, noted German soprano, as *Elizabeth* in "Tannhäuser" at the Metropolitan Opera House. She had appeared in May 1882, in oratorio at the Cincinnati (O.) Festival.

1885. Jan. 10. Nicodé's Symphonic Variations given in New York City, by Theodore Thomas.

1885. Jan. 23. Chaikovsky's "Serenade" for string orchestra, given by the Symphony Society of New York City.

1885. Jan. 31. Bach's "Three Sonata Movements" (arranged for orchestra by W. Gericke) given by the Boston Symphony Orchestra.

1885. Feb. 5. Berlioz's "Tristia" given in New York City, by Theodore Thomas; also Rameau's gavotte, tambourine, and minuet, from the opera "Castor and Pollux."

1885. Mar. 14. Volkmann's overture to "Richard III" given by the Boston Symphony Orchestra.

1885. Mar. 16. J. Strauss' opera "Die Fledermaus" presented at the Casino, New York City, with De Wolf Hopper in the cast.

1885. Mar. 31. Production of Dudley Buck's symphonic overture "Marmion" at a concert of American music, given in New York City, by Frank van der Stucken. Also Templeton Strong's symphonic poem "Undine," and E. C. Phelps's "American Legend" for violin and orchestra.

1885. April 11. Cowen's "Welsh Symphony" (Fourth, in B minor) given by Theodore Thomas, in New York City.

1885. April 16. Mackenzie's oratorio "The Rose of Sharon" given in New York City, under Theodore Thomas.

1885. April 28. Rubinstein's "Fantasia Eroica" given in Brooklyn, N. Y., by Theodore Thomas.

1885. Oct. 30. Gounod's oratorio "Mors et Vita" given in St. Louis, Mo., by Theodore Thomas.

1885. Oct. 30. Ecker's Concert Overture, Schubert's "Trauermarsch" and R. Fuchs's Symphony in C major, given by the Boston Symphony Orchestra.

1885. Nov. 4. American début of Felia Litvinne, as *Leonora* in "Il Trovatore" at the Academy of Music, New York City, under Colonel Mapleson.

1885. Nov. 14. Mozart's "Haffner Serenade" given by the Boston Symphony Orchestra.

1885. Nov. 23. Anton Seidl appeared as conductor at the Metropolitan Opera House, New York City.

1885. Nov. 24. Chaikovsky's Third Suite given by Theodore Thomas, in New York City.

1885. Nov. 25. American début of Lilli Lehmann, noted German soprano, as *Carmen*, also of Max Alvary as *Don José*,

ANNALS OF MUSIC IN AMERICA

in Bizet's opera "Carmen" at the Metropolitan Opera House, New York City.

1885. Dec. 2. Goldmark's opera "Die Königen von Saba" presented at the Metropolitan Opera House, New York City, with Lehmann and Fischer.

1885. Dec. 3. Maude Powell, noted American violinist, made her début on her return from European study and concertizing, under Theodore Thomas, at Orange, N. J. On Dec. 5 she appeared at Philadelphia. Played Max Burch's First Violin Concerto.

1885. Dec. 12. Scharwenka's Symphony in C minor, given by Theodore Thomas, in New York City.

1885. Dec. 23. Massenet's opera "Manon" presented at the Academy of Music, New York City, by Mapleson, with Minnie Hauck, Del Puente, and Giannini in leading parts.

1885. Walter Damrosch appointed conductor of the New York Symphony and Oratorio Societies, on the death of his father, Dr. Leopold Damrosch.

1885. The American Institute of Applied Music established in New York City, by Miss Kate Chittenden.

1885–1916. The Kneisel Quartet organized in Boston. Became well known throughout the United States and Europe.

1886. Jan. 2. Saint-Saëns's "Rhapsodie d'Auvergne" given by the Boston Symphony Orchestra.

1886. Jan. 4. Herman Goetz's opera "The Taming of the Shrew" given in New York City (in English) by the American Opera Company, Theodore Thomas conductor, at the Academy of Music. At this performance Pauline Allemand made her début.

1886. Jan. 4. Wagner's opera "Die Meistersinger" presented at the Metropolitan Opera House, New York City, with Frau Seidl-Krauss as *Eva*, Marianne Brandt as *Magdalena*, Emil Fischer as *Hans Sachs*, Stritt as *Walther*, Staudigl as *Pogner*, Kemlitz as *Beckmesser*, Krämer as *David*, and Anton Seidl as conductor.

1886. Jan. 9. Dvořák's Second Symphony (D minor) given by the Philharmonic Society, New York City.

1886. Jan. 9. E. Barnard's Violin Concerto in G major, given by the Boston Symphony Orchestra with T. Adamowski as soloist.

1886. Jan. 12. Svendsen's "Norwegian Artists' Carnival" given by Theodore Thomas, in New York City.

1886. Jan. 15. Lalo's "Rhapsodie and Scherzo" played by the Symphony Society, New York City.

1886. Jan. 16. W. Gericke's "Chorus of Homage" given by the Boston Symphony Orchestra, conducted by the composer.

1886. Jan. 20. American début of William Candidus, tenor, in a performance of "Lohengrin" (in English) at the Academy of Music, New York City, with the American Opera Company.

1886. Jan. 21. Jensen's "Wedding Music" given by Theodore Thomas at a concert in Jersey City, N. J.

1886. Jan. 23. H. Reinhold's "Prelude, Menuet, and Fugue" for strings given by the Boston Symphony Orchestra.

1886. Jan. 30. Horatio Parker's "Scherzo" for orchestra played at a concert given in New York City, by Alexander Lambert, with F. van der Stucken as conductor.

1886. Feb. 15. Johann Strauss's opera "The Gipsy Baron" (Die Zigeunerbaron) presented in English, by H. Conried, at the Casino, New York City.

1886. Mar. 1. Delibes's opera "Lakmé" presented by the American Opera Company, at the Academy of Music, New York City (in English) with Pauline Allemand in the title-rôle. (It had been given inadequately by Emma Abbott in 1883.)

1886. Mar. 13. Scholz's Symphony in B flat given in New York City, by Theodore Thomas.

1886. Mar. 13. Three movements from Gericke's "Serenade" given by the Boston Symphony Orchestra, conducted by the composer.

1886. Mar. 16. Liszt's "Concerto Pathétique" given in New York City, by Theodore Thomas.

1886. Mar. 20. Dvořák's cantata "The Spectre Bride" given in Brooklyn, N. Y., under Theodore Thomas; also Raff's "Die Jahreszeiten" for chorus, pianoforte and orchestra.

1886. Mar. 23. Borodin's symphonic poem "On the Steppes of Central Asia," and the tarantella from Gernsheim's Symphony in F, given by the Philharmonic Society in Brooklyn, N. Y.

1886. Mar. 23. Pratt's "Court Minuet" produced, and Delibes's ballet music "Sylvia," given by Theodore Thomas, in New York City.

1886. April 30. Delibes's "Scène de Bal" given in New York City, by Theodore Thomas.

1886. July 5. Rubinstein's "Bal Costumé" (Second Series) given in New York City, by Theodore Thomas.

1886. July 21. Schytte's "Pantomimes" given in Chicago, by Theodore Thomas.

1886. July 29. Bruckner's Seventh Symphony (E major) played by the Theodore Thomas Orchestra, in Chicago.

1886. Oct. 26. Massenet's "Marche Héroique," and Gadsby's orchestral scene "The Forest of Arden," given in New York City, by Theodore Thomas.

1886. Oct. 28. Nicodé's "Jubilee March," César Cui's "Tarantella," and Massenet's "La Vierge" for string orchestras, given in New York City, by Theodore Thomas.

1886. Nov. 1. Chaikovsky's "Italian Caprice" for orchestra, played by the Philharmonic Society in New York City.

1866. Nov. 4. Schumann's "Marche Funèbre" and Arthur Sullivan's overture "In Memoriam" given in New York, by Theodore Thomas. Also Raff's "Festival March."

1886. Nov. 5. Arthur Bird's First Symphony played by the Symphony Society in New York City.

1886. Nov. 6. Brahms's Serenade in A for strings, and Dvořák's "Legends" (Opus 59, first collection), given by the Boston Symphony Orchestra.

1886. Nov. 10. American début of Albert Niemann, noted Wagnerian tenor, in "Die Walküre" at the Metropolitan Opera House, New York City.

1886. Nov. 13. R. Henberger's overture to Byron's "Cain" given by the Boston Symphony Orchestra.

1886. Nov. 19. Brüll's opera "Das Goldene Kreuz" presented at the Metropolitan Opera House, New York City.

1886. Dec. 1. Wagner's opera "Tristan und Isolde" presented at the Metropolitan Opera House, New York City, with Lilli Lehmann as *Isolde*, M. Brandt as *Brangäne*, Niemann as *Tristan*, Robinson as *Kurwenal*, von Milde as *Melot*, Emil Fischer as *King Mark*. Anton Seidl, conductor.

1886. Dec. 4. Chaikovsky's "Manfred Symphony" played by the Philharmonic Society, in New York City, Theodore Thomas conducting.

1886. Dec. 11. Production of Chadwick's Second Symphony (B flat) by the Boston Symphony Orchestra.

1886. Dec. 11. Brahms's Fourth Symphony (E minor, Op. 98) given by the Symphony Society, New York City.

1886. Dec. 23. Dvořák's "Slavonic Rhapsodie" (Op. 45) given by the Boston Symphony Orchestra.

1886. Dec. 30. Massé's opera "Galatea" presented at the Brooklyn Academy of Music, by Arthur Mees.

1886. The American Opera Company established in New York City, by Mrs. Jeannette Thurber, with Theodore Thomas as conductor. Lasted two seasons.

1886. Norfolk Festivals of the Litchfield County (Conn.) Choral Union commenced.

1886. American Conservatory of Music established in Chicago, by J. J. Hattstaedt.

1886. Chicago Symphony Orchestra organized with Hans Balatka as director.

1887. Jan. 3. Goldmark's opera "Merlin" presented at the Metropolitan Opera House, New York City, under Walter Damrosch.

1887. Jan. 15. A. Krug's symphonic prologue to "Otello" given by the Boston Symphony Orchestra.

1887. Jan. 15. The music of Delibes's ballet "Coppelia" given in New York City, by Theodore Thomas.

1887. Jan. 19. Saint-Saëns's Third Symphony (C minor) given by Theodore Thomas, in New York City.

1887. Jan. 27. Mendelssohn's cantata "Athalie" (Racine's text) given by the Cecilia Society in Boston.

1887. Feb. 5. Production of Arthur Foote's overture "In the Mountains" by the Boston Symphony Orchestra.

1887. Feb. 10. Hans von Bülow's symphonic poem, "The Minstrel's Curse," given by the Symphony Society, in New York City.

1887. Feb. 19. A. C. Mackenzie's ballad "La belle dame sans merci" given by the Boston Symphony Orchestra.

1887. Feb. 24. The Music of the "Flower Girl" Scene from Wagner's opera "Parsifal" given in Philadelphia, by Theodore Thomas.

1887. Feb. 26. Berlioz's "The Trojans in Carthage" arranged as a dramatic cantata by H. E. Krehbiel, performed in English in Chickering Hall, New York City. Chief singers were M. Gramm, M. Groebl, F. Hirsch, M. Alvary, W. Dennison, G. Prehn and F. Remmertz; Narrator, Charles Roberts. F. van der Stucken, conductor.

1887. Mar. 1. Dvořák's "Legende" given by Theodore Thomas in New York City. Also Svendsen's "Festival Polonaise."

1887. Mar. 3. Liszt's oratorio "Christus" given (complete) by the Oratorio Society of New York City.

1887. Mar. 12. Rubinstein's oratorio "Paradise Lost" given in Brooklyn, under the direction of Theodore Thomas.

1887. Mar. 14. Rubinstein's opera "Nero" given by the American Opera Company, in New York City.

1887. Mar. 23. Moszkowski's First Suite for orchestra; and on the 31st Dvořák's Suite (Opus 39), given in New York City, by Theodore Thomas.

1887. April 23. Arthur Bird's "Carnival Scene" given at a Symphony Concert in New York City, under the direction of F. van der Stucken, at Chickering Hall. Also Rubinstein's Sixth Symphony (A minor).

1887. July 21. Huber's "Römische Karneval," and on the 28th Scharwenka's fantasia "Liebesnacht," given by Theodore Thomas in Chicago, Ill.

1887. July. Production of Harry Rowe Shelley's "Dance of Egyptian Maidens"; and H. H. Huss's rhapsody for the pianoforte and orchestra at the convention of the Music Teachers' National Association in New York City.

1887. Oct. 22. Dvořák's Suite in D given by the Boston Symphony Orchestra.

1887. Oct. 12. Reinecke's Variations on "Ein' Feste Burg" given by Theodore Thomas in New York City. Also Dvořák's "Slavonic Dances" (Second Series).

1887. Oct. 12. Lalo's "Symphony Espagnole" given by the Boston Symphony Orchestra.

1887. Oct. 12. Smetana's overture to "The Bartered Bride" given by Theodore Thomas, in New York City.

1887. Nov. 15. L. A. Russell's "Pastoral" given at a concert of American Music in New York City, conducted by the composer. Also Arthur Whiting's Pianoforte Concerto in D minor

1887. Nov. 23. Nessler's opera "Der Trompeter von Säckingen" presented at the Metropolitan Opera House, New York City.

1887. Nov. 24. Templeton Strong's Symphony in F major performed at a concert of American Music in New York City, under F. van der Stucken.

1887 Nov. 25. Eugen d'Albert's First Symphony played by the Symphony Society of New York.

1887. Nov. 29. American début of Josef Hofmann (pianist) at a concert given in the Metropolitan Opera House, New York City.

1887. Dec. 23. Noteworthy revival of Weber's opera "Euryanthe" at the Metropolitan Opera House, New York City, with Lilli Lehmann, Marianne Brandt, Max Alvary and Emil Fischer.

1887. Dec. 24. Production of G. W. Chadwick's "Melpomene Overture" by the Boston Symphony Orchestra.

1887. Teresina Tua, noted violinist, visited America.

1888. Jan. 4. Wagner's Nibelungen Trilogy given in America for the first time beginning on this date with a performance of "Das Rheingold," at the Metropolitan Opera House, New York City, with Emil Fischer as *Wotan*, Max Alvary as *Loge*, Grienaur as *Donner*, Mittelhauer as *Froh*, Beck as *Alberich*, Sedlmayer as *Mime*, Weiss as *Fafner*, Modlinger as *Fasolt*, Madame Moran-Olden as *Fricka*, Bettaque as *Freia*, and Traubmann, Koschoska, and Reil as the *Rhine-Daughters*. Anton Seidl conductor.

1888. Jan. 30. " Die Walküre." (See 1877, April 12.)
1888. Feb. 1. " Siegfried," with Lilli Lehmann, Marianne Brandt, Max Alvary, and Emil Fischer.
1888. Jan. 6. Spontini's opera " Ferdinand Cortez " presented at the Metropolitan Opera House, New York City.
1888. Jan. 17. Schubert's " Divertissement à la Hongroise " given by Theodore Thomas in New York City.
1888. Jan. 25. Wagner's opera " Götterdämmerung " presented at the Metropolitan Opera House, New York City, with Lilli Lehmann, Seidl-Krauss, Marianne Brandt, Albert Niemann, and Emil Fischer in the cast. Anton Seidl conducting.
1888. Jan. 26. Production of Arthur Foote's cantata " The Wreck of the Hesperus " by the Cecilia Society in Boston.
1888. Jan. 28. C. Villiers Stanford's " Irish Symphony " given by the Symphony Society in New York City.
1888. Jan. 28. Otto Floersheim's " Elevation " given by the Boston Symphony Orchestra.
1888. Jan. 28. Scharwenka's " Arkadische Suite " given in New York City, by Theodore Thomas.
1888. Feb. 4. Chaikovsky's suite " Mozartiana " given by Theodore Thomas in New York City.
1888. Feb. 16. Rubinstein's Second Concerto for cello given by the Philadelphia orchestra, with Victor Herbert as soloist. Theodore Thomas conductor.
1888. Feb. 18. H. Grädener's Overture given by the Boston Symphony Orchestra.
1888. Feb. 24. Liszt's psalm " O Salutaris " for mezzo-soprano, chorus and orchestra, given by the Symphony Society in New York City, with Marianne Brandt as soloist.
1888. Feb. 25. Wagner's only Symphony (in C) given by the Boston Symphony Orchestra.
1888. Feb. 28. Bungert's symphonic poem " Auf der Wartburg," and F. Cowen's Fifth Symphony (in F) given by Theodore Thomas in New York City.
1888. Mar. 2. Harry Rowe Shelley's " Grand Sonata " given by Theodore Thomas in New York City.
1888. Mar. 8. R. Strauss's symphonic fantasia " Aus Italien " given by Theodore Thomas in Philadelphia.

1888. Mar. 16. A. Bruckner's Fourth (Romantic) Symphony (E flat) given at a concert in Chickering Hall, New York City, under direction of Anton Seidl.

1888. Mar. 17. Mozart's Violoncello Concerto (Op. 193) given in New York City by Theodore Thomas.

1888. April 3. MacDowell's First Pianoforte Concerto given at a concert under direction of B. J. Lang, with B. F. Whelpley as soloist, in Boston.

1888. April 6. Haydn's "Bear Symphony" (C major) given by Anton Seidl at a concert in Chickering Hall, New York City.

1888. April 7. Karl Goldmark's Second Symphony (E flat major) given by the Boston Symphony Orchestra.

1888. April 14. Rheinberger's "Passacaglia" and Praeger's symphonic poem "Life and Love, Battle and Victory" given in New York City, by Theodore Thomas.

1888. April 16. Verdi's opera "Otello" presented at the Academy of Music, New York City, under the management of Italo Campanini, with Eva Tetrazzini as *Desdemona*, Campanini as *Otello*, Scalchi as *Emilia*, and Galassi as *Iago*. Conductor Cleofonte Campanini.

1888. July 19. Dvořák's Symphonic Variations (Op. 78) given in Chicago, by Theodore Thomas.

1888. Oct. 27. Overture to Peter Cornelius's opera "The Barber of Bagdad" given by the Boston Symphony Orchestra.

1888. Nov. 10. The entr'acte to von Weber's "The Three Pintos," also Liszt's "Vogelpredigt des Heiligen Franz von Assisi," given at a concert at Chickering Hall, New York City, under Anton Seidl. At this concert Fritz Kreisler, noted Austrian violinist, made his American début.

1888. Nov. 13. American début of Moritz Rosenthal, noted pianist, at Steinway Hall, New York City.

1888. Nov. 17. Dvořák's "Slavonic Dances" (third and fourth series) given by the Boston Symphony Orchestra.

1888. Nov. 22. Felix Draeseke's "Serenata" given by the Symphony Society, in New York City.

1888. Nov. 24. Schubert's overture in E minor, and Bruch's Fantasia for Violin and Orchestra (Opus 46) given by the Boston Symphony Orchestra.

1888. Nov. 24. Grieg's concert-overture "In Autumn" given at a concert of the Brooklyn Philharmonic Society, Theodore Thomas conducting.

1888. Dec. 1. Vincent d'Indy's "Wallenstein Trilogy" and Victor Herbert's "Serenade," given at a concert in Chickering Hall, New York City, by Anton Seidl.

1888. Dec. 8. Reyer's "Waking of the Valkyrie" given by Theodore Thomas, in New York City.

1888. Dec. 29. A. Lindner's Concerto for Violoncello (Opus 34) given by the Boston Symphony Orchestra.

1888. Dudley Buck's oratorio "The Light of Asia" given by the Newark, N. J., Harmonic Society. This work was produced in England in 1885.

1889. Jan. 12. Gounod's opera "La Reine de Saba" presented in New Orleans, La.

1889. Jan. 17. Wagner's "Traüme" given by Theodore Thomas in Chicago.

1889. Jan. 19. First complete performance of Chaikovsky's Violin Concerto given in New York City, by Maud Powell.

1889. Jan. 24. Grieg's first suite "Peer Gynt," and Chaikovsky's Introduction and Fugue, given by Theodore Thomas in New York City.

1889. Mar. 5. MacDowell's Second Pianoforte Concerto (D minor) and Chaikovsky's Fifth Symphony (E minor) given at a concert in Chickering Hall, New York City, by Theodore Thomas.

1889. Mar. 6. Bristow's overture "The Jibbenainosay" given by the Harlem Philharmonic Society, New York City, conducted by the composer.

1889. Mar. 9. Mackenzie's overture to "Twelfth Night" given by Theodore Thomas, in New York City.

1889. Mar. 14. Mackenzie's "Benedictus" given in New York City by Theodore Thomas.

1889. Mar. 15. Chaikovsky's First Suite given in Brooklyn by Theodore Thomas.

1889. Mar. 27. Edward Grell's "Missa Solemnis" performed by the Oratorio Society in New York City.

1889. Mar. 28. Schumann's Fantasia for violin and orchestra

given at a concert in New York City, under Theodore Thomas.

1889. Mar. 30. Schubert's Overture in B given by the Boston Symphony Orchestra.

1889. April 4. Brahms's Waltzes given by the Boston Symphony Orchestra.

1889. April 20. J. K. Paine's symphonic poem, "An Island Fantasy" given by the Boston Symphony Orchestra.

1889. Aug. E. C. Phelps's "Elegy" for orchestra, produced at Brighton Beach, New York, N. Y., by Anton Seidl.

1889. Sept. 29. Brooklyn Symphony Orchestra organized by Carl Venth. Was in existence several years and produced a number of minor compositions by American composers.

1889. Nov. 16. Eckert's Concerto for Violoncello (A minor), Max Bruch's "Kol Nidrei" for 'cello and orchestra given by the Boston Symphony Orchestra.

1889. Nov. 23. Arthur Foote's Suite for Strings produced by the Boston Symphony Orchestra.

1889. Dec. 4. Karl Goldmark's overture "In the Spring" given at a concert of the Symphony Society in New York City.

1889. Dec. 7. Brahms's Violin Concerto in D played by the Boston Symphony Orchestra with Franz Kneisel as soloist.

1889. Auditorium dedicated, in Chicago, Ill.

CHAPTER VII

1890 — 1900

THE decade covered in this chapter was remarkable for progress in many directions.

Large orchestras were established all over the country — Pittsburgh, Cincinnati, San Francisco, Los Angeles, widely scattered cities, were among those which made serious efforts in the orchestral line, and performed large orchestral works.

America became in a still greater degree the hunting ground of the musical star who came from Europe, and swept the country of its loose dollars, appearing both as soloist with these orchestras, and giving recitals in the various cities.

Among pianists we had Busoni, who was, for a time, resident in Boston, Vladimir de Pachmann, the great interpreter of Chopin, who was immensely popular for some twenty-five years, and Paderewski, whose progress through the country was marked by previously unheard of demonstrations. It is said that thousands of people traveled many miles to see the train pass in which he was traveling. Alfred Reisenauer came in 1895, Slivinski, Alberto Jonás, Raoul Pugno, Siloti and Dohnanyi, were among those who made their first appearances in America during this decade.

There was also a large list of violin virtuosi beginning with Adolf Brodsky, who was followed by Henri Marteau, César Thomson, Ondriczek, Burmester, Halir, Gregorovitch, Marsick, Maud MacCarthy, Petschnikof and Madame Normann Neruda, who had been prominent in England for many years, and was long past her prime when she visited America. But the greatest artist of all was Eugen Ysaye, who first appeared in 1894, and who, since the great war, has been conductor of the Cincinnati Orchestra.

Opera continued to flourish on misfortune. Henry Abbey, who had ruined himself in driving out Mapleson, formed a partnership with John B. Schoeffel and Maurice Grau, and for some years provided opera for the country. Signor Luigi Arditi, who first appared as conductor of the Havana Company in about 1848, and had seen more operatic service in America than any other conductor, made a brief but interesting estimate of the impresarios under whom he had traveled during those years. " I have come to the conclusion," he writes, " that Don Francesco Marty (of the Havana Company) was the most generous of men, and Max Maretzek the cleverest. Colonel Mapleson was decidedly the astutest of all directors, . . . while to Henry Abbey must be attributed every straightforward and honorable quality. Maurice Grau was the cleverest of *entrepreneurs*."

Among the singers brought here by this combination was Tamagno, who appeared in 1890. The following season came Jean and Edouard de Reszke, who reigned supreme for a number of years. Also two American singers who had made reputations abroad, — Emma Eames and Marie van Zandt. In 1893 Nellie Melba and Emma Calvé came; and in 1894 Pol Plançon. In 1896 the Abbey and Grau combination collapsed. Abbey died soon after, and Grau continued alone until 1903.

In 1895 Walter Damrosch made an effort, which extended over several years, to reëstablish German opera, at the Metropolitan Opera House. This house, by the way, had been burned down in 1892, but was rebuilt and opened again in the following year. Several new singers were brought over from Germany, among them being Johanna Gadski.

In 1897 and 1898 Walter Damrosch joined forces with Charles A. Ellis, the manager of the Boston Symphony Orchestra, who had already been managing a company of which Melba was the star.

In 1896 Ernestine Schumann-Heink made her first American appearance in Chicago, and the following year joined the Metropolitan Company. Also Milka Ternina, an excellent artist, made her first appearance in Boston.

In 1898 Maurice Grau was the leading operatic impresario once more and introduced several new singers, including Marie Brema, Suzanne Adams, an American, and Marie Engle, also in 1900 another American, Louise Homer, while of the men Albert

Alvarez, a French tenor, and Antonio Scotti, an Italian baritone, were the most brilliant stars.

Italian opera was now being pushed hard by German opera, while French opera was very little heard. The table of performances published in New York at the end of the season 1900–1901 shows that Wagner had thirty-four performances out of a total of eighty-six. Gounod was next with twelve performances, Verdi with eight, Puccini with eight, Meyerbeer with five, Mascagni with four, Reyer and Massenet three each, Boito, Mozart and Donizetti two each, and Beethoven, Leoncavallo and Bizet one each.

American composers were seeking new themes indigenous to the soil. Many had already written something under the title of "Rip van Winkle," and Walter Damrosch had brought out an opera based on Hawthorne's novel "The Scarlet Letter." Anton Dvořák composed his "New World Symphony" making use of negro melodies for his themes. The resources of the Indians, the prairies and the mountains have been tapped more or less successfully. The oil fields still offer a thrilling subject for the composer.

1890. Jan. 4. Peter Cornelius's opera "Der Barbier von Bagdad" presented at the Metropolitan Opera House, New York City, under Walter Damrosch, also J. Bayer's ballet "Die Puppensee," with Frank Damrosch conducting.

1890. Jan. 4. Saint-Saëns's Third Violin Concerto (B minor) given by the Boston Symphony Orchestra with T. Adamowski as soloist; also Borodin's First Symphony (E flat).

ANNALS OF MUSIC IN AMERICA

1890. Jan. 11. Production of MacDowell's symphonic tone poem "Lancelot and Elaine," given by the Boston Symphony Orchestra.

1890. Jan. 23. Edouard Lalo's opera "Le Roy d'Ys," presented at New Orleans, La., with Furst, Balleroy, Geoffroy, Rossi, Butat, Miss Leavinson and Mrs. Beretta in the caste.

1890. Jan. 31. Brahms's "Liebeslieder Waltzes" given by the Symphony Society, in New York City.

1890. Feb. 1. Chaikovsky's Fourth Symphony (F minor) given at a concert of the Symphony Society in New York City. W. Damrosch conducting.

1890. Mar. 24. Début of Tamagno, great Italian tenor, as *Otello* at the Metropolitan Opera House, New York City.

1890. Mar. 25. Dvořák's Pianoforte Concerto in G minor, given at a concert in Chickering Hall, Boston, under B. J. Lang, with Benjamin L. Whelpley as soloist.

1890. April 8. J. C. D. Parker's oratorio "St. John" produced by the Handel and Haydn Society in Boston.

1890. Nov. 1. Goldmark's overture "Prometheus," and Sgambati's Pianoforte Concerto in G minor, given by the Boston Symphony Orchestra.

1890. Nov. 15. Moszkowski's Second Suite given in New York City, by Theodore Thomas.

1890. Nov. 20. Raff's overture to "Romeo and Juliet" given at a concert of the Cecilia Society in Boston.

1890. Nov. 22. Haydn's Concerto for Violoncello given by the Boston Symphony Orchestra, with Anton Hekking as soloist, also Smetana's symphonic poem "Vltava."

1890. Nov. 26. Franchetti's opera "Asraële," presented at the Metropolitan Opera House, New York City.

1890. Dec. 6. Goldmark's Violin Concerto in A minor given by the Boston Symphony Orchestra. F. Kneisel, soloist.

1890. Dec. 10. Production of H. W. Parker's overture "Count de Paris" by the Manuscript Society in New York City. Also E. C. Phelps's "Meditation" for orchestra.

1890. Dec. 12. Smareglia's opera "Der Vassall von Szigeth" presented at the Metropolitan Opera House, New York City.

1890. Dec. 12. Richard Burmeister's Pianoforte Concerto given by the Symphony Society in New York City, with the composer as soloist.

1890. Dec. Leopold Godowski, who had previously toured America as accompanist for Ovide Musin, made his first recital-tour.

1890. Grand opera given by Abbey and Schoeffel with a company including Adelina Patti, Emma Albani, Lillian Nordica, Fabbri, Carbone, Ravelli, Tamagno and others.

1891. Jan. 9. The Duke of Saxe-Coburg Gotha's opera "Diana von Solange," presented at the Metropolitan Opera House, New York City.

1891. Jan. 10. Joachim's Violin Concerto in G given by Theodore Thomas in New York City, and on the 17th, Rubinstein's overture to "Antony and Cleopatra" in Brooklyn, N. Y.

1891. Jan. 23. Début of Xaver Scharwenka in concert at Metropolitan Opera House, New York City.

1891. Jan. 24. Arthur Foote's symphonic prologue "Francesca da Rimini" produced by the Boston Symphony Orchestra.

1891. Feb. 4. Chaikovsky's overture fantasia "Hamlet" given by Theodore Thomas in Brooklyn, N. Y.

1891. Feb. 5. Massenet's cantata "Eve" given by the New York Chorus Society at Lenox Lyceum, New York City.

1891. Feb. 23. Dudley Buck's Romance, for Four Horns and Orchestra, played at an American Composers' Concert in New York City, under Mortimer Wiske. Also H. R. Shelley's Concerto for Violin.

1891. Mar. 7. Klughardt's Third Symphony (D major) given by the Boston Symphony Orchestra.

1891. Mar. 14. Paderewski's Pianoforte Concerto in A minor given by the Boston Symphony Orchestra, with Madame Julie Rivé-King as soloist.

1891. April 2. G. W. Chadwick's ode, "The Pilgrims' Hymn," produced by the Cecilia Society, Boston.

1891. April 10. Dudley Buck's overture "The Star Spangled Banner" produced at the "Tribune" Celebration in New York City.

1891. April 15. Massenet's suite "Esclarmonde" given in Chicago, by Theodore Thomas.

1891. April 29. Balakirev's oriental fantasia "Islamei" given by the Boston Symphony Orchestra, with Arthur Friedheim, soloist.

1891. May 5. Berlioz's "Te Deum" given by the Oratorio-Society in New York City, at the opening of Carnegie Hall.

1891. May 8. Chaikovsky's "Legend" and "Paternoster" given by the Oratorio Society, New York City, conducted by the composer.

1891. Sept. 9. Mascagni's opera "Cavalleria Rusticana" given in Philadelphia, under Gustav Hinrichs.

1891. Sept. 23. Dr. J. F. Bridge's dramatic oratorio "The Repentance of Nineveh" given at the Worcester (Mass.) Musical Festival.

1891. Sept. 24. Also Victor Herbert's dramatic cantata "The Captive."

1891. Sept. 24. MacDowell's suite in A minor, and

1891. Sept. 25. Handel's "Overture to an Occasional Oratorio."

1891. Oct. 31. Richard Strauss's tone poem "Don Juan" given by the Boston Symphony Orchestra, A. Nikisch conducting.

1891. Nov. 3. American début of Adolf Brodsky, noted violinist, with the New York Symphony Society, in Brahms's concerto.

1891. Nov. 5. Liszt's symphonic poem "Hungaria" given at a concert of the Philharmonic Orchestra in the Tremont Theatre, Boston, with Bernhard Listemann as conductor.

1891. Nov. 13. American début of Ferruccio Busoni, pianist, with the Boston Symphony Orchestra in Beethoven's Fourth Concerto.

1891. Nov. 18. American début of Ignace Paderewski, noted Polish pianist, in Carnegie Hall, New York City.

1891. Nov. 21. Production of C. M. Loeffler's suite for violin and orchestra, "Les Viellées de l'Ukraine," by the Boston Symphony Orchestra.

1891. Nov. 29. Berlioz's "Le 5 Mai," for bass solo, chorus and orchestra given by the Cecilia Society in Boston.

1891. Dec. 8. Rimsky-Korsakof's second symphony "Antar"

given by the Arion Society, New York City, F. van der Stucken, conductor.

1891. Dec. 14. American début of Jean (tenor) and Edouard (bass) de Reszke in "Roméo et Juliette" at the Metropolitan Opera House, New York City.

1891. Dec. 21. American début of Marie van Zandt, American soprano, as *Amina* in "La Sonnambula" at the Metropolitan Opera House, New York City.

1891. Dec. 25. Reyer's opera "Sigurd" presented at the French Opera House, New Orleans, La.

1891. Dec. 26. Handel's Concerto in F major for strings and two wind instruments, given by the Boston Symphony Orchestra.

1891. Dec. 31. Chaikovsky's fantasia "Francesca da Rimini" given by the Boston Symphony Orchestra.

1891. The Chicago Symphony Orchestra established, with Theodore Thomas as conductor.

1892. Jan. 6. Litolff's overture to "King Lear" played at a Young People's Concert of the Boston Symphony Orchestra.

1892. Jan. 9. Strauss's tone poem "Tod und Verklärung" given by the Philharmonic Society, New York City, Theodore Thomas conducting.

1892. Jan. 10. Chadwick's "A Pastoral Prelude" produced by the Boston Symphony Orchestra.

1892. Jan. 15. American début of Jean Lasalle, noted French baritone, as *Nelusko* in "L'Africaine" at the Metropolitan Opera House, New York City.

1892. Jan. 29. P. Scharwenka's symphonic poem "Frühlingswogen" given by the Chicago Symphony Orchestra. Theodore Thomas conductor.

1892. Feb. 5. Max Bruch's Second Concerto for Violin given by the New York Symphony Society with Geraldine Morgan, soloist.

1892. Feb. 6. First recital of Vladimir de Pachmann, Russian pianist, at Chickering Hall, New York City.

1892. Feb. 13. Massenet's opera "Hérodiade" presented at the French Opera House, New Orleans. (Given in New York, Nov. 8, 1909, by Hammerstein.)

1892. Feb. 20. F. Busoni's Symphonic Suite (Op. 23), three movements, given by the Boston Symphony Orchestra.

1892. Feb. 27. A. Dvořák's Fourth Symphony (G major) and Borodin's "A Prairie Scene" given by the Boston Symphony Orchestra.

1892. April 1. R. Strausss's symphonic poem "Macbeth" given by the Boston Symphony Orchestra.

1892. April 16. Suite from G. Henschel's music to "Hamlet" played by the Boston Symphony Orchestra, conducted by the composer.

1892. May 5. G. W. Chadwick's cantata "Phoenix Expirans" produced at the Springfield, Mass., Festival.

1892. Aug. 1. John Philip Sousa, noted bandmaster, resigned from the Marine Corps, and organized his band, which gained a world-wide reputation.

1892. Aug. 27. Metropolitan Opera House, New York City, destroyed by fire.

1892. Oct. 21. A. Dvořák's "Carnival" and "Otello" overtures presented at a concert given under the auspices of the National Conservatory of Music in New York City, in honor of the composer's first appearance in America.

1892. Oct. 21. The music of Moritz Moszkowski's opera "Boabdil" given by the Chicago Symphony Orchestra. Also J. Strauss's waltz "Seid umschlugen Millionen."

1892. Oct. 22. Chaikovsky's suite "Le Casse-Noisette" given by the Chicago Symphony Orchestra.

1892. Oct. 22. Saint-Saëns's Second Symphony (A minor) given by the Boston Symphony Orchestra.

1892. Oct. 22. Production of J. K. Paine's "Columbus March and Hymn," and George W. Chadwick's "Columbian Ode," at the dedication of the Music Building at the World's Fair in Chicago, Ill., under Theodore Thomas.

1892. Nov. 11. Hamish McCunn's concert overture "The Land of the Mountain and Flood" given by the Chicago Symphony Orchestra.

1892. Dec. 2. Cherubini's Overture given in New York City.

1892. Dec. 17. P. Gilson's symphonic sketches, "La Mer," given by the Philharmonic Society, New York City.

1892. Peoples' Choral Union organized in New York City, by Frank Damrosch.

1893. Jan. 4. Saint-Saëns's opera "Samson et Dalila" presented at the French Opera House, New Orleans, with Renaud and Madame Mounier in the leading parts.

1893. Jan. 24. Moritz Moszkowski's opera "Boabdil" presented at the Manhattan Opera House, New York.

1893. Jan. 31. P. Mascagni's opera "L'Amico Fritz" given its first complete stage performance in America by Walter Damrosch at Carnegie Hall, New York City. (A performance had been given June 8, 1892, by Gustav Heinrichs, in Philadelphia.)

1893. Feb. 3. Fuchs's Serenade for Strings and Two Horns given by the New York Symphony Society.

1893. Feb. 4. Arthur Foote's ballad "The Skeleton in Armor" for chorus, quartet and orchestra, produced by the Boston Symphony Orchestra.

1893. Mar. 4. G. Riemenschneider's "Tödtentanz" given by the Boston Symphony Orchestra.

1893. Mar. 7. Volkmann's Violoncello Concerto given by the Chicago Symphony Orchestra.

1893. Mar. 17. Edgar Tinel's oratorio "St. Francis d'Assisi" given by the Oratorio Society, New York City.

1893. April 8. Margaret Ruthven Lang's "Dramatic Overture" produced by the Boston Symphony Orchestra.

1893. April 15. F. Busoni's Symphonic Tone Poem produced by the Boston Symphony Orchestra.

1893. May 3. H. W. Parker's oratorio "Hora Novissima" produced by the Church Choral Society in New York City.

1893. June. Musorgsky's "Une Nuit sur le Mont Chauvée" said to have been played in a series of Russian concerts at the World's Columbian Exposition (June 5–13) with V. T. Hlavac, conductor.

1893. June 6. Balakiref's Overture on Russian Themes given at the Chicago Exposition at a concert of Russian music, and on June 7, Glazunof's "Triumphal March."

1895. June 12. Arthur Bird's Third Orchestral Suite given at the Chicago (Ill.) Exposition.

ANNALS OF MUSIC IN AMERICA

1893. July 7. Harry Rowe Shelley's "Carnival Overture" produced at the Chicago Exposition, and on the 19th his suite "The Ruined Castle."

1893. July 29. Margaret Ruthven Lang's overture "Witches" produced at the Chicago Exposition.

1893. Aug. Bizet's opera, "The Pearl Fishers," given in English in Philadelphia.

1893. Nov. 16. Scholz's suite, "Wanderings," given by the Chicago Symphony Orchestra.

1893. Nov. 16. Gounod's opera "Philémon et Baucis" given in English by the Duff Opera Company, at Herrman's Theatre, New York City.

1893. Nov. 24. G. Charpentier's orchestral suite "Impressions d'Italie" given by the Chicago Symphony Orchestra.

1893. Nov. 27. New Metropolitan Opera House, New York City, opened with a performance of "Faust," at which Pol Plançon, noted French basso, made his American début.

1893. Nov. 29. American début of Emma Calvé, noted French mezzo-soprano, as *Santuzza*, in "Cavalleria Rusticana" at the Metropolitan Opera House, New York City.

1893. Dec. 2. American début of Richard Burmeister, pianist, at Carnegie Hall, New York City, with the Damrosch Orchestra.

1893. Dec. 3. F. A. Lamond's overture "From the Highlands" given by the Chicago Symphony Orchestra.

1893. Dec. 4. American début of Nellie Melba, great Australian soprano, in "Lucia di Lammermoor" at the Metropolitan Opera House, New York City.

1893. Dec. 5. First appearance in America of Josef Slivinski, Polish pianist, at a concert in Madison Square Hall, New York City.

1893. Dec. 9. Alberto Jonás, noted Spanish pianist, made his American début in Carnegie Hall, New York City.

1893. Dec. American début of Sigrid Arnoldson, soprano, in Gounod's opera "Philémon et Baucis," at the Metropolitan Opera House, New York City.

1893. Dec. 9. Sinding's First Symphony (D minor) given by the Chicago Symphony Orchestra.

1893. Dec. 15. Dvořák's symphony in E minor "From the New World" produced by the Philharmonic Society in New York City. (Played from MS.)

1893. Dec. 28. Sgambati's "Te Deum" performed in Chicago, Ill., under directorship of Theodore Thomas.

1893. Dec. 30. Chaikovsky's "1812" overture given by the Boston Symphony Orchestra.

1893. Henri Marteau, violinist, made his first American concert tour.

1893. The Pittsburgh (Pa.) Symphony Orchestra organized under Frederick Archer.

1893. Emil Paur appointed conductor of the Boston Symphony Orchestra.

1893–4. Abbey and Grau presented grand opera with a company which included as newcomers, Emma Calvé, Nellie Melba, Sigrid Arnoldson, Pol Plançon, Gurin, Dufriche and Vignas.

1894. Jan. 5. Dvořák's Concerto for Violin given by the New York City Symphony Society, with Henri Marteau as soloist.

1894. Jan. 27. Liszt's rhapsody "Espagnole" given by the Boston Symphony Orchestra.

1894. Feb. 3. Moszkowski's "Torchlight Dance" given by the Chicago Symphony Orchestra.

1894. Feb. 3. Loeffler's "Concerto Fantastique" for Violoncello, produced by the Boston Symphony Orchestra, and at the same concert d'Albert's overture to "Esther" was played for the first time in America.

1894. Feb. 7. Hartmann's overture "Nordische Meerfahrt," Bruch's "Romanza" (Opus 42), and Saint-Saëns's "Morceau de Concert," given by the Boston Symphony Orchestra.

1894. Mar. 16. Chaikovsky's Sixth Symphony given by the Symphony Society in New York City, and Victor Herbert's Second Violoncello Concerto, with the composer as soloist.

1894. April 7. Hans von Bülow's "Funerale" given by the Boston Symphony Orchestra.

1894. April 20. Massenet's opera "Werther" given at the Metropolitan Opera House, New York City, with Eames, Arnoldson and Jean de Reszke in leading parts; Mancinelli conducting.

1894. May 23. Goldmark's overture to "Sappho" given in Cincinnati, O., under Theodore Thomas.

1894. May 25. Second and third tableaux from Rubinstein's sacred opera "Moses," given by Theodore Thomas in Cincinnati, O.

1894. June 15. Leoncavallo's opera "I Pagliacci" presented in New York with Kronold, Montegriffo and Campanari.

1894. Aug. 29. Puccini's opera "Manon Lescaut" presented at the Grand Opera House, Philadelphia, with Selma Kronold and Montegriffo.

1894. Sept. 27. Handel's Concerto (No. 7, in B flat) for organ and orchestra given at the Worcester (Mass.) Festival, with William C. Carl as soloist.

1894. Oct. 19. G. W. Chadwick's Third Symphony (F major) produced by Boston Symphony Orchestra. (This work won the prize offered by the National Conservatory.)

1894. Oct. 30. American début of César Thomson, noted Belgian violinist, at Carnegie Hall, New York City.

1894. Nov. 17. P. Benoit's Symphonic Poem for flute and orchestra given by the Boston Symphony Orchestra.

1894. Nov. 25. American début of Eugen Ysaye, great Belgian violinist, in a concert at the Metropolitan Opera House, New York City.

1894. Dec. 7. Joachim's "Theme and Variations" for violin, given by the Symphony Society, New York City, with Eugen Ysaye as soloist.

1894. Dec. 17. Bemberg's opera "Elaine" (libretto by Paul Ferrier) presented at the Metropolitan Opera House, New York City, with Melba, Mantelli, J. and E. de Reszke, Plançon and Castelmary.

1894. Dec. 28. Goldmark's Scherzo (Op. 45) given by the Chicago Symphony Orchestra.

1894. Dec. 29. Henry Holden Huss's Pianoforte Concerto in B major produced by the Boston Symphony Orchestra, with the composer as soloist.

1895. Jan. 5. C. M. Loeffler's Divertimento in A minor, produced by the Boston Symphony Orchestra.

1895. Jan. 15. American début of Sybil Sanderson, American

soprano, as *Manon*, at the Metropolitan Opera House, New York City.

1895. Jan. 25. A. Mackenzie's nautical overture "Britannica" given by the Chicago Symphony Orchestra.

1895. Feb. 4. Verdi's opera "Falstaff" presented at the Metropolitan Opera House, New York City, with Emma Eames, Zelie de Lussan, Scalchi, Campanari, and Maurel. Mancinelli conducting.

1895. Feb. 8. Cecile Chaminade's "Concertstücke," for orchestra, given by the Chicago Symphony Orchestra.

1895. Feb. 16. Gustav Strube's overture to "The Maid of Orleans" produced by the Boston Symphony Orchestra.

1895. Feb. 21. Howard LeGrand's oratorio "The Resurrection" given by the Church Choral Society, New York City.

1895. Feb. 22. Rheinberger's Concerto in G minor, for organ, given by the Chicago Symphony Orchestra.

1895. Feb. 28. Maurice Arnold's "American Plantation Dances" given by the American Symphony Orchestra, New York City.

1895. Mar. 1. American début of Johanna Gadski, soprano, as *Elsa* in "Lohengrin" at the Metropolitan Opera House, New York City.

1895. Mar. 23. Marschner's overture to "Hans Heiling," and Reinecke's entr'acte of "Der Gouverneur von Tours" given by the Boston Symphony Orchestra; also R. Kahn's overture in C minor "Elegie" produced (from MS.).

1895. Mar. 30. H. Goetz's "Spring Overture"; Knorr's "Variations on an Ukraine Folk Song," and H. W. Parker's Rhapsody for baritone and orchestra, given by the Boston Symphony Orchestra.

1895. April 14. J. C. D. Parker's oratorio "The Life of Man" produced by the Handel and Haydn Society in Boston.

1895. Oct. 6. Humperdinck's opera "Hänsel und Gretel" given in English in New York City at Daly's Theatre, with Alice Gordon, Marie Elba, Louise Meisslinger, Jacques Bars, C. Brané and E. Johnson. A. Seidl, conductor.

1895. Oct. 19. Mozart's Andante and Variations in D minor given by the Boston Symphony Orchestra.

1895. Oct. 25. Smetana's symphonic poem " Sarka," and Edward German's " Three Dances of the Time of Henry VIII," given by the Chicago Symphony Orchestra.

1895. Nov. 1. The *Vorspiel* to R. Strauss's opera " Guntram " given by the Chicago Symphony Orchestra.

1895. Nov. 1. Rameau's suite de ballet from " Acanthe et Céphisse " and the Prelude to the third act of R. Strauss's opera " Guntram " given by the Symphony Society in New York City.

1895. Nov. Symphony Orchestra organized in San Francisco, Cal., with Fritz Scheel as conductor.

1895. Nov. 4. Paderewski's " Polish Fantasia " given at a concert in Carnegie Hall, New York City.

1895. Nov. 8. César Franck's symphonic poem " Les Sylphides," given by the Chicago Symphony Orchestra.

1895. Nov. 15. The ballet music from Massenet's opera " Thaïs," and Strauss's tone poem " Till Eulenspiegel," given by the Chicago Symphony Orchestra.

1895. Nov. 15. American début of Franz Ondriczek, violinist, at a concert of the Philharmonic Society, New York City, in Dvorák's A minor Concerto for violin.

1895. Nov. 29. American début of Giuseppe Cremonini, tenor, at the Metropolitan Opera House, New York City.

1895. Nov. 30. The Prelude to d'Albert's opera " Der Rubin " played by the Boston Symphony Orchestra.

1895. Dec. 7. Reznicek's overture to the opera " Donna Diana " given by the Boston Symphony Orchestra.

1895. Dec. 11. Massenet's opera " La Navarraise " presented at the Metropolitan Opera House, New York city, with Emma Calvé in the title-rôle.

1895. Dec. 17. American début of Yvette Guilbert at Hammerstein's Music Hall, New York. N. Y.

1895. Willy Burmester, violinist, toured the United States.

1895. Alfred Reisenaur, pianist, first appeared in America.

1895. Cincinnati Orchestral Association founded, with Frank van der Stucken as conductor.

1895–6. German opera given in New York and several of the large cities by Walter Damrosch, with a company including

Johanna Gadski, Marie Brema, Rose Sucher, Rothmühl (tenor) and others.

1896. Jan. 4. Lalo's Suite "Namouna," given by the Boston Symphony Orchestra.

1896. Jan. 23. Edward MacDowell's "Indian Suite" given by the Boston Symphony Orchestra at the Metropolitan Opera House, New York City.

1896. American début of Milka Ternina, soprano, as *Brunnhilde* in "Die Walküre" in Boston.

1896. Feb. 7 Chaikovsky's First Symphony (G minor) given by the Philharmonic Society, New York City.

1896. Feb. 11. Stage production of Walter Damrosch's opera "The Scarlet Letter," at the Boston Theatre, Boston, Mass., with Gadski, Berthald and Mertens.

1896. Feb. 13. Scharwenka's opera "Mataswintha" given in concert form by the Manuscript Society in New York City.

1896. Feb. 22. H. Zöllner's orchestral fantasia "Midnight at Sedan" given by the Boston Symphony Orchestra.

1896. Mar. 21. "Three Hungarian Dances" by Brahms, given by the Boston Symphony Orchestra.

1896. April 4. Production of Gustav Strube's Symphony in C minor, by the Boston Symphony Orchestra.

1896. April 17. Handel's Concerto in F, for strings, given by the Chicago Symphony Orchestra, and on the 24th Smetana's symphonic poem "Vysehrad."

1896. April 24. Henschel's "Stabat Mater" given by the Oratorio Society, New York City, conducted by the composer.

1896. Oct. 17. Bourgault-Ducoudray's "L'Interrement d'Ophélie" given by the Boston Symphony Orchestra.

1896. Oct. 23. Balakireff's symphonic poem "Thamar" given by the Chicago Symphony Orchestra.

1896. Oct. 24. Chabrier's Overture to "Gwendoline" given by the Boston Symphony Orchestra.

1896. Oct. 31. Production of Mrs. H. H. A. Beach's "Gaelic Symphony" (from MS.) by the Boston Symphony Orchestra.

1896. Nov. 7. The "Sevilliana" from Massenet's opera "Don César de Bazan" given by the Boston Symphony Orchestra.

1896. Nov. 8. American début of Karl Halir, violinist, in Beethoven's Violin Concerto, with the Philharmonic Society, New York City.

1896. Nov. 13. Giordano's opera "Andrea Chénier" given at the Academy of Music, New York City, by Mapleson, with Bonaplato-Bau, Scalchi and Durot.

1896. Nov. 13. Smetana's symphonic poem "Richard III," Duparc's symphonic poem "Lenore," and Glazunof's "Oriental Rhapsody," given by the Chicago Symphony Orchestra.

1896. Nov. 21. The Intermezzo from Goldmark's opera "Das Heimchen am Herd" given by the Boston Symphony Orchestra.

1896. Nov. 24. American début of C. Gregorovitch, violinist, at Chickering Hall, New York City, with the American Symphony Orchestra.

1896. Dec. 11. Roentgen's "Ballad on a Norwegian Folk Song" given by the Chicago Symphony Orchestra.

1896. Dec. 19. Dvořák's Violoncello Concerto in B minor, given by the Boston Symphony Orchestra. Schroeder, soloist.

1896. Dec. 26. Selections from Gluck's ballet, "Don Juan," and from Humperdinck's opera "Königskinder," also Handel's First Overture, in D minor, given by the Boston Symphony Orchestra.

1896. American début of Jacques Bars, tenor, in "Hänsel und Gretel" at Daly's Theatre, New York City.

1896. Margaret Ruthven Lang's "Sappho's Prayer" produced in New York City.

1896. Los Angeles (Cal.) Symphony Orchestra organized.

1896. Martin Marsick, violinist, made his first tour in America.

1897. Jan. 1. Dvořák's tone poem "The Golden Spinning Wheel" given by the Chicago Symphony Orchestra.

1897. Jan. 2. Smetana's symphonic poem "Wallenstein's Lager" given by the Boston Symphony Orchestra.

1897. Jan. 8. Rimsky-Korsakof's suite "Mlada" given by the Chicago Symphony Orchestra.

1897. Jan. 16. Dittersdorf's Symphony in C major, given by the Boston Symphony Orchestra.

1897. Feb. 4. Dvořák's symphonic poem "The Water Fay" given at a concert of the Seidl Society at the Academy of Music, New York City.

1897. Feb. 5. R. Strauss's tone poem, "Also sprach Zarathustra," given by the Chicago Symphony Orchestra.

1897. Feb. 12. Massenet's opera "Le Cid" given at the Metropolitan Opera House, New York City, with Felia Litvinne, Clementine de Vere, J. Bars, J. de Reszke, Pol Plançon, J. Lasalle and E. de Reszke. Mancinelli conducting.

1897. Mar. 6. Arthur Whiting's Fantasy for pianoforte and orchestra in B flat minor, given by the Boston Symphony Orchestra.

1897. Mar 17. J. W. Glover's oratorio "St. Patrick at Tara" given at the Lexington Opera House, New York City.

1897 Mar. 24. Mozart's Symphony in A major given by the American Symphony Society in Chickering Hall, New York City. Sam Franko, conductor.

1897. April 3. Dvořák's Rondo for Violoncello (Op. 94) given by the Boston Symphony Orchestra.

1897. April 17. Rimsky-Korsakof's symphonic suite "Scheherazade" given by the Boston Symphony Orchestra.

1897. June 25. H. R. Shelley's Symphony in E flat played at the Music Teachers National Association Convention in New York City.

1897. Sept. 22. Production of Gustav Strube's Violin Concerto (Op. 13) at the Worcester (Mass) Festival, with F. Kneisel as soloist.

1897. Oct. 16. Glazunof's "Poème Lyrique" (Op. 42) given by the Boston Symphony Orchestra.

1897. Oct. 23. Rimsky-Korsakof's overture on Russian church themes, "La Grand Paque Russe," and Gernsheim's Violin Concerto in D major, given by the Boston Symphony Orchestra.

1897. Oct. 29. Glazunof's Second Concert Waltz given by the Chicago Symphony Orchestra, and on the 4th Nov. Glazunof's tableaux musicales "Printemps."

1897. Nov. 26. Chaikovsky's symphonic ballad "Voyvode" given by the Symphony Society in New York City.

1897. Dec. 3. Introduction to Act II of d'Albert's opera "Gernot," given by the Pittsburgh Symphony Orchestra. Frederick Archer conductor.

1897. Dec. Production of Henry K. Hadley's First Symphony under direction of Anton Seidl, in New York City.

1897. Dec. 10. Raoul Pugno, French pianist, first appeared in the United States.

1897. Dec. 13. Massenet's opera "Le Portrait de Manon" given in French by the Society of Musical Arts, at the Astoria, New York City. Also C. Chaminade's ballet "Callirhoë," and on Dec. 21, an opera by V. Thompson and Aïme Lachaume, "In Old Japan," was produced.

1897-8. The Damrosch-Ellis Opera Company gave grand opera throughout the country with artists including Melba, Nordica, Gadski, soprani; van Cauteren and Mattfeld, contralti; Kraus, Salignac, Rothmühl and Ibos, tenors; Stehman, Fischer, and Boudouresque, basses.

1898. Jan. 7. Hugo Kaun's "Festival March and Hymn" given by the Chicago Symphony Orchestra.

1898. Jan. 8. Siegfried Wagner's symphonic poem "Sehnsucht" given by the Philharmonic Society in New York City.

1898. Jan. 8. Production of C. M. Loeffler's dramatic poem, "La mort de Tintagiles" by the Boston Symphony Orchestra.

1898. Jan. 14. Hugo Kaun's Symphony in D minor given by the Chicago Symphony Orchestra.

1898. Jan. 15. Paganini's "Caprice" for violin, in A minor, given by the Boston Symphony Orchestra.

1898. Jan. 25. American début of Alexander Siloti, famous Russian pianist, as a concert given by Anton Seidl at the Astoria, New York City.

1898. Jan. 27. Production of Gustav Strube's overture for trumpets, horns, tuba and kettledrums, at a concert of the Apollo Club in Boston.

1898. Jan. 27. Dubois's Concerto for Violin, in D minor, given by the Pittsburgh Symphony Orchestra with Henri Marteau as soloist.

1898. Jan. 29. César Franck's symphonic poem "The Wild

Huntsman" given at Cincinnati, O., by Theodore Thomas.

1898. Feb. 5. Chaikovsky's Second Pianoforte Concerto (G major) given by the Boston Symphony Orchestra. Alexander Siloti, soloist.

1898. Feb. 26. A. Goring Thomas's cantata "The Swan and the Skylark" given at a Seidl Concert in the Metropolitan Opera House, New York City.

1898. Mar. 1. H. H. Huss's dramatic scene, "Cleopatra's Death," given by the Philharmonic Society, New York City, under A. Seidl.

1898. Mar. 5. Glazunof's Fifth Symphony (B flat major) given by the Philharmonic Society in New York City. A Seidl conductor.

1898. Mar. 7. Saint-Saëns's Fifth Pianoforte Concerto given by the Chicago Symphony Orchestra in New York City, with Raoul Pugno as soloist. Also César Franck's "Variations Symphoniques."

1898. Mar. Puccini's opera "La Bohème" presented in San Francisco, Cal., by the Royal Italian Opera Company. (Given by same company in New York, May 10.)

1898. April 7. F. Weingärtner's symphonic poem, "The Elysian Fields," given by the Philharmonic Society, New York City.

1898. Horatio Parker's oratorio "St. Christopher" given by the Oratorio Society, New York City.

1898. April 23. D'Indy's symphonic variations "Istar" given by Chicago Symphony Orchestra. Theodore Thomas, conductor.

1898. Oct. 22. Chausson's symphonic poem "Viviane," and Mackenzie's three dances for "The Little Minister" given by the Chicago Symphony Orchestra.

1898. Nov. 7. American début of Ernestine Schumann-Heink, as *Ortrud* in "Lohengrin," in Chicago.

1898. Nov. 8. American début of Albert Saléza, tenor, as *Romeo*, in Chicago.

1898. Nov. 29. American début of Ernest van Dyck, as *Tannhäuser*, at the Metropolitan Opera House, New York City.

1898. Dec. 3. First performance of Walter Damrosch's

ANNALS OF MUSIC IN AMERICA

"Manilla Te Deum" given by the Oratorio Society of New York City.

1898. Dec. 14. American début of Anton van Rooy, as *Wotan* in "Die Walküre" at the Metropolitan Opera House, New York City.

1898. Dec. 25. American début of Maud MacCarthy, violinist, at the Metropolitan Opera House, New York City.

1898. Borodin's Symphony in B minor first played in America by the Cincinnati Orchestra.

1898. Victor Herbert appointed conductor of the Pittsburgh Symphony Orchestra.

1899. Jan. 4. American début of Suzanne Adams, American soprano, at the Metropolitan Opera House, New York City.

1899. Jan. 7. R. Strauss's tone poem "Don Quixote," given by the Chicago Symphony Orchestra.

1899. Jan. 12. Gounod's opera "La Reine de Saba," presented at the French Opera House, New Orleans, La.

1899. Jan. 17. F. S. Converse's Symphony in D minor (first movement) given by the Boston Symphony Orchestra. The first full performance was not given till Jan. 30, 1920.

1899. Jan. 17. Grieg's Symphonic Dances given by the Chicago Symphony Orchestra.

1899. Feb. 3. Hugo Kaun's overture "Der Maler von Antwerpen" given by the Chicago Symphony Orchestra.

1899. Feb. 7. American début of Albert Alvarez, French operatic tenor, as *Romeo*, in Boston, at the Boston Theatre.

1899. Feb. 8. American début of Lady Halle (Normann Neruda), noted violinist, with the Boston Symphony Orchestra. She played Spohr's Violin Concerto in C minor.

1899. Mar. 4. Chabrier's "Bourrée Fantastique" given by the Boston Symphony Orchestra.

1899. Mar. 10. Mancinelli's opera "Ero e Leandro" presented at the Metropolitan Opera House, New York City, conducted by the composer.

1899. Mar. 22. American début of E. Dohnanyi, Hungarian pianist, with Boston Symphony Orchestra at Carnegie Hall, New York City.

1899. Mar. 25. César Franck's oratorio "The Beatitudes" given by the Liederkranz Society of New York City.

1899. April. 15. César Franck's Symphony in D. Minor given by the Boston Symphony Orchestra.

1899 April 24. Perosi's oratorio "The Transfiguration of Christ" given by the Cecilia Society of Boston.

1899. Oct. 14. Arensky's Pianoforte Concerto in F minor, given by the Boston Symphony Orchestra with Katherine Goodson as soloist.

1899. Oct. 20. Dvořák's tone poem, "The Wild Dove," given by the Chicago Symphony Orchestra.

1899. Oct. 21. Lalo's Violoncello Concerto in D minor, and Glazunof's Sixth Symphony (G minor) given by the Boston Symphony Orchestra.

1899. Oct. The Society of American Musicians and Composers organized to succeed the MS. Society of New York City.

1899. Nov. 3. American début of Mark Hambourg, pianist, in Boston with the Boston Symphony Orchestra.

1899. Nov. 4. Siegfried Wagner's opera "Der Barenhäuter," and W. Berger's Symphony in B flat major, given by the Boston Symphony Orchestra.

1899. Nov. 17. American début of A. Petchnikof, violinist, with the Philharmonic Orchestra, New York City.

1899. Nov. 18. Dvořák's symphonic poem (Op. 111), "Pisen Bohatyrská" given by the Boston Symphony Orchestra.

1899. Dec. 9. F. Draeseke's "Jubel Overture" given by the Boston Symphony Orchestra.

1899. Dec. 23. American début of Antonio Scotti, noted baritone, as *Don Giovanni* at the Metropolitan Opera House, New York City.

1899. Dec. 30. H. W. Parker's "Northern Ballad" given by the Boston Symphony Orchestra.

CHAPTER VIII

1900

THE first decade of the twentieth century was noteworthy for the establishment of orchestras throughout the land. During the nineteenth century the development of the resources of the country and the increase of its wealth and population was phenomenal. In 1900 the population of the United States was about seventy-five millions. Chicago, which was practically non-existent in 1800, had a population of about two millions and was already a rival of New York. Railroads, unknown at the beginning of the nineteenth century, had covered the country with a network of communications and caused the growth of large cities in places far remote from the civilization of the year 1800.

We find Minneapolis establishing an orchestra in 1902, St. Paul in 1905, New Orleans in 1906, Seattle in 1908, while the Symphony Society of New York was reorganized in 1905, and a Russian Symphony orchestra established in New York City. The term "Symphony Orchestra" has been universally adopted, till we have symphony orchestras even in the moving picture houses. In Grove's Dictionary (edition of 1890) the only symphony orchestra mentioned is "the Boston Symphony Orchestra," though the "Symphony Society" of New York is also listed. It seems then that the term "symphony" applied to an orchestra is an American qualification signifying complete equipment, and at least good intentions.

During this period the New York Philharmonic Society adopted the plan, for three successive years, of engaging visiting, or guest conductors, and in this way a number of the most prominent European conductors were introduced to the American public.

A few American composers emerged, and of them the most frequently found were Frederick S. Converse and Henry K. Hadley, of whose works several were produced by the leading orchestras and opera companies.

The list of virtuosi is also long. Among pianists Harold Bauer and Ossip Gabrilovitsch appeared in 1900, and later came Rudolf Ganz, Josef Lhevinne, Katherine Goodson, and Serge Rachmaninof. Among violinists, Kubelik, Kocian, Hugo Heerman, Jacques Thibaud, Efrem Zimbalist and Arthur Spalding, only the last being of American birth.

The list of singers is long, and is chiefly associated with opera. Louise Homer, an American, made her début in 1900, and Geraldine Farrar, another American, in 1906. Among other noted singers we find, Lucienne Breval, Caruso, Fremstad, Tetrazzini, Bonci, Renaud, Chaliapine, Morena, Destinn,

Mary Garden, John McCormack, Edouard Clément, and Slezak, — samples of many nationalities.

This brings us to the opera. Maurice Grau resigned from the directorship of the Metropolitan Opera House in 1903. Grau brought the star system to a climax, and gave opera with "all star casts," but few new operas were presented under his management. In 1903 Heinrich Conried succeeded to the management of the Metropolitan Opera House, and set himself to work to abolish the star system, as far as possible, and produce a good ensemble. The abolition of the star system proved an impossibility, because people had been fed upon it since the musical life of the country began, and New York audiences would not go to hear singers who had not already made European reputations. But Mr. Conried succeeded in producing many works new to the American public. Of these "Parsifal" stands forth conspicuously, though he found a competitor in Henry W. Savage, who produced "Parsifal" in English a few days in advance of Mr. Conried's production. This was followed in 1906 by Strauss's "Salome." Conried died in 1908 and was succeeded by the dual control of Signor Gatti-Casazza and Andreas Dippel, but Dippel soon resigned and went to Chicago, and from that date until the present (1922) Signor Gatti-Casazza has been sole manager of the Metropolitan Opera House.

In 1906 Oscar Hammerstein opened the Manhattan Opera House in New York City and instituted a strong rivalry with the Metropolitan. He brought to America some excellent singers and presented many works new to the American public. While the Metropolitan company gave more German than French or Italian opera, the Manhattan seemed to tend towards a preponderance of French opera. The rivalry was beneficial to the public if not to the stockholders.

We find during this period an opera, "The Pipe of Desire," by Frederick S. Converse, the first American opera to be presented at the Metropolitan Opera House. All the principals, with one exception, were also of American birth, — Louise Homer, Riccardo Martin, Clarence Whitehill and Herbert Witherspoon. The other principal was Lenora Sparks, an English singer.

The most notable feature of the decade seems to have been the spread of musical enterprise throughout the country. Distant cities were organizing choral societies and orchestras to a greater extent than ever before. It is necessary not only to develop composers, support a few fine orchestras and produce a few operas, but the nation must grow musically as a whole. The support given to musical enterprise depends on the education of the rising generation, and must begin with the schools.

1900. Jan. 5. Sinding's "Rondo Infinito" given by the Chicago Symphony Orchestra. Also Weidig's "Scherzo Capriccioso."
1900. Jan. 13. R. Goldmark's overture to "Hiawatha" produced (from MS.) by the Boston Symphony Orchestra.

ANNALS OF MUSIC IN AMERICA

1900. Jan. 19. Sinding's "Episodes Chevaleresques" given by the Chicago Symphony Orchestra.

1900. Jan. 22. Spinelli's opera "A Basso Porto" presented by the Castle Square Opera Company in New York City.

1900. Jan. 24. American début of Fritz Friedrichs, as *Beckmesser* in "Die Meistersinger" at the Metropolitan Opera House, New York City.

1900. Jan. 25. Reyer's opera "Salammbô" presented at the French Opera House, New Orleans.

1900. Feb. 3. G. W. Chadwick's "Elegiac Overture" produced (from MS.) by the Boston Symphony Orchestra.

1900. Feb. 10. V. d'Indy's suite for orchestra "Médée" given by the Boston Symphony Orchestra.

1900. Feb. 11. E. Pessard's "Danses Espagnoles," and Dubois's "Marche des Batteurs" from the opera "Xavière," given at a concert of the Orchestral Club, in Boston.

1900. Feb. 17. C. Franck's symphonic poem "Les Éolides" given by the Boston Symphony Orchestra.

1900. Mar. 10. R. Strauss's symphonic poem "Ein Heldenleben" given by the Chicago Symphony Orchestra.

1900. Mar. 10. Sinding's Violin Concerto in A major given by the Philharmonic Society in New York City, with Henri Marteau as soloist. Also Guiraud's "Caprice" for violin.

1900. Mar. 10. J. K. Paine's ballet music from his opera "Azara" given by the Boston Symphony Orchestra.

1900. Mar. 14. The overture to Coleridge Taylor's "The Song of Hiawatha" given at a concert of the Cecilia Society, Boston.

1900. Mar. 25. C. Franck's symphonic poem, with chorus, "The Beatitudes," given by the German Liederkranz, in New York City.

1900. April 7. Mrs. H. H. A. Beach's pianoforte concerto in C sharp minor produced (from MS.) by the Boston symphony Orchestra; also Rameau's "Ballet Suite" given for the first time in America.

1900. April 27. The Overture to Saint-Saëns's opera "La Princesse Jaune"; Becker's "Scenes Luxembourgeoises"; Dubois's "Rigaudon" and "Danses Cénénoles," and E.

Tavan's " Noce Arabe " given by the Orchestral Club, Boston.

1900. July 2 Production of Frank von der Stucken's symphonic festival prologue, " Pax Triumphans," at a Saengerfest in Brooklyn, N. Y.

1900. Oct. Philadelphia Symphony Orchestra established by the Orchestral Association, with Fritz Scheel as conductor.

1900. Oct. 19. Chaikovsky's suite de ballet " La Belle au Bois Dormant " and G. Schumann's " Symphonic Variations " for organ and orchestra given by the Chicago Symphony Orchestra; also d'Indy's " Wallenstein's Camp."

1900. Oct. 20. Handel's Fourth Concerto for Organ (B minor) given by the Chicago Symphony Orchestra.

1900. Oct. 20. Edouard Strauss and his Vienna Orchestra made American début at the Waldorf Astoria, New York City. Made an extensive tour of the United States.

1900. Nov. 2. Berlioz's overture to " Rob Roy " given by the Chicago Symphony Orchestra.

1900. Nov. 12. American début of Charles Gilibert (baritone) in " Roméo et Juliette " in San Francisco, Cal. His New York début took place at the Metropolitan Opera House on Dec. 18, in the same opera, as the *Duke of Verona*.

1900. Nov. 17. American début of Ossip Gabrilowitsch, Russian pianist, at Carnegie Hall, New York City.

1900. Nov. 13. American début of Robert Blass (tenor), as *Herman* in " Tannhäuser," in San Francisco, Cal. New York début Dec. 24.

1900. Nov. 14. American début of Louise Homer (contralto) as *Amneris* in " Aida," and Imbart de la Tour (tenor) as *Rhadames*, at San Francisco, Cal. New York début same opera, Metropolitan Opera House, Dec. 22.

1900. Nov. 16. Josef Suk's symphony in E major given by the Philharmonic Society, New York City.

1900. Nov. 17. American début of Marcel Journet (baritone) in " Lucia " at San Francisco, Cal.

1900. Nov. 19. American début of Fritzi Scheff (lyric soprano) as *Mimi* in " La Bohème " at San Francisco, Cal. New York début as *Fidelio*, Metropolitan Opera House, Dec. 29.

1900. Nov. 19. Goring Thomas's opera " Esmeralda " given

ANNALS OF MUSIC IN AMERICA

by the Metropolitan English Grand Opera Company at the Metropolitan Opera House, New York City.

1900. Nov. 24. F. Cowen's sixth symphony "Idyllic" (F major) given by the Boston Symphony Orchestra.

1900. Nov. 30. Henri Rabaud's symphonic poem, "La Procession Nocturne" played by the Cincinnati Symphony Orchestra, Frank van der Stucken conducting.

1900. Dec. 1. Tanaief's symphony in C, and Brahms's first pianoforte concerto (D minor), with Harold Bauer (début) as soloist, given by the Boston Symphony Orchestra.

1900. Dec. 2. Scriabin's "Reverie" given by the Cincinnati Symphony Orchestra.

1900. Dec. 5. Coleridge Taylor's cantata "Hiawatha's Departure" given by the Cecilia Society in Boston.

1900. Dec. 8. Smetana's fourth symphonic poem "Má Vlast" given by the Boston Symphony Orchestra.

1900. Dec. 10. F. X. Arens's "Salve Regina" given by the Musical Arts Society, in New York City.

1900. Dec. 22. F. S. Converse's "Festival of Pan" produced by the Boston Symphony Orchestra.

1900. Dec. Bach's B minor Mass given by the Bach Choir at Bethlehem, Pa., at one of the Bach Festivals which were inaugurated this year.

1901. Jan. Death of Edmund C. Stanton, manager of the Metropolitan Opera House, New York City, from 1884 to 1891.

1901. Jan. 11. Rimsky-Korsakof's "Fantaisie de Concert" for violin given by the Philharmonic Society in New York City with Maud Powell as soloist.

1901. Jan. 14. New York début of Margaret McIntyre, soprano, as *Marguerite* in Boito's opera "Mefistofele" at the Metropolitan Opera House.

1901. Jan. 16. New York début of Lucienne Breval, noted French soprano, in Massenet's opera "Le Cid," at the Metropolitan Opera House.

1901 Jan. 18. Victor Herbert's symphonic poem "Hero and Leander" produced by the Pittsburgh Symphony Orchestra, conducted by the composer.

1901. Jan. 23. Luigini's "La Voix des Cloches" given at a concert of the Orchestral Club in Boston.

1901. Jan. 27. H. R. Shelley's overture "Santa Claus" given at a concert in the Metropolitan Opera House, New York City, under Walter Damrosch.

1901. Jan. 29. C. M. Loeffler's "Divertissement Espagnol" for saxophone and orchestra (written for Mrs. Richard J. Hall) produced at a concert of the Orchestral Club in Boston, with Mrs. Hall as soloist.

1901. Feb. 2. I. Brüll's overture to "Macbeth" (Op. 46), and van der Stucken's symphonic prologue to "William Ratcliffe," given by the Boston Symphony Orchestra.

1901. Feb. 4. Puccini's opera "La Tosca" presented at the Metropolitan Opera House, New York City, with Milka Ternina as *La Tosca*, Cremonini as *Cavaradossi*, Scotti as *Scarpia*, Gilibert as the *Sacristan*, and Mancinelli conducting.

1901. Mar. 1. Philharmonic Orchestra of Leipzig visiting America, gave its first concert in New York City, Hans Winderstein, conductor.

1901. Mar. 9. Bruckner's Third Symphony (D minor) given by the Boston Symphony Orchestra.

1901. Mar. 15. Elgar's overtures "Cockaigne" and "In London Town," also Glazunof's "Ruses d'Amor," given by the Chicago Symphony Orchestra.

1901. Mar. 30. Schumann's overture "Julius Caesar" (Op. 128), given by the Boston Symphony Orchestra.

1901. April 6. H. Brockway's "Sylvan Suite" for orchestra produced by the Boston Symphony Orchestra.

1901. April 13. F. Weingärtner's symphony in G major, given by the Boston Symphony Orchestra.

1901. April 20. Gustav Strube's Rhapsody for Orchestra (Op. 17) produced by the Boston Symphony Orchestra.

1901. Sept. 26. G. W. Chadwick's oratorio "Judith" produced at the Worcester (Mass.) Festival.

1901. Sept. 27. Mackenzie's orchestral suite "Coriolanus" given at the Worcester (Mass.) Festival.

1901. Oct. 14. Eugen d'Albert's overture "Der Improvisatore" given by the Chicago Symphony Orchestra.

1901. Nov. 15. Dvořák's overture "Mein Heim," given by the Chicago Symphony Orchestra.
1901. Nov. 16. S. von Hausegger's symphony "Barbarossa" given by the Symphony Society in New York City.
1901. Nov. 22. J. Suk's march "Pohadka" given by the Chicago Symphony Orchestra.
1901 Dec. 2. American début of Jan Kubelik, violinist, at a concert in Carnegie Hall, New York City.
1901. Dec. 6. Production of Victor Herbert's "Woodland Fancies," orchestral suite, by the Pittsburgh Symphony Orchestra, conducted by the composer.
1901. Dec. 7. Glazunof's "Ouverture Solennelle" given by the Chicago Symphony Orchestra, also Sibelius's "Two Legends" from "Kalevala."
1901. Dec. 20. Production of Henry K. Hadley's symphony "The Four Seasons" by the Philharmonic Society in New York City. This work won the New England Conservatory and Paderewski prizes. Was played in Chicago Jan. 24, 1902, and Pittsburgh, Nov. 27, 1903.
1901. Dec. 28. Bruckner's Fifth Symphony (D flat major), and Bach's concerto for trumpet, flute, oboe, and violin, in F major, given by the Boston Symphony Orchestra.
1901. Century Musical Club formed in Atlanta, Ga.
1901. F. van der Stucken resigned conductorship of the Cincinnati Symphony Orchestra and was succeeded by L. Stokowski.
1902. Jan. 3. Production, by the Pittsburgh Symphony Orchestra, of Fritz Stahlberg's suite, "Die Brautschau."
1902. Jan. 3. Elgar's "Variations" for orchestra given by the Chicago Symphony Orchestra.
1902. Jan. 7. Chauvet's suite "Feuillets d'Album" (orchestrated by Henri Maréchal); the introduction to the first act of d'Indy's music drama "Fervaal"; and Enesco's symphonic suite "Poème Roumain" given at a concert of the Orchestral Club in Boston.
1902. Jan. 10. Production of R. Burmeister's dramatic tone poem "The Sisters" by the Philharmonic Society, New York City.

1902. Jan. 11. Liszt's "Tödten-Tanz," for pianoforte and orchestra, given by the Boston Symphony Orchestra.

1902. Jan. 22. Isidore de Lara's opera "Messaline" presented at the Metropolitan Opera House, New York City, with Emma Calvé, Alvarez and Scotti. Flon conducting.

1902. Jan. 25. Orchestral suite from Glazunof's ballet "Raymonda" given by the Boston Symphony Orchestra.

1902. Jan. 31. Sibelius's symphonic poem "Journeys Homewards" given by the Philharmonic Society, New York City.

1902. Feb. 9. Gounod's lamentation "Gallia" (1871) given by the Handel and Haydn Society in Boston.

1902. Feb. 14. Paderewski's opera "Manru" presented at the Metropolitan Opera House, New York City, with Marcella Sembrich, Louise Homer, David Bispham, and Bandrowski.

1902. Feb. 14. The love scene from R. Strauss's opera "Feuernot" given by the Chicago Symphony Orchestra.

1902. Feb. 28. C. M. Loeffler's "By the Waters of Babylon," for women's voices with harp, two flutes, cello, and organ, given by the Choral Art Society, Boston.

1902. Mar. 1. Schilling's symphonic prologue to "Oedipus Rex" given by the Boston Symphony Orchestra.

1902. Mar. 14. H. K. Hadley's "Suite Orientale" produced by the Pittsburgh Symphony Orchestra.

1902. Mar. 15. H. Koessler's "Symphonic Variations" given by the Boston Symphony Orchestra.

1902. Mar. 27. Bridge's cantata "The Forging of the Anchor" given at the Baptist Temple, Brooklyn, N. Y., under the direction of E. M. Bowman.

1902. April 1. Rabaud's "Fantaisie sur des Chansons Russes"; Mozart's adagio and minuet from the second "Divertissement"; and Debussy's prelude to "L'Aprèsmidi d'un Faune," given by the Orchestral Club, Boston.

1902. April 5. D'Indy's Second Symphony (B flat major) given by the Boston Symphony Orchestra, with Harold Bauer as soloist.

1902. April 8. Massenet's cantata "The Promised Land" given by the Cecilia Society, Boston.

1902. April 12. Production (from MS.) of C. M. Loeffler's

ANNALS OF MUSIC IN AMERICA

two poems for orchestra, " Lebonne Chansson " and Villanelle au Diable," by the Boston Symphony Orchestra.

1902. Oct. 8. Mascagni's opera " Zanetto " presented at the Metropolitan Opera House, New York City, by a special company conducted by the composer.

1902. Oct 16. Mascagni's opera " Iris " given at the Metropolitan Opera House, New York City, by a special company conducted by the composer.

1902. Oct. 25. H. Huber's Second Symphony (E minor) given by the Boston Symphony Orchestra.

1902. Oct. 28. F. Cowen's overture " The Butterfly's Ball " given by the Chicago Symphony Orchestra, and on the 31st Saint-Saëns's overture " Les Barbares."

1902. Nov. 4. Järnefelt's symphonic poem " Korsholm " given by the Chicago Symphony Orchestra.

1902. Nov. 14. Boellman's " Variations Symphoniques," and Sibelius's suite " King Christian II," given by the Chicago Symphony Orchestra.

1902. Nov. 15. Caetani's " Symphonic Prelude in A minor " given by the Philharmonic Society, in New York City.

1902. Nov. 15. Rimsky-Korsakof's overture " To the Betrothed of the Tsar " given by the Boston Symphony Orchestra.

1902. Nov. 19. American début of Elsa Ruegger, cellist, at a Wetzler concert in Carnegie Hall, New York City.

1902. Nov. 22. American début of J. Kocian, violinist, at a concert given by Walter Damrosch in Carnegie Hall, New York City.

1902. Nov. 28. Widor's Chorale and Variations for harp and orchestra given by the Chicago Symphony Orchestra; also Elgar's military marches, " Pomp " and " Circumstance."

1902. Nov. 29. J. Suk's suite " A Fairy Tale " given by the Boston Symphony Orchestra.

1902. Dec. 2. Production of Georg Henschel's " Requiem " by the Cecilia Society, Boston, conducted by the composer.

1902. Dec. 5. F. Weingärtner's Second Symphony (in E flat) given by the Philharmonic Society, New York City.

1902. Dec. 6. Bach's Concerto in A minor for violin and

orchestra, and Berlioz's overture "Les Francs Juges" given by the Boston Symphony Orchestra.

1902. Dec. 19. American début of Madame Kirkby-Lunn, contralto, as *Brangäne* in "Tristan und Isolde" at the Metropolitan Opera House, New York City.

1902. Dec. 23. Massenet's opera "Cendrillon" presented at the French Opera House, New Orleans.

1902. Dec. 27. H. W. Parker's Concerto in E flat for organ and orchestra produced by the Boston Symphony Orchestra.

1902. Heinrich Conried became manager of the Metropolitan Opera House, and Alfred Herz appeared as conductor.

1902. Minneapolis Symphony Orchestra established in Minneapolis, Minn.

1903. Jan. 2. Production of Victor Herbert's orchestral suite "Columbus," by the Pittsburgh Symphony Orchestra.

1903. Jan. 2. Urspruch's overture "Der Sturm" given by the Chicago Symphony Orchestra.

1903. Jan. 5. D'Indy's "Fantasia on French Folk Themes," given by the Longy Club at Chickering Hall, Boston.

1903. Jan. 7. Chevillard's "Le Chêne et le Roseau," G. Longy's "Impression" for saxophone (dedicated to Mrs. R. J. Hall), d'Ambrosio's "Quatre Pièces d'Orchestre," and Jan Blockx's "Danse Flamande" given by the Orchestral Club, Boston.

1903. Jan. 23. Volbach's "Es waren zwei Königskinder" given by the Chicago Symphony Orchestra.

1903. Jan. 24. Arensky's Introduction to the opera "Nala and Damayanti" given by the Boston Symphony Orchestra.

1903. Jan. 25. Production of G. Strube's "Hymn to Eros" at a concert given in Boston, for the Germanic Museum.

1903. Jan. 27. C. W. von Gluck's Symphony in A major (probably not previously heard in America) given by Sam Franko's orchestra in New York City.

1903. Jan. 30. Ritter's "Symphonic Waltz," and Wagner's "Coronation March" given by the Chicago Symphony Orchestra.

1903. Jan. 31. Fibich's overture in F major to Vrehlicky's comedy "A Night on Karlstein," and Mackenzie's suite for violin and orchestra, " Pibroch," given by the Boston Symphony Orchestra.

1903. Feb. 5. L. von Gaertner's tone poem " Macbeth " given by the Wetzler orchestra in Carnegie Hall, New York City. Also Hugo Heermann, noted violinist, made his American début, playing the Beethoven Violin Concerto.

1903. Feb. 7. Hugo Kaun's symphonic poems, " Minnehaha " and " Hiawatha " given by the Chicago Symphony Orchestra.

1903. Feb. 7. Sibelius's symphonic poem " The Swan of Tuenela " given by the Cincinnati Symphony Orchestra.

1903. Feb. 8. Dubois's oratorio " Paradise Lost " given by the Handel and Haydn Society in Boston.

1903. Feb. 13. Coleridge Taylor's Ballad in D minor given by the Chicago Symphony Orchestra.

1903. Mar. 14. Production of F. Stahlberg's tone poem " To the Memory of Abraham Lincoln " by the Pittsburgh Symphony Orchestra.

1903. Mar. 14. G. Schumann's overture " The Dawn of Love " given by the Boston Symphony Orchestra.

1903. Mar. 23. Elgar's cantata " The Dream of Gerontius " given by the Apollo Musical Club, Chicago. H. M. Wild conductor.

1903. April 4. G. M. Witkowski's Symphony in D minor given by the Boston Symphony Orchestra.

1903. April 11. F. S. Converse's symphonic poem " Endymion's Narrative " produced by the Boston Symphony Orchestra.

1903. April 15. The " Marche Funèbre " from the last scene of Berlioz's " Hamlet " given by the Orchestral Club, Boston.

1903. April 18. R. Strauss's " Burleske " in D minor for pianoforte and orchestra, given by the Boston Symphony Orchestra.

1903. Oct. 17. The " Entr'acte Symphonique " from Bruneau's opera " Messidor " given by the Boston Symphony Orchestra.

1903. Oct. 24. Variations on a Russian Theme, by six Russian composers, given by the Chicago Symphony Orchestra.

1903. Oct. 24. E. F. Arbos's morceau de concert "Tango," and Glazunof's "Fourth Symphony" (E flat) given by the Boston Symphony Orchestra.

1903. Oct. 30. American début of Jacques Thibaud, French violinist, at a Wetzler concert in Carnegie Hall, New York City.

1903. Oct. 31. V. d'Indy's symphonic introduction to "L'Étranger" given by the Chicago Symphony Orchestra.

1903. Oct. Symphony Society of New York City, reorganized with Walter Damrosch as conductor.

1903. Nov. 7. Bruneau's symphonic poem "La Belle aux Bois Dormant" also Elgar's incidental music for "Granis and Diarmid" given by the Chicago Symphony Orchestra.

1903. Nov. 20 Glazunof's Seventh Symphony given by the Pittsburgh Symphony Orchestra.

1903. Nov. 23. American début of Enrico Caruso, noted Italian tenor, as the *Duke* in "Rigoletto" at the Metropolitan Opera House, New York City.

1903. Nov. 25. American operatic début of Olive Fremstad as *Sieglinde* at the Metropolitan Opera House, New York City. She had appeared in concert in 1892, but had gone abroad and now appeared as an operatic artist.

1903. Nov. 27. Frank Guerney Cauffman's tone poem "Salammbô" given by the Philadelphia Symphony Orchestra.

1903. Nov. 28. E. Dohnanyi's Symphony in D minor given by the Boston Symphony Orchestra.

1903. Nov. 30. Carl Busch's cantata "King Olaf" produced by the Apollo Musical Club of Chicago. H. M. Wild, conductor.

1903. Dec. 8. Bruno Oscar Klein's Suite for violoncello and orchestra, in F, given by the Philharmonic Society, New York City.

1903. Dec. 10. Debussy's lyric poem "La Demoiselle Élue" given at a concert of the pupils of Madame Salisbury, in Boston, with Helen Allen Hunt as soloist, and Heinrich Gebhardt, pianist. A full performance with orchestra was given by the Cecilia Society April 4, 1905, when Isabelle Bouton and Bertha Cushing Child were soloists.

ANNALS OF MUSIC IN AMERICA

1903. Dec. 18. Cowen's "Indian Rhapsody" given by the Pittsburgh Symphony Orchestra.

1903. Dec. 24. First performance in German, outside of Bayreuth, of Wagner's "Parsifal" given by the Metropolitan Opera Company, New York City, under Heinrich Conried, with Milka Ternina as *Kundry;* Alois Burgstaller as *Parsifal;* Anton Van Rooy as *Amfortas;* Robert Blass as *Gurnemanz;* Marcel Journet as *Titurel;* Otto Goritz as *Klingsor,* and Alfred Hertz conductor.

1903. Dec. 26. G. Schumann's "Variationen und Doppelfuge" given by the Chicago Symphony Orchestra.

1903. Dec. Edythe Walker, contralto, made her American début at the Metropolitan Opera House, in "Aïda."

1903–4. Guest conductors of the Philharmonic Society of New York City:

Edouard Colonne	of Paris, France
Gustav F. Kogel	" Frankfort am Main, Germany
Henry J. Wood	" London, England
Victor Herbert	" Pittsburgh, Pa.
Felix Weingartner	" Munich, Bavaria
Vasili Safonof	" Moscow, Russia
Richard Strauss	" Berlin, Germany

1904. Jan. 1. Lemare's "Rhapsody and Caprice Orientale" given by the Pittsburgh Symphony Orchestra.

1904. Jan. 2. Sibelius's Second Symphony (D major) given by the Chicago Symphony Orchestra.

1904. Jan. 5. Moussorgsky's fantaisie for orchestra,[1] "Une Nuit sur le Mont Chauve"; V. d'Indy's "Choral Varié" for saxophone (dedicated to Mrs. R. J. Hall), Mrs. Hall soloist; Rabaud's eclogue "Poëme Virgilien"; and Augusta Holmès's symphonic poem "Irlande," given by the Orchestral Club in Boston, G. Longy, conductor.

1904. Jan. 8. F. Stahlberg's Suite (Opus 10) produced by the Pittsburgh Symphony Orchestra.

[1] Said to have been played at the World's Fair, Chicago, under Theodore Thomas in a series of concerts of Russian music from June 5–13th, 1893.

1904. Jan. 12. American début of Pablo Casals, noted violoncellist, at a concert given by Sam Franko in the New Lyceum, New York City.

1904. Jan. 23. Glazunof's suite "Moyen Age" given by the Chicago Symphony Orchestra.

1904. Jan. 23. Schumann's suite for orchestra "In Carnival Time" given by the Boston Symphony Orchestra.

1904. Jan. 28. First concert of the Russian Symphony Orchestra, organized by Modest Altschuler, in Cooper Union Hall, New York City. Rachmaninof's "The Cliff" was played for the first time in America.

1904. Feb. 6. Dubois's overture "Frithjof" given by the Boston Symphony Orchestra.

1904. Feb. 9. Elgar's oratorio "The Apostles" given by the Oratorio Society, New York City.

1904. Feb. 10. Debussy's three nocturnes, "Images," "Fêtes," and "Sirens," given at a Chickering production concert in Boston, B. J. Lang conducting.

1904. Feb 11. Ippolitof-Ivanof's "Caucasian Sketches" given by the Russian Symphony Orchestra, New York City.

1904. Feb. 20. Bruckner's Ninth Symphony (unfinished) given by the Chicago Symphony Orchestra.

1904. Feb. 26. Frederick Stock's "Symphonic Variations" given by the Chicago Symphony Orchestra.

1904. Feb. 27. Th. Akimenko's "Lyric Poem" for orchestra given by the Boston Symphony Orchestra.

1904. Mar. 3. Arensky's "Variations on an Original Theme," and Tanaief's "First Symphony," given by the Russian Symphony Orchestra at the Cooper Union, New York City.

1904. Mar. 12. G. Strube's "Fantastic Overture" produced by the Boston Symphony Orchestra.

1904. Mar. 21. Richard Strauss's "Symphonia Domestica" given by the Philharmonic Society, New York City, conducted by the composer.

1904. April 9. Glazunof's overture "Carneval" given by the Boston Symphony Orchestra.

1904. April 11. Widor's "Ouverture Espagnol," Rameau's opera ballet "Les Indes Galantes," and Ten Brink's

ANNALS OF MUSIC IN AMERICA

"Première Suite d'Orchestre," given by the Orchestral Club in Boston.

1904. April 16. Madame Helen Hopekirk's Concert Piece in D minor given by the Boston Symphony Orchestra, with Madame Hopekirk as soloist.

1904. April 17. Gleason's symphonic poem "Edris" produced by the Chicago Symphony Orchestra.

1904. April 23. Hugo Wolf's symphonic poem "Penthesilea" given by the Chicago Symphony Orchestra.

1904. April 23. Chadwick's concert overture "Euterpe" produced by the Boston Symphony Orchestra.

1904. April 30. Sibelius's tone poem "Eine Saga" given by the Chicago Symphony Orchestra.

1904. Production of Leo Schulz's "American Festival Overture" at the St. Louis Exposition.

1904. Oct. A Symphony Orchestra formed in New York City by Arnold Volpe.

1904. Oct. 22. P. Dukas's scherzo "The Sorcerer's Apprentice" given by the Boston Symphony Orchestra.

1904. Nov. 5. Elgar's overture "In the South" given by the Chicago Symphony Orchestra.

1904. Nov. 6. Mahler's Fourth Symphony given by the Symphony Society, New York City.

1904. Nov. 11. E. Boehe's "Wanderings of Odysseus" given by the Philadelphia Symphony Orchestra, also Max Schilling's tone poem "The Witch Song."

1904. Nov. 18. Chausson's "Poëme" for solo violin with orchestra, given by the Symphony Society in New York City. (It was played in Boston April 25 by Miss Jessie Davis, piano, and Hugh Codman, violin).

1904. Nov. 19. Rimsky-Korsakof's third act of the ballet "Mlada," and Rachmaninof's dances from "Aleko" given by the Russian Symphony Orchestra, New York City.

1904. Nov. 26. Saint-Saëns's First Symphony (E flat major) and Massenet's "Hungarian Scenes" given by the Boston Symphony Orchestra.

1904. Dec. 3. Carl Goldmark's overture "In Italy" given by the Chicago Symphony Orchestra.

1904. Dec. 3. Bach's Second Violin Concerto (in E major) given by the Boston Symphony Orchestra.
1904. Dec. 17. Rachmaninof's Pianoforte Concerto in F sharp minor given by the Boston Symphony Orchestra.
1904. Dec. 24. Chaikovsky's symphonic description of "The Battle of Poltava," and the hopak from "Mazeppa," also Glazunof's symphonic poem "Stenka Razine," and Rimsky-Korsakof's overture "May Night" given by the Russian Symphony Orchestra, in New York City.
1904. Dec. 31. D'Indy's Symphony in B flat major (Op. 57) given by the Philadelphia Symphony Orchestra.
1904. The Chicago Orchestra permanently endowed and Orchestra Hall built.
1904. American début of Luisa Tetrazzini took place at the Tivoli, in San Francisco, Cal.
1904. Coleridge Taylor visited America as the guest of the Coleridge Taylor Society of Washington, D. C.
1904. Emil Paur appointed conductor of the Pittsburgh Symphony Orchestra (1904–1910).
1904–5. Johann Strauss's opera "Die Zigeunerbaron" given at the Metropolitan Opera House, New York City. This was produced in English at the Casino Feb. 15, 1886.
1904–5. Guest conductors of the Philharmonic Society, New York City, for this season were:

Frederic H. Cowen	of London, England
Arthur Nikisch	of Vienna, Austria
E. Schuch	of Dresden, Germany
B. Glazunof	of St. Petersburg, Russia
C. V. Stanford	of London, England
E. Colonne	of Paris, France
Sir E. Elgar	of Malvern, England

1905. Jan. 4. E. Chabrier's "Danse Slave" from the opera "Le Roi Malgré Lui"; A. Georges's "Prèlude d'Axël"; H. Sitt's "Andante" for violin and orchestra; G. Sparck's symphonic poem, "Boabdil"; C. Forsyth's "Concerto in G minor" (first movement); Erik Satie's "Gymnopèdies" numbers 1 and 2, orchestrated by C. Debussy; and J. Bordier's "Meditation on the seventh prelude of Bach," given by the Orchestral Club in Boston.

1905. Jan. 20. Simandl's concert piece for doublebass and orchestra given by the Pittsburgh Symphony Orchestra.

1905. Jan. 20. Elgar's concert overture "Froissart" given by the Chicago Symphony Orchestra.

1905. Jan. 21. Rimsky-Korsakof's suite "Tsar-Saltan" given by the Russian Symphony Orchestra in New York City.

1905. Jan. 21. Hugo Wolf's "Italian Serenade" given by the Chicago Symphony Orchestra.

1905. Jan. 21. F. S. Converse's two poems "Night" and "Day" given by the Boston Symphony Orchestra.

1905. Feb. 3. Rimsky-Korsakof's Pianoforte Concerto in C sharp minor given by the Philadelphia Symphony Orchestra.

1905. Feb. 4. Eugen d'Albert's Second Pianoforte Concerto (in E major) given by the Boston Symphony Orchestra.

1905. Feb. 8. Elgar's "Benedictus" given by the New York Oratorio Society.

1905. Feb. 11. Bruch's Serenade in A minor for violin given by the Boston Symphony Orchestra.

1905. Feb. 25. Arensky's suite "Silhouettes," excerpts from Mussorgsky's opera "Khovanstchina," and Kalinnikof's "Symphony in A," given by the Russian Symphony Orchestra in New York City.

1905. Mar. 3. Converse's fantasia "The Mystic Trumpeter" produced by the Philadelphia Symphony Orchestra.

1905. Mar. 25. Gustav Mahler's Fifth (Giant) Symphony given by the Cincinnati Symphony Orchestra.

1905. Mar. 25. Rimsky-Korsakof's musical picture "Sadko" given by the Boston Symphony Orchestra.

1905. Mar. 30. Ysaye's "Poëme Elegiaque" for violin and orchestra given by the New York Symphony Society with Ysaye as soloist.

1905. April 1. Chaikovsky's fantasia "Night" given by the Russian Symphony Orchestra in New York City. Also Rubinstein's "Romance et Caprice Russe."

1905. April 4. Charpentier's symphonic drama "La Vie du Poëte" given by the Cecilia Society in Boston.

1905. April 14. R. Strauss's cantata "Taillefer" given by the Oratorio Society in New York City.

1905. April 18. E. Chausson's "Hymn Védique," and G. Hüe's symphonic suite "Titania" given by the Orchestral Club in Boston.

1905. April 22. Gustav Strube's symphonic poem "Longing" produced by the Boston Symphony Orchestra.

1905. April 29. G. Ropartz's "Fantasia in D minor" produced by the Boston Symphony Orchestra.

1905. Sept. 29. G. W. Chadwick's symphonic poem "Cleopatra" produced at the Worcester (Mass) Festival.

1905. Oct. 21. Smetana's overture "Libussa" given by the Boston Symphony Orchestra.

1905. Oct. 27. Liadof's "Baba Yaga" given by the Philadelphia Symphony Orchestra.

1905. Nov. 18. Rimsky-Korsakof's suite "Snow Maiden" given by the Russian Symphony Orchestra, New York City. Also, Rachmaninof's "Second Pianoforte Concerto" (won Glinka Prize 1904) with Raoul Pugno as soloist.

1905. Nov. 18. Busoni's "Comedy Overture" in C major given by the Boston Symphony Orchestra.

1905. Nov. 25. American début of Madame Jeanne Jomelli, at the Metropolitan Opera House, New York City, as *Elizabeth* in "Tannhäuser."

1905. Dec. 2. César Franck's symphonic poem "Psyche and Cupid" given by the Boston Symphony Orchestra.

1905. Dec. 4. Magnard's "Chant Funèbre" given by the Boston Symphony Orchestra in Philadelphia, with Vincent d'Indy as guest conductor.

1905. Dec. 22. Production of Wassily Leps's Japanese reincarnation theme "Andon," for soprano, tenor, and orchestra, by the Philadelphia Symphony Society.

1905. Dec. 23. Gustav Strube's Violin Concerto in F sharp minor produced by the Boston Symphony Orchestra.

1905. Dec. 24. Sibelius's symphonic poem "Finlandia" given at a concert at the Metropolitan Opera House, New York City, with A. Vigna as conductor. It was played by the Russian Symphony Orchestra on Dec. 30.

1905. Dec. 30. Zolotaref's "Rhapsodie Hebraique" given by the Russian Symphony Orchestra in New York City. Also Arensky's Violin Concerto (Op. 54), with Maud Powell as soloist.

1905. Dec. 30. Webber's Symphony in C minor given by the Boston Symphony Orchestra.

1905. The St. Paul (Minn.) Symphony Orchestra formed under Walter Rothwell.

1905. Frederick Stock appointed conductor of the Chicago Symphony Orchestra.

1905. The Institute of Musical Art established in New York City by Frank Damrosch.

1905–6. The guest conductors of the New York Philharmonic Society this season were:

Willem Mengelberg	of Amsterdam, Holland.
Victor Herbert	of Pittsburgh, Pa.
Max Fiedler	of Hamburg, Germany.
Vasily Safonof	of Moscow, Russia.
Ernst Kunwald	of Frankfort am Main, Germany
Fritz Steinbach	of Cologne, Germany

1906. Jan. 2. Guiraud's "Chasse Fantastique"; Faure's "Pavane"; Massenet's "Pastorale Mystique," from the opera "Le Jongleur de Notre Dame"; Lalo's "Valse de Cigarette, Namouna"; Bruneau's "Préludes de l'Ouragan"; Sparck's "Légende," for saxophone and orchestra (production); Tiersot's "Danses Populaires Françaises," given by the Orchestral Club in Boston.

1906. Jan. 9. First American appearance of Rudolph Ganz, noted pianist, with the Kneisel Quartet, in Boston.

1906. Jan. 20. Chausson's Symphony in B flat major given by the Boston Symphony Orchestra.

1906. Jan. 26. Tirindelli's symphonic poem "Tragi-Commedia" given by the Cincinnati Symphony Orchestra.

1906. Jan. 27. American début of Josef Lhevinne, noted pianist, at a concert of the Russian Symphony Orchestra in Carnegie Hall, New York City.

1906. Jan. 27. Glazunof's symphonic picture "The Kremlin" given by the Boston Symphony Orchestra.

1906. Jan. 31. Giordano's opera "Siberia" presented at the French Opera House, New Orleans, La.

1906. Jan. 31. F. S. Converse's opera "The Pipe of Desire," produced at Jordan Hall, Boston. (It was presented at the Metropolitan Opera House, New York, Mar. 18, 1908.)

1906. Feb. 6. V. d'Indy's oratorio "St. Mary Magdalene" given by the Cecilia Society in Boston.

1906. Feb. 11. J. Suk's Scherzo for Orchestra given by the New York Symphony Society.

1906. Feb. 24. Konius's suite "Childhood" given by the Russian Symphony Orchestra in New York City.

1906. Mar. 2. Adolf Weidig's symphonic fantaisie "Semiramis" given by the Chicago Symphony Orchestra.

1906. Mar. 3. F. Boehe's "First Four Episodes for Orchestra" given by the Boston Symphony Orchestra.

1906. Mar. 3. Production of F. S. Converse's ballads for baritone and orchestra by the Boston Symphony Orchestra at Providence, R. I., with David Bispham as soloist.

1906. Mar. 10. J. Dalcroze's "Violin Concerto in C minor" given by the Boston Symphony Orchestra.

1906. Mar. 10. Arthur Shepherd's "Ouverture Joyeuse" also H. F. Gilbert's "Salammbo's Invocation" given at a concert of the New Music Society in New York City, and at the same concert Ruth Deyo, pianist, made her début.

1906. Mar. 17. R. M. Glier's First Symphony; Serof's "Cossack Dances"; César Cui's "Waltz"; and Mlynarsky's "Violin Concerto," given by the Russian Symphony Orchestra, New York City.

1906. Mar. 31. Busoni's suite "Geharnischte" given by the Boston Symphony Orchestra.

1906. April. 2. Production of H. H. Huss's Violin Concerto in D minor by the New Music Society in Carnegie Hall, New York City.

1906. April 7. Max Schilling's prelude to act III of "The Piper's Holiday" produced by the Boston Symphony Orchestra.

1906. April 17. Widor's "Les Pêcheurs de Saint-Jean"; Bourgault-Decoudray's "Rhapsodie Cambodgienne"; A. Caplet's "Impression d'Automne" (Elegie for saxaphone, written for and played by Mrs. R. J. Hall); M. Moszkowski's "Larghetto" and "Intermezzo," and R. Schumann's "Two Pieces in Canon Form" (orchestrated by Th. Dubois), given by the Orchestral Club in Boston.

1906. April 21. First concert of the Chicago Musical Art Society, organized under Clarence Dickinson.

1906. May 3. Production of W. H. Humiston's "Southern Fantasy" for orchestra, at the Mendelssohn Union, Orange, N. J.

1906. Oct. 8. First appearance of the "La Scala" orchestra of Milan (Italy) at Carnegie Hall, New York City, with Leoncavallo as conductor.

1906. Oct. 15. Production of F. S. Converse's incidental music to Percy Mackaye's play "Jeanne d'Arc," given by Sothern and Julia Marlowe in Philadelphia.

1906. Oct. 15. Puccini's opera "Madame Butterfly" presented by the Henry Savage Opera Company (in English) at Washington, D. C.

1906. Oct. Vassily Safonof appointed conductor of the Philharmonic Society, New York City.

1906. Nov. 3. Saint-Saëns's fantasia "Africa" for pianoforte and orchestra given by the Symphony Society in New York City with the composer as soloist.

1906. Nov. 12. Puccini's opera "Madama Butterfly" given by the Savage Opera Company in Washington, D. C.

1906. Nov. 15. Glazunof's "Scène Dansante" given by the Russian Symphony Orchestra in New York City.

1906. Nov. 20. American début of F. Constantino, tenor, also Fely Dereyne, Riccardo Martin, and A. Segurola, with the San Carlo Opera Company in New Orleans, La.

1906. Nov. 26. American operatic début of Geraldine Farrar, soprano, as *Juliette* in Gounod's "Roméo et Juliette." at the Metropolitan Opera House, New York City.

1906. Nov. 27. Elgar's cantata "The Banner of St. George" given at a Musurgia Concert, at Carnegie Hall, New York City, with the assistance of one hundred members of the Brooklyn Oratorio Society.

1906. Nov. 30. J. Sibelius's Violin Concerto in D minor given by the Philharmonic Society, New York City, with Maud Powell as soloist.

1906. Dec. 3. American début of Alessandro Bonci, Italian tenor, in "I Puritani," at the Manhattan Opera House, New York City.

1906. Dec. 4. Piérné's oratorio "The Children's Crusade" given by the Oratorio Society, New York City.

1906. Dec. 5. American début of Maurice Renaud, great French baritone, as *Rigoletto*, at the Manhattan Opera House, New York City.

1906. Dec. 5. Giordano's opera "Fedora" given at the Metropolitan Opera House, New York City, with Lina Cavalieri (début), Caruso, Scotti. A. Vigna conducting.

1906. Dec. 7. Début of Donalda as *Marguerite* in "Faust" at the Manhattan Opera House, New York City.

1906. Dec. 15. César Franck's morceau symphonique, "Redemption," given by the New York Symphony Society.

1906. Dec. 19. Début of de Cisneros and Bassi in "Aïda" at the Manhattan Opera House, New York City.

1906. Dec. 20. Glazunof's Third Symphony; Rachmaninof's capriccio "Tzigane"; and Scriabin's Pianoforte Concerto with the composer as soloist, given by the Russian Symphony Orchestra, in New York City.

1906–7. Oscar Hammerstein opened the Manhattan Opera House in New York City with a company including Melba, Gilibert-LeJeune, Mazarin Kate d'Arta, Farnetti, and Luisa Tetrazzini, soprani; Bressler-Gianoli, and Maria Gay, mezzi; Eleanora de Cisneros and Zacchari, contralti; A. Bonci, Bassi, Dalmores, Altchevski, tenori; M. Renaud, M. Sammarco, Ancona, Mendolfi, baritoni; E. de Reszke, Braz, and Maglinez, bassi.

1906. The Philharmonic Society of New Orleans, La., organized. (Reorganized in 1917.)

1906. St. Paul (Minn.) Symphony Orchestra organized with E. B. Emanuel as conductor. Walter H. Rothwell became conductor in 1908.

1907. Jan. 5. Sibelius's First Symphony (E minor) given by the Boston Symphony Orchestra.

1907. Jan. 17. Sibelius's overture "Karelia" given by the Russian Symphony Orchestra in New York City.

1907. Jan. 17. A. Oldberg's dramatic overture "Paolo and Francesca" produced by the Chicago Symphony Orchestra.

ANNALS OF MUSIC IN AMERICA

1907. Jan. 19. American début of Katherine Goodson, English pianist, with the Boston Symphony Orchestra. She played Grieg's concerto in A minor.

1907. Jan. 20. Production of Arthur Foote's "Four Character Pieces" by the Chicago Symphony Orchestra.

1907. Jan. 22. R. Strauss's opera "Salome" presented at the Metropolitan Opera House, New York City with Olive Fremstad, and C. Burrian in leading parts, and Alfred Hertz conducting.

1907. Jan. 25. Paul Juon's fantasie "The Watchman's Song" (after Danish Folk Songs) given by the Philadelphia Symphony Orchestra.

1907. Feb. 1. American début of Mario Sammarco, noted baritone, in "Pagliacci" at the Manhattan Opera House, New York City.

1907. Feb. 7. Sibelius's orchestral suite "Karelia" given by the Russian Symphony Orchestra in New York City.

1907. Feb. 7. Elgar's "Romance" for orchestra given by the Symphony Society in New York City.

1907. Feb. 9. Tinel's three symphonic pictures from the enr'acte music to Corneille's "Polyeucte" given by the Boston Symphony Orchestra.

1907. Feb. 26. Scriabin's First Symphony, and Ippolitof-Ivanof's Second "Caucasian Suite" for orchestra given by the Russian Symphony Orchestra in New York City.

1907. Mar. 2. Debussy's orchestral sketches "La Mer" given by the Boston Symphony Orchestra.

1907. Mar. 9. Bach's "Brandenburg Concerto" in C major, for three violins, three celli, and three basses, given by the Boston Symphony Orchestra.

1907. Mar. 14. Scriabin's third symphony "The Divine Poem," and Davidof's "Violoncello Concerto" (Alwin Schroeder, soloist) given by the Russian Symphony Orchestra, in New York City.

1907. Mar. 16. Moszkowsky's symphonic poem "The Steppe" (Op. 66) given by the Boston Symphony Orchestra.

1907. Mar. 19. American début of Sir Edward Elgar as conductor of his oratorio, "The Apostles" with the Oratorio Society in New York City.

1907. Mar. 26. Elgar's oratorio "The Kingdom" given by the Oratorio Society, New York City.

1907. Mar. 27. Pietro Floridia's Symphony in D minor given by the Cincinnati Symphony Orchestra.

1907. Mar. 30. O. Fried's Prelude and Double Fugue for Strings, given by the Boston Symphony Orchestra.

1907. Mar. 31. Handel's oratorio "Belshazzar" given by the Handel and Haydn Society in Boston, with Madame Kileski-Bradbury, Misses Bouton, Kellogg, Mr. George Hamlin, and Mr. Watkin Mills as soloists.

1907. April 1. X. Scharwenka's opera "Mataswintha" presented at the Metropolitan Opera House, New York City.

1907. April 3. Dr. P. Hartmann's oratorio "St. Peter" produced at Carnegie Hall, New York City.

1907. April 6. Howard Brockway's Symphony in D major produced by the Boston Symphony Orchestra.

1907. April 9. J. K. Paine's opera "Azara" presented, in concert form, by the Cecilia Society in Boston.

1907. April 13. Reger's "Serenade" (Op. 59) given by the Boston Symphony Orchestra; also production of Henry K. Hadley's tone poem "Salome."

1907. April 27. Victor Bendix's Fourth Symphony (D minor) given by the Boston Symphony Orchestra.

1907. Oct. 2. F. S. Converse's dramatic poem "Job" produced at the Worcester (Mass.) Festival.

1907. Oct. 4. A. Hinton's Second Pianoforte Concerto.

1907. Oct. 19. V. d'Indy's symphonic poem "Jour d'été à la Montagne" given by the Boston Symphony Orchestra.

1907. Nov. 1. F. Stock's "Symphonic Waltz" given by the Chicago Symphony Orchestra.

1907. Nov. 4. American début of Jeanne Gerville-Reache, French contralto, as the *Blind Mother* in "La Giaconda" at the Manhattan Opera House, New York City.

1907. Nov. 14. Glazunof's Eighth Symphony (E flat) given by the Russian Symphony Orchestra in New York City.

1907. Nov. 16. The overture to Pfitzner's Christmas play "The Little Christ Elf" given by the Boston Symphony Orchestra.

1907. Nov. 17. Edward German's "Welsh Rhapsody" given by the Symphony Society in New York City, conducted by the composer.

1907. Nov. 18. Francesco Cilea's opera "Adrienne Lecouvreur" presented at the Metropolitan Opera House, New York City, with Cavalieri, Caruso and Scotti in the leading parts.

1907. Nov. 20. American début of the Russian basso Chaliapin in "Mefistofele" at the Manhattan Opera House, New York City.

1907. Nov. 23. C. M. Loeffler's symphonic poem "A Pagan Poem" produced by the Boston Symphony Orchestra. Also Reznicek's adagio, scherzo and finale from "Symphonic Suite in E minor," given for the first time in America.

1907. Nov. 30. E. Boehe's symphonic poem "Taormina" given by the Boston Symphony Orchestra.

1907. Dec. 1. Dr. L. Damrosch's "Silver Wedding" produced by the Symphony Society, New York City.

1907. Dec. 4. Wolf-Ferrari's oratorio "Vita Nuova" given by the Oratorio Society, New York City.

1907. Dec. 7. Liapunof's Pianoforte Concerto given by the New York Symphony Society with Josef Hoffman as soloist.

1907. Dec. 12. Ilyinsky's suite "Mir und Antra," and Arensky's "First Symphony," given by the Russian Symphony Orchestra in New York City.

1907. Dec. 20. Max Reger's "Variations and Fugue" (Op. 100) given by the Philadelphia Symphony Orchestra.

1907. Dec. 21. D'Ambrosio's Violin Concerto in B minor, with R. Czerwonski as soloist; the "Goldonian Intermezzo" from Bassi's "Suite Variée," and Humperdinck's overture to "The Forced Marriage," given by the Boston Symphony Orchestra.

1907. First Beethoven Festival given by the Symphony Society, New York City,

Carl Pohlig appointed conductor of the Philadelphia Symphony Orchestra (1907–1912).

1907. Max Zach appointed conductor of the St. Louis Symphony Orchestra.

1908. Jan. 1. American début of Gustav Mahler as conductor of a performance of "Tristan und Isolde" at the Metropolitan Opera House, New York City.

1908. Jan. 3. Charpentier's opera "Louise" presented at the Manhattan Opera House, New York City, with Mary Garden in leading part. Campanini conducting.

1908. Jan. 14. H. Bischoff's Symphony in E major given by the Boston Symphony Orchestra.

1908. Jan. 15. New York début of Luisa Tetrazzini, great soprano, in "La Traviata" at the Manhattan Opera House. (She had previously been heard in San Francisco.)

1908. Jan. 15. Beethoven's "Twelve Dances" given under Sam Franko at Mendelssohn Hall, New York City.

1908. Jan. 16. Sibelius's Third Symphony (C major) given by the Russian Symphony Orchestra in New York City.

1908. Jan. 18. Mozart's "Three German Dances" given by the Boston Symphony Orchestra.

1908. Jan. 21. Henri Rabaud's Second Symphony (E minor); E. Chausson's "Poëme de l'Amour et de la Mer" for voice and orchestra, (1) "La Fleur des Faux," "Interlude," (2) "La Mort de l'Amour"; and Balakiref's symphonic poem "En Bohème" given at an orchestral concert in Boston by Mrs. Richard J. Hall.

1908. Jan. 25. Schelling's "Fantastic Suite" for pianoforte and orchestra given by the Boston Symphony Orchestra.

1908. Jan. 29. Dohnanyi's Violoncello Concerto in D given by the Boston Symphony Orchestra in Indianapolis, Ind., with H. Warnke as soloist.

1908. Feb. 2. Chaikovsky's opera "Eugen Onegin" given in concert form, by the Symphony Society in New York City.

1908. Feb. 13. The scene "Winter" from Glazunof's ballet, "The Seasons," given by the Russian Symphony Orchestra in New York City.

1908. Feb. 14. Richard Wagner's "Columbus" overture given by the Philadelphia Symphony Orchestra.

1908. Feb. 15. Rimsky-Korsakof's "Caprice on Spanish Themes"; and Schielderup's "Sunrise on the Himalayas" from the stage music to Gjellerup's "Opferfeuer"; also

Schjelderup's symphonic poem "A Summer Night on the Fjord" given by the Boston Symphony Orchestra.
1908. Feb. 19. Debussy's opera "Pelléas et Mélisande" presented at the Manhattan Opera House, New York City, with Mary Garden, Jeanne Gerville-Reache, and Perier in the cast. Campanini conducting.
1908. Feb. 22. Production of Chadwick's "Symphonic Sketches" by the Boston Symphony Orchestra.
1908. Feb. 28. Josef Hofmann's Third Pianoforte Concerto given by the Philharmonic Society in New York City.
1908. Feb. 29. E. Dohnanyi's Concert Piece in D major given by the Boston Symphony Orchestra.
1908. Mar. 4. American début of Madame Berta Morena as *Sieglinde* at the Metropolitan Opera House, New York City.
1908. Mar. 14. Balakiref's Symphony in C major given by the Boston Symphony Orchestra.
1908. Mar. 26. Stahlberg's symphonic suite "Ueber's Weltenmeer" given by the Volpe Orchestra in New York City.
1908. Mar. 28. Gustav Strube's "Fantastic Dance," for orchestra, produced by the Boston Symphony Orchestra
1908. April 7. M. Reger's "Unaccompanied Violin Sonata" given in New York City by Dora Valesca Becker.
1908. April 11. C. P. E. Bach's Second Symphony, in E Flat, given, and H. K. Hadley's Third Symphony (B minor) produced by the Boston Symphony Orchestra.
1908. April 18. E. Moór's Pianoforte Concerto (Op. 57) and Ertel's symphonic poem "The Midnight Review" given by the Boston Symphony Orchestra.
1908. June. Production of H. W. Parker's "Ballade" for chorus and orchestra, by the Litchfield County Choral Union at Norfolk, Conn. Conducted by the composer.
1908. Sept. 16. New building of the Academy of Music in Brooklyn, N. Y., opened.
1908. Sept. 25. American début of Blanche Arral in San Francisco, Cal., under the management of M. Grau.
1908. Oct. 17. E. Sauer's First Pianoforte Concerto (E minor) given by the Boston Symphony Orchestra with the composer as soloist.

1908. Oct. 24. MacDowell's third symphonic poem "Lamia" (Op. 29) produced by the Boston Symphony Orchestra.

1908. Oct. 31. Chaikovsky's "Variations on a Rococo Theme" for cello and orchestra, given by the Boston Symphony Orchestra.

1908. Nov. 7. Début of Albert Spalding, violinist, with the New York Symphony Society.

1908. Nov. 9. American début of Maria Labia in "Tosca" at the Manhattan Opera House, New York City.

1908. Nov. 14. Grètry's three dances from "Céphale et Procris" given by the Boston Symphony Orchestra.

1908. Nov. 14. American début of Dr. Ludwig Wüllner, lieder singer, at Mendelssohn Hall, New York City.

1908. Nov. 16. American début of Emmy Destinn as *Aïda* at the Metropolitan Opera House, New York City, on which occasion A. Toscanini made his first appearance as conductor.

1908. Nov. 21. Sibelius's symphonic poem "A Spring Day" given by the Boston Symphony Orchestra.

1908. Nov. 23. Eugen d'Albert's opera "Tiefland" presented at the Metropolitan Opera House, New York City.

1908. Nov. 25. Massenet's opera "Thaïs" presented at the Manhattan Opera House, New York City, with Mary Garden (her American début), Emma Trentini, J. Gerville-Reache, and Maurice Renaud. G. Campanini conducting.

1908. Nov. 27. Massenet's opera "Le Jongleur de Notre Dame" presented at the Manhattan Opera House, New York City, with Mary Garden in the title rôle, supported by Renaud and Dufranne.

1908. Dec. 2. Debussy's cantata "The Blessed Damosel" given by the Oratorio Society in New York City.

1908. Dec. 8. Gustav Mahler's Second Symphony (C minor) given by the Symphony Society in New York City, conducted by the composer.

1908. Dec. 10. Scriabin's fourth symphony "Ecstasy" given by the Russian Symphony Orchestra in New York City.

1908. Dec. 10. American début of Mischa Elman, violinist, playing Chaikovsky's Violin Concerto.

1908. Dec. 11. Rubinstein's Pianoforte Fantasia in C major

(Op. 84) given by the New York Philharmonic Society with Josef Lhevinne as soloist.

1908. Dec. 12. Noren's "Kaleidoscope" (theme and variations) given by the Boston Symphony Orchestra.

1908. Dec. 17. Puccini's opera "Le Villi" presented at the Metropolitan Opera House, New York City.

1908. Dec. 19. Pierné's cantata "The Children of Bethlehem" given at a Young People's Concert in New York City. Frank Damrosch, conductor.

1908. Dec. 19. Rubinstein's Fifth Piano Concerto (E flat major) given by the Boston Symphony Orchestra.

1908. Seattle (Wash.) Symphony Orchestra organized, with Michael Kegrizi as conductor.

1908. Signor Gatti-Casazza engaged as manager of the Metropolitan Opera House, New York City.

1908. Oscar Hammerstein's Opera House in Philadelphia opened.

1909. Jan. 2. O. Nicolai's "Religious Festival" overture on the chorale "Eine Feste Burg" given by the Boston Symphony Orchestra.

1909. Jan. 3. Elgar's First Symphony (A flat) given by the New York Symphony Society.

1909. Jan. 6. Catalani's opera "La Wally" presented at the Metropolitan Opera House, New York City, with Emmy Destinn and Riccardo Martin in the leading parts.

1909. Jan. 14. Rachmaninof's Second Symphony (E minor) given by the Russian Symphony Orchestra in New York City, conducted by the composer.

1909. Jan. 15. Emil Paur's Symphony in A major produced by the Pittsburgh Symphony Orchestra, conducted by the composer.

1909. Jan. 16. Schilling's "Harvest Festival" from the opera "Moloch" given by the Boston Symphony Orchestra.

1909. Jan. 22. American début of Carl Jörn, tenor, in "Die Meistersinger" at the Metropolitan Opera House, New York City.

1909. Jan. 23. Paul Scheinpflug's "Overture to a Comedy of Shakespeare" given by the Boston Symphony Orchestra.

1909. Feb. 13. Paderewski's Symphony in B minor (Op. 24) produced by the Boston Symphony Orchestra.

1909. Feb. 19. Smetana's opera "Prodoná nevěsta" presented at the Metropolitan Opera House, New York City, with Destinn, Jörn, Didur and Reiss. G. Mahler, conductor.

1909. Mar. 10. Jan Blockx's opera "La Princesse d'Auberge" presented at the Metropolitan Opera House, New York City, with Maria Labia and Jeanne Gerville-Reache in the leading rôles.

1909. Mar. 12. A. Bruckner's Eighth Symphony (C minor) given by the Boston Symphony Orchestra.

1909. Mar. 27. A. Maquarre's overture "On the Sea Cliffs" given by the Boston Symphony Orchestra.

1909. April 29. First public performance of P. G. Clapp's tone poem "Norge" given by the Boston Symphony Orchestra in Sanders Theater, Cambridge, Mass. Had been performed by the Pierian Sodality May 22, 1908.

1909. April 1. Production of W. W. Gilchrist's passion oratorio "The Lamb of God" at the Cathedral of St. John the Divine, New York City.

1909. April 3. Strube's Symphony in B minor played from MS. by the Boston Symphony Orchestra.

1909. April 17. Arthur Foote's Suite in E major for string orchestra produced by the Boston Symphony Orchestra.

1909. May 28. Henry K. Hadley's prize composition "The Culprit Fay" produced at the Powers Theatre, Grand Rapids, Mich. Played by the Chicago Orchestra Oct. 29, and the Boston Symphony Orchestra Nov. 14.

1909. June. G. W. Chadwick's' Christmas pastoral "Noël" produced by the Litchfield County Choral Union at Norfolk, Conn., conducted by the composer.

1909. Oct. 9. Saint-Saëns's ballad on Victor Hugo's "La Fiancée du Timbalier" given by the Boston Symphony Orchestra.

1909. Oct. 16. Reger's symphonic "Prologue to a Tragedy" (Op. 108) given by the Boston Symphony Orchestra.

1909. Oct. 23. Granville Bantock's comedy overture, "The Pierrot of a Minute," given by the Boston Symphony Orchestra.

ANNALS OF MUSIC IN AMERICA

1909. Oct. 25. American début of Tilly Koenen (Dutch lieder singer) at a recital in Mendelssohn Hall, New York City.

1909. Nov. 4. American début (as pianist) of S. Rachmaninof at a recital at Smith College, Northampton, Mass.

1909. Nov. 7. The ballet music from Mozart's pantomime "Les Petits Riens" given by the Symphony Society in New York City. Also Rimsky-Korsakof's "Russian Song."

1909. Nov. 8. American début of Eric Schmedes, tenor, in "Die Walküre" at the Metropolitan Opera House, New York City.

1909. Nov. 8. Opening of the Boston Opera House under the management of Henry Russell, with a performance of "La Gioconda" with Lillian Nordica, Louise Homer, Madame Meitschek, F. Constantino, Baklanof, Mardones, Pulcini, Stroesco.

1909. Nov. 10. American operatic début of John McCormack, noted tenor, as *Alfredo* in "La Traviata," at the Manhattan Opera House, New York City.

1909. Nov. 12. J. M. Ravel's "Rhapsodie Espagnole" given by the Chicago Symphony Orchestra.

1909. Nov. 15. Massenet's opera "Sappho" presented at the Manhattan Opera House, New York City, with Mary Garden in the title rôle.

1909. Nov. 15. Debussy's "Rondes de Printemps" (Image pour Orchestre) given by the Philharmonic Society in New York City.

1909. Nov. 16. Operatic début of Alma Gluck as *Sophie* in "Werther" at the New Theatre, New York. She appeared on Dec. 3 at the Metropolitan Opera House as the *Blessed Spirit* in "Orfeo."

1909. Nov. 16. American début of Edmond Clément, noted French tenor, in "Werther," at the Manhattan Opera House, New York City.

1909. Nov. 17. American début of Otto Slezak, Russian tenor, as *Otello* at the Metropolitan Opera House, New York City.

1909. Nov. 18. Arensky's "Variations" for strings, given by the Russian Symphony Orchestra, New York City.

1909. Nov. 27. Delius's symphony poem, "Paris, a Night Piece," given by the Boston Symphony Orchestra.

1909. Nov. 28. Rachmaninof's Third Pianoforte Concerto (Op. 30) given by the Symphony Society in New York City with the composer as soloist. Also Lalo's "Arlequin."

1909. Dec. 3. Rachmaninof's tone poem "The Isle of the Dead" given by the Chicago Symphony Orchestra, conducted by the composer.

1909. Dec. 5. American début of Josef Malkin, cellist, as soloist in Haydn's "Concerto in D" with the Symphony Society in New York City. (N. B. Malkin played at a concert Nov. 28 at the Manhattan Opera House.)

1909. Dec. 14. American début of Jeanne Maubourg in "Madame Angot" at the New Theatre, New York City.

1909. Dec. 16. Mahler's First Symphony given by the Philharmonic Society in New York City.

1909. Dec. 23. Gluck's opera "Orfeo ed Eurydice" presented at the Metropolitan Opera House, New York City, with Homer, Gadski, Alson, Gluck. Toscanini conducting.

1909. Dec. Henry K. Hadley appointed conductor of the Seattle (Wash.) Symphony Orchestra.

1910. Jan. 5. Liza Lehmann, noted song-writer, gave her first concert in America at Symphony Hall, Boston, Mass.

1910. Jan. 5. Production of Wm. Berwald's "Dramatic Overture" by the New York Symphony Orchestra, Walter Damrosch, conductor, at Syracuse, N. Y.

1910. Jan. 7. H. K. Hadley's "Symphonic Fantasia" produced by the Symphony Orchestra in St. Louis, Mo.

1910. Jan. 10. Massenet's opera "Griselidis" given at the Manhattan Opera House, New York City.

1910. Jan. 18. F. Volbach's Symphony in B minor given by the Philadelphia Symphony Orchestra.

1910. Jan. 23. Franchetti's opera "Germania" given at the Metropolitan Opera House, New York City, with Emmy Destinn, Caruso, and Amato in the leading parts.

1910. Jan. 26. Debussy's "Marche Ecossais"; d'Indy's "Souvenirs"; Rameau's "Dardanus"; P. Dukas's "Ariane et Barbe Bleue" (excerpts); G. Pierné's "Ramuntcho," given by the Orchestral Club in Boston.

1910. Feb. 1. R. Strauss's opera "Elektra" given at the Manhattan Opera House, New York City, with Madame Mazarin as *Elektra*, and Jeanne Gerville-Reache as *Klytemnestra*.

1910. Feb. 7. Georg Schumann's cantata "Ruth" given by the Apollo Musical Society, Chicago.

1910. Feb. 8. H. Bruneau's opera "l'Attaque du Moulin" presented at the New Theatre, Harlem, N. Y.

1910. Feb. 12. Chadwick's Sinfonietta in D major produced by the Boston Symphony Orchestra.

1910. Feb. 13. Sullivan's oratorio "The Golden Legend" given by the Handel and Haydn Society in Boston.

1910. Feb. 15. Max Schilling's symphonic fantasy "Meerguss" given by the St. Paul (Minn.) Symphony Orchestra.

1910. Feb. 20. Moszkowski's Third Orchestral Suite given by the Symphony Society in New York City.

1910. Mar. 4. Glazunof's Violin Concerto in A minor given by the Russian Symphony Orchestra in New York City with Mischa Elman as soloist.

1910. Mar. 5. Chaikovsky's opera "Pique Dame" presented at the Metropolitan Opera House, New York City, with Emmy Destinn, Leonora Sparkes, Alma Gluck, Slezak, and Didur.

1910. Mar. 6. Granville Bantock's "Fine Old English Tunes" arranged for small orchestra; and Haydn's Concerto for Violin with A. Saslafsky as soloist, given by the Symphony Society in New York City.

1910. Mar. 11. Busoni's orchestral suite "Turandot" given by the Philharmonic Society in New York City.

1910. Mar. 19. G. Strube's comedy overture "Puck" produced by the Boston Symphony Orchestra.

1910. Mar. 27. E. Bossi's "Paradise Lost" given by the Handel and Haydn Society in Boston.

1910. April 16. Ducasse's "Suite Française" in D minor, given by the Boston Symphony Orchestra.

1910. April 19. Balakiref's "Ouverture"; C. Franck's "Quatres Pièces Brèves"; Ducasse's "Variations Plaisantes sur un Thême Grave" (harp obbligato); L. Moreau's "Pastorale" for saxophone and orchestra (written for Mrs. R.

J. Hall, and produced at this concert with Mrs. Hall as soloist); and S. Lazzari's symphonic poem " Effet de Nuit," given by the Orchestral Club, in Boston.

1910. April 23. Aug. Halm's Symphony in D minor for string orchestra given by the Boston Symphony Orchestra.

1910. April 28. Oscar Hammerstein's withdrawal from opera in New York and Philadelphia announced. The Metropolitan Opera Company purchased rights in opera, contracts with artists, scenic equipment, etc.

1910. June 2. Production of S. Coleridge Taylor's rhapsodie dance, "The Bamboula," at Norfolk, Conn.

1910. Aug. 17. H. F. Gilbert's "Comedy Overture on Negro Themes" produced at an open air concert in Central Park, New York City.

1910. Aug. 29. P. Floridia's opera "Paoletta" produced in Cincinnati, O.

1910. Sept. 29. The first part of Granville Bantock's "Omar Khayyàm" given at the Worcester (Mass.) Festival.

1910. Oct. 6. Wallace's symphonic poem "Villon," and Saint-Saëns's March "Occident and Orient" given by the Symphony Society, New York City.

1910. Oct. 28. Delius's English rhapsody "Brigg Fair" given by the Symphony Society, New York City.

1910. Oct. 29. American début of Anton Witek, violinist (concert-master of the Boston Symphony Orchestra), as soloist.

1910. Nov. 5. Opening of the Chicago Opera Company under the management of Andréas Dippel, with a performance of "Aïda."

1910. Nov. 14. Gluck's opera "Armide" given at the Metropolitan Opera House, New York City, with Olive Fremstad, Louise Homer, Caruso and Amato.

1910. Nov. 16. Production at the Boston Opera House of F. S. Converse's opera "The Sacrifice."

1910. Nov. 16. Debussy's opera "L'Enfant Prodigue" given at the Boston Opera House, with Alice Neilson, Blanchart, Lasalle, etc.

1910. Nov. 16. Liadov's "Kikimora" and "Le Lac Enchanté," given by the Russian Symphony Orchestra, in New York City.

ANNALS OF MUSIC IN AMERICA

1910. Nov. 20. Excerpts from Chaikovsky's opera "Jeanne d'Arc" given by the Symphony Society, New York City.

1910. Nov. 26. Mozart's Adagio and Fugue for string orchestra given by the Boston Symphony Orchestra.

1910. Dec. 1. American début of Kathleen Parlow (Canadian violinist) with the Russian Symphony Orchestra, in New York City.

1910. Dec. 1. I. F. Stravinsky's "Feuerwerk" given by the Russian Symphony Orchestra in New York City.

1910. Dec. 4. Dvořák's "In the Spinning Room" given by the Symphony Society, New York City.

1910. Dec. 4. R. Laparra's opera "La Habañera" given by the Boston Opera Company.

1910. Dec. 10. Puccini's opera "La Fanciulla" ("The Girl of the Golden West") presented at the Metropolitan Opera House, New York City, with Emmy Destinn, Caruso and Amato in the leading parts.

1910. Dec. 28. Production (first performance on any stage) of Humperdinck's opera "Königskinder" with Geraldine Farrar, Marie Mattfeld, H. Jadlowker, Otto Goritz, A. Didur and A. Reiss in the leading parts. Metropolitan Opera House, New York City.

1910. Sept. MacDowell Festivals at Peterboro, N. H., instituted under the auspices of the MacDowell Memorial Association.

1910. Gatti-Casazza became sole director of the Metropolitan Opera House, on the withdrawal of Andreas Dippel.

1910. Philadelphia-Chicago Opera Company formed with Andreas Dippel as manager.

1911. Jan. 3. G. Enesco's Suite for Orchestra (Op. 9) given by the Philharmonic Orchestra, New York City.

1911. Jan. 6. Debussy's "Iberia" (second of the third series of "Images") given by the Philharmonic Society in New York City. Also Chabrier's "Ode à la Musique."

1911. Jan. 20. Leo Blech's opera "Versiegelt" presented at the Metropolitan Opera House, New York City.

1911. Jan. 25. Saint-Saëns's "Ouverture de Fête"; G. Lekue's Adagio for Strings"; Rhené-Baton's "Variations" for pianoforte and orchestra; P. Dukas's overture to "Polyeucte";

H. Woollett's "Siberia" for saxophone and orchestra (written for Mrs. R. J. Hall) (production); Lazzari's (*a*) "Armor," (*b*) "Marche pour une Fête Joyeuse," given by the Orchestral Club in Boston.

1911. Jan. 27. Production of Arthur Foote's Serenade in E major for strings, by the St. Louis Symphony Orchestra.

1911. Jan. 28. Gernsheim's tone poem "To a Drama" (Op. 82) given by the Boston Symphony Orchestra.

1911. Feb. 3. Paul Dukas's opera "Ariana et Barbe Bleue" presented at the Metropolitan Opera House, New York City, with Geraldine Farrar in the title rôle.

1911. Feb. 5. Paul Dukas's Symphony in C given by the Symphony Society in New York City.

1911. Feb. 11. Scharwenka's Fourth Pianoforte Concerto (F minor) given by the Boston Symphony Orchestra with the composer as soloist.

1911. Feb. 15. Dvořák's posthumous symphony given by the Philharmonic Society in New York City.

1911. Feb. 16. Rachmaninof's "Fantasia" for two pianos and orchestra given by the New York Symphony Society.

1911. Feb. 17. Enesco's Symphony in E flat major given by the Symphony Society in New York City.

1911. Feb. 25. Production of Victor Herbert's opera "Natoma" by the Chicago-Philadelphia Opera Company in Philadelphia, with Mary Garden, L. Grenville, and John McCormack in the leading rôles.

1911. Feb. 27. F. Stock's Suite for String Orchestra given by the St. Louis Symphony Orchestra.

1911. Feb. 27. J. Stransky's "Symphonic Song" given by the Philharmonic Society, New York City.

1911. Feb. Symphony by F. Delius produced by the New York Symphony Society.

1911. Mar. 3. Chabrier's unfinished opera "Briseis" given, in concert form, by the MacDowell Chorus in New York City.

1911. Mar. 3. Victor Kolar's symphonic poem "Hiawatha" given by the Symphony Society, New York City.

1911. Mar. 4. R. Mandl's "Overture to a Gascon Comedy" given by the Boston Symphony Orchestra.

1911. Mar. 6. A. Perelli's opera "A Lover's Quarrel" given at Philadelphia.

1911. Mar. 11. Sinigaglia's overture "Le Baruffe Chiozzotte" given by the Boston Symphony Orchestra.

1911. Mar. 14. Production of the opera "Mona," libretto by Brian Hooker and music by H. W. Parker, at the Metropolitan Opera House, New York City.

1911. Mar. 24. Wolf-Ferrari's opera "The Secret of Suzanne" presented by the Philadelphia-Chicago Opera Company in Philadelphia.

1911. Mar. 25–30. Brahms Festival held in New York City by the Symphony and Oratorio Societies.

1911. Mar. 25. Jean Nouguès's opera "Quo Vadis" presented in Philadelphia by the Chicago-Philadelphia Opera Company.

1911. April. The Minneapolis Symphony Orchestra visited New York for the first time, as guest of the Philharmonic Society.

1911. April 10. Felix Woyrsch's Mystery for soli, chorus, orchestra and organ, "Tödtentanz" given by the Apollo Musical Society in Chicago.

1911. April 15. Production of G. W. Chadwick's "Suite Symphonique" by the Boston Symphony Orchestra.

1911. April 22. Production of Arthur S. Curry's symphonic poem "Attala" by the Boston Symphony Orchestra, conducted by the composer.

1911. May 19. Death, in Vienna, of Gustav Mahler, conductor of the Philharmonic Orchestra of New York City.

1911. June 6. Production of Horatio Parker's "Collegiate Overture," and Henry K. Hadley's symphony, "North, South, East and West," by the Litchfield County Choral Union at Norfolk, Conn., under the direction of the composers.

1911. Aug. 10. Production of Henry K. Hadley's tone poem "The Atonement of Pan" by the Bohemian Club at San Francisco, Cal.

1911. Sept. 27. Max Reger's "The Nuns" given at the Worcester (Mass.) Festival.

1911. Oct. 7. Production of Max Reger's "A Comedy Overture" by the Boston Symphony Orchestra.

1911. Oct. 28. Granville Bantock's poem " Dante and Beatrice " given by the Boston Symphony Orchestra, and at the same concert Efrem Zimbalist, violinist, made his American début, playing Glazunof's Concerto (Op. 82).

1911. Nov. 2. Josef Stransky made his appearance as conductor of the Philharmonic Society in New York City.

1911. Nov. 2. Aeolian Hall (New York City) opened with a recital by Gottfried Galston, pianist.

1911. Nov. 4. Margarete Matzenauer made her American début as *Aïda* at the Metropolitan Opera House, New York City.

1911. Nov. 18. Ludwig Thuille's opera " Lobetanz " presented at the Metropolitan Opera House, New York City, with Gadski, Jadlowker, etc.

1911. Nov. 18. Grieg's " Old Norwegian Romance " with variations, given by the Boston Symphony Orchestra.

1911. Nov. 24. Elgar's Second Symphony (E flat) given by the Cincinnati Symphony Orchestra.

1911. Nov. 25. Balakiref's overture on the theme of a Spanish March given by the Boston Symphony Orchestra.

1911. Nov. 26. Laucella's symphonic poem " Consalvo " produced by the Philharmonic Society, New York City.

1911. Dec. 10. Début of Arthur Shattuck, pianist, in the Rachmaninof concerto, with the Symphony Society of New York City.

1911. Dec. 11. Liszt's oratorio " The Legend of St. Elizabeth " given by the MacDowell Chorus at Carnegie Hall, New York City.

1911. Dec. 17. Production of J. van der Pals's two symphonic pieces " Autumn " and " Spring " by the Philharmonic Society, New York City.

1911. Dec. 28. Weingärtner's Third Symphony (E major) given by the Philharmonic Society, New York City.

1911. A Symphony Orchestra formed in Kansas City, Mo., under Carl Busch.

1911. Symphony Orchestra in San Francisco, Cal., formed, and Henry K. Hadley appointed conductor.

1912. Jan. 3. Wolf Ferrari's opera " Le Donne Curiose " presented at the Metropolitan Opera House, New York City, with Farrar, Maubourg, Jadlowker, Scotti and Didur.

1912. Jan. 7. American début of Wilhelm Bachaus, pianist, in Beethoven's "Emperor" Concerto, with the Symphony Society, New York City.

1912. Jan. 9. American début of Elena Gerhardt, lieder singer in New York City.

1912. Jan. 10. American début of Vanni Marcoux, French baritone, as *Golaud* in "Pelléas et Mélisande" at the Boston Opera House.

1912. Jan. 16. Production of P. G. Clapp's prelude "In Summer" by the St. Louis Symphony Orchestra.

1912. Jan. 16. Wolf-Ferrari's opera "The Jewels of the Madonna" given at the Auditorium by the Chicago Opera Company, with Carolina White in the leading rôle, Sammarco, Dufau, Daddi, etc., assisting.

1912. Jan. 26. Production of F. S. Converse's symphonic poem "Ormazd" by the St. Louis Symphony Orchestra.

1912. Jan. 26. Delius's tone poem "In a Summer Garden" given by the Philharmonic Society, New York City.

1912. Jan. 27. Massenet's opera "Don Quichotte" presented at the French Opera House, New Orleans, La.

1912. Feb. 2. Production of Geo. F. Boyle's "Pianoforte Concerto in D minor" by the Philharmonic Society, New York City, with Ernest Hutcheson as soloist.

1912. Feb. 4. Production of two symphonic sketches from F. Stahlberg's "Im Hochland," by the Philharmonic Society, New York City.

1912. Feb. 11. Production of Mary Lawrence Townsend's "Serenade" by the Russian Symphony Orchestra, New York City.

1912. Feb. 12. Debussy's mystery "Le Martyre de St. Sébastien" given by the MacDowell Chorus, in New York City.

1912. Feb. 14. American début of Lucille Marcel as *Tosca*, in Boston.

1912. Feb. 16. Victor Kolar's symphonic poem "A Fairy Tale" produced by the Symphony Society in New York City.

1912. Mar. 3. Saint-Saëns's "Hymn to Pallas Athene" given by the Symphony Society, New York City.

1912. Mar. 11. F. Schmitt's "Rhapsodie Viennoise" (production); P. Gaubert's "Poëme Elegiaque" for saxophone and orchestra (production written for and played by Mrs. R. J. Hall); A. Roussel's "Poëme de la Forêt" (production); Roger Ducasse's "Petit Suite" (production), given at an Orchestral Concert in Boston under the management of Mrs. R. J. Hall.

1912. Mar. 15. J. G. Mraczek's "Symphonic Burlesque" for grand orchestra given by the Boston Symphony Orchestra.

1912. Mar. 16. Production of F. Stahlberg's "Symphonic Scherzo" by the Philharmonic Society, New York City.

1912. Mar. 25. Brahms's "Triumphlied" for chorus and orchestra given in New York City.

1912. April 7. Max Reger's "Romantic" and "Ballet" Suites, given by the Philharmonic Society, New York City.

1912. April 8. First appearance in America of the London (England) Symphony Orchestra, A. Nikisch, conductor, at Carnegie Hall, New York City.

1912. April 14. Production of P. G. Clapp's "Dramatic Poem," by the Pierian Sodality of Harvard University, at the Hotel Astor, New York City.

1912. April 14. Monteverde's opera "Orfeo" given in concert form at the Metropolitan Opera House, New York City, with Rita Fornia, M. Duchène, Anna Case, H. Weil, H. Witherspoon and Basil Ruysdael.

1912. May. Production of Arne Oldberg's "Symphonic Variations" at the North Shore Festival, Evanston, Ill.

1912. May 16. Production of Wm. Berwald's overture "Walthari" by the New York Symphony Orchestra, Walter Damrosch, conductor, at the Central New York Music Festival, Syracuse, N. Y.

1912. June 4. Production of G. W. Chadwick's symphonic fantasie "Aphrodite" by the Litchfield County Choral Union, at Norfolk, Conn.

1912. June 5. Production of Henry F. Gilbert's "Negro Rhapsody," also Coleridge Taylor's Concerto for Violin, his "Negro Air" for solo violin and orchestra, and "A Tale of Old Japan," by the Litchfield County Choral Union, at Norfolk, Conn.

1912. Oct. Leopold Stokowski, having severed his connection with the Cincinnati Symphony Orchestra in March, appeared as conductor of the Philadelphia Symphony Orchestra.

1912. Oct. 30. A. Schoenberg's "Five Pieces for Orchestra" given by the Chicago Symphony Orchestra.

1912. Oct. 30. E. Schelling's "Legende Symphonique" given by the Philadelphia Symphony Orchestra.

1912. Nov. 4. Début of Titta Ruffo as the *Duke* in "Rigoletto," with the Chicago-Philadelphia Company at Philadelphia, Pa.

1912. Nov. 7. Delius's symphonic poem "Life's Dance" given by the Chicago Symphony Orchestra.

1912. Nov. 7. Goldmark's opera "Das Heimchen am Herd" presented at the Metropolitan Opera House, Philadelphia, with Maggie Teyte, Mabel Riegelman, Helen Stanley, Riccardo Martin, and Henri Scott, in the leading parts, and Arnold Winternitz conducting.

1912. Nov. 8. Maurice Ravel's orchestral suite "Ma Mère l'Oye" given at a concert in Aeolian Hall, New York City. And at the same concert William Becher's "Pianoforte Concerto" was produced.

1912. Nov. 13. R. Strauss's "Festival Prelude" given by the Philharmonic Society, New York City.

1912. Nov. 14. Weingärtner's "Lustige Overture" given by the Philharmonic Society, New York City.

1912. Nov. 15. Dr. Ernest Kunwald appeared as conductor of the Cincinnati Symphony Orchestra.

1912. Nov. 16. Ernest Fanelli's symphonic pictures "Thebes" given by the Symphony Society, New York City.

1912. Nov. 19. Max Reger's "Concerto in Ancient Style" given at the Waldorf-Astoria Hotel, New York City, by the Philharmonic Society.

1912. Nov. 21. Bruckner's Sixth Symphony (A major), and Korngold's "Overture to a Play," given by the Philharmonic Society, New York City.

1912. Nov. 21. Ippolitof-Ivanof's "Armenian Rhapsodie," given by the Russian Symphony Orchestra at its tenth anniversary concert in New York City.

1912. Dec. 3. Cornelius Dopper's third symphony "Rembrandt" (in C minor) given by the St. Paul (Minn.) Symphony Orchestra.

1912. Dec. 3. Louis Koemmenich made his first appearance as conductor of the Oratorio Society of New York City, at a performance of "Elijah," on the resignation of Frank Damrosch.

1912. Dec. 6. G. Fitelberg's tone poem "Das Lied vom Falken" given by the St. Louis Symphony Orchestra.

1912. Dec. 13. Production of David S. Smith's Symphony in F minor by the Cincinnati Symphony Orchestra.

1912. Dec. 14. Borodin's Second Symphony (D minor) given by the Boston Symphony Orchestra.

1912. Dec. 21. Klughardt's "Concerto for Violoncello" (Op. 59) given by the Boston Symphony Orchestra.

1912. Dec. 27. American début of Frieda Hempel, noted soprano, as *Marguerite* in "Les Huguenots" at the Metropolitan Opera House, New York City.

1912. Dec. 29. The "Jena Symphony" (ascribed to Beethoven, and discovered in the archives of the University of Jena) given by the Boston Symphony Orchestra. This work was played publicly for the first time at St. Petersburg, Dec. 1911.

1912. Philharmonic Society of New York reorganized in such a manner as to secure the Pulitzer bequest of $500,000.

1913. Jan. 11. Joseph Holbrook's symphonic poem "Queen Mab" given by the Boston Symphony Orchestra.

1913. Jan. 16. Arensky's "Serenade" given by the Russian Symphony Orchestra, New York City.

1913. Jan. 16. American début of Max Pauer, noted pianist, in New York City.

1913. Jan. 25. Production of Gustav Strube's symphonic poems "Narcissus" and "Echo" by the Boston Symphony Orchestra.

1913. Feb. 6. Zandonai's opera "Conchita" presented at the Metropolitan Opera House, Philadelphia, with Tarquina Tarquini in the title rôle, by the Philadelphia-Chicago Opera Company.

1913. Feb. 15. Ernest Lendvai's "Symphony in D major" given by the Boston Symphony Orchestra.

1913. Feb. 20. Perelli's opera "A Lover's Quarrel" given by the Chicago-Philadelphia Company, in Philadelphia, with Zepelli, Sammarco, and Berat.

1913. Feb. 24. Wilhelm Kienzl's opera "Les Ranz des Vaches" given at the Metropolitan Opera House, Philadelphia, by the Chicago-Philadelphia Opera Company.

1913. Feb. 27. Production of Walter Damrosch's opera "Cyrano de Bergerac" at the Metropolitan Opera House, New York City, with Amato and Frances Alda in the leading rôles, and Alfred Hertz conducting.

1913. Feb. 27. Production of J. Stransky's two symphony songs, "Moonrise" and "Requiem," by the Philharmonic Society, New York City.

1913. Mar. 2. Sibelius's Symphony No. 4 given by the New York Symphony Society.

1913. Mar. 8. Vivaldi's "Concerto in G minor" for violin, organ and orchestra, given by the Boston Symphony Orchestra.

1913. Mar. 8. Louis Aubert's opera "La Forêt Bleue" given at the Boston Opera House with Carmen Melis, Bernice Fisher, Elizabeth Amsden, Jeska Swartz, Riddez and Potter. Caplet conducting.

1913. Mar. 8. Mussorgsky's opera "Boris Godunof" presented at the Metropolitan Opera House, New York City, with Anna Case, Jeanne Maubourg, Louise Homer, Paul Althouse and Didur.

1913. Mar. 23. Leoncavallo's opera "Zingari" presented by the Chicago Opera Company, conducted by the composer, at Chicago.

1913. Mar. 28. O. Taubmann's "A Choral Service" given by the Oratorio Society, New York City.

1913. April 17. R. Strauss's "Der Abend" (16 parts), and Granville Bantock's choral symphony "Atalanta in Calydon" (20 parts), also Percy Grainger's "Folk Tune Settings," given by the MacDowell Chorus in New York City.

1913. June 3. Production of Edgar S. Kelley's second symphony "New England" by the Litchfield County Choral Union at Norfolk, Conn.

1913. Oct. 2. G. Pierné's oratorio "St. Francis of Assisi" given at the Worcester (Mass.) Festival.

1913. Nov. 11. Florent Schmitt's *drame muet* "La Tragédie de Salome" given by the Boston Symphony Orchestra.

1913. Nov. 14. Jarnefelt's "Praeludium" given by the Russian Symphony Orchestra in New York City.

1913. Nov. 20. Franchetti's opera "Cristoforo Colombo" presented at the Metropolitan Opera House, Philadelphia, by the Chicago-Philadelphia Opera Company, with Rosa Raisa, Titta Ruffo, and Bassi in the leading rôles, and Campanini conducting.

1913. Nov. 21. Production of Gustav Strube's symphonic poem "Loreley" by the St. Louis Symphony Orchestra.

1913. Nov. 21. Arthur Hinton's Second Symphony (C minor) given by the Minneapolis (Minn.) Symphony Orchestra.

1913. Nov. 28. Operatic début of Sophie Braslau (contralto) at the Metropolitan Opera House, New York City, as *Prince Feodor* in "Boris Godounov."

1913. Nov. 28. F. Arbos's "Guajiras" for violin and orchestra given by the Philadelphia Symphony Orchestra, with Bonarios Grimson as soloist.

1913. Dec. 5. H. Février's opera "Monna Vanna" presented at the Boston Opera House, with Mary Garden, Jeska Swartz, L. Muratore and Vanni Marcoux.

1913. Dec. 9. R. Strauss' opera "Der Rosenkavalier" given at the Metropolitan Opera House, New York City, with Frieda Hempel, M. Ober, H. Weil, Carl Jörn and Otto Goritz. Hertz conducting.

1913. Dec. 12. Elgar's symphonic study "Falstaff" given by the Symphony Society, New York City.

1913. Dec. 18. F. Schmitt's "Psaulme XLVI" given by the Cecilia Society in Boston.

1913. Dec. 27. Ravel's fantasy "Juon" and "Vaegtervise" (Watchman's Song) given by the Boston Symphony Orchestra.

1914. Jan. 2. Albert Roussel's evocation "La Ville Rose" given by the Philadelphia Symphony Orchestra.

1914. Jan. 2. Montemezzi's opera "L'Amore di Tre Rè" presented at the Metropolitan Opera House, New York City, with Bori, Braslau, Amato and Didur. Toscanini conducting.

1914. Jan. 6. W. Stenhammer's "Midwinter" given by the Minneapolis Symphony Orchestra.

1914. Jan. 16. Gabriel Pierné's orchestration of C. Franck's "Prelude, Chorale, and Fugue" for pianoforte, given by the Symphony Society, New York City.

1914. Jan. 20. R. Zandonai's "O Padre Nostro" for male voices, organ and orchestra, from "Purgatory," given by the Schola Cantorum in New York City.

1914. Jan. 24. Production of Victor Herbert's one-act opera "Madeline" at the Metropolitan Opera House, New York City, with Alda, Sparkes, Althouse, Segurola and Pini-Corsi.

1914. Jan. 25. Production of G. Hüe's "Fantasie" for flute and orchestra, with G. Barrère as soloist; also V. Kolar's "Suite" for orchestra, and Lekew's "Adagio" for strings, by the Symphony Society in New York City.

1914. Feb. 6. Production of M. Kernochan's cantata "The Foolish Virgins" by the Orange Musical Art Society at East Orange, N. J.

1914. Feb. 12. J. G. Ropartz's symphonic étude "The Hunt of Prince Arthur" given by the Philharmonic Society, New York City.

1914. Feb. 17. Spendiarof's symphonic poem "The Three Palms" given by the Russian Symphony Orchestra, New York City.

1914. Feb. 19. Production of Mabel W. Daniels's "The Guests of Sleep" by the Cecilia Society in Boston.

1914. Feb. 26. Vittorio Gnecchi's opera "Cassandra" given at the Metropolitan Opera House, Philadelphia, by the Chicago-Philadelphia Opera Company, with Rosa Raisa, J. Claussen, and Dalmores. Sturani, conductor.

1914. Feb. 26. Charpentier's opera "Julien" presented at the Metropolitan Opera House, New York City, with Farrar, Caruso, and Gilly.

1914. Mar. 7. Production of Otto Urack's first symphony (E

major) by the Boston Symphony Orchestra, conducted by the composer.

1914. Mar. 14. Production of R. Goldmark's tone poem "Samson" by the Boston Symphony Orchestra.

1914. Mar. 25. Wolf-Ferrari's opera "L'Amore Medico" presented at the Metropolitan Opera House, New York City, with L. Bori, B. Alten, L. Rothier, Pini-Corsi, Segurola. Toscanini conducting.

1914. April 2. Production of Francis Pauly's Pianoforte Concerto in E flat, by the Minneapolis Symphony Orchestra, with Florence Pauly as soloist.

1914. April 3. Production of Eric Korngold's Sinfonietta (Op. 5) by the Chicago Symphony Orchestra.

1914. April 5. Production of Wm. Berwald's cantata "The Seven Last Words of Christ" by the St. Thomas Church Choir, New York City. Tertius Noble, organist and director.

1914. April 11. Production of P. G. Clapp's "Symphony in E minor" by the Boston Symphony Orchestra, conducted by the composer.

1914. April 19. The Fort Worth (Texas) Symphony Orchestra organized under Carl Venth. Produced several works by American composers, including Carl Venth's "Prologue to an Indian Drama."

1914. April 25. Reznicek's Symphonishes Lebensbild "Schlemihl" given by the Boston Symphony Orchestra.

1914. May 28. Production of "Cahokia," the pageant and masque of St. Louis (music by F. S. Converse), at Forest Park, St. Louis, Mo.

1914. June 2. Production of H. K. Hadley's tone poem "Lucifer" at the Litchfield County Choral Union Festival, Norfolk, Conn., conducted by the composer.

1914. June. Production of Coleridge Taylor's orchestral rhapsody "From the Prairie" (Arthur Mees, conductor), and J. Sibelius's orchestral tone poem "Aalloteret," by the Litchfield County Choral Union, at Norfolk, Conn., conducted by the composer.

1914. Aug. 20. Production of Arthur Nevin's suite "Love Dreams" at the MacDowell Festival, Peterboro, N. H.

1914. Aug. Henry F. Gilbert's music to Synge's play "Riders to the Sea" produced at a MacDowell Festival, Peterboro, N. H., conducted by the composer.

1914. Oct. 23. Roussel's ballet pantomime "Le Festin de l'Araignée" given by the Symphony Society of New York City.

1914. Oct. 23. Dohnanyi's Suite for Orchestra (Op. 19) given by the Minneapolis Symphony Orchestra.

1914. Oct. 24. Ropartz's Fourth Symphony (C major) given by the Boston Symphony Orchestra.

1914. Nov. 6. Hugo Alfvén's Third Symphony (E minor) given by the Minneapolis Symphony Orchestra.

1914. Nov. 29. Symphonic fragment from Ravel's Ballet "Daphnis and Chloe" given by the Symphony Society of New York City.

1914. Dec. 13. Hugo Alfvén's "Festspel-Polonaise" given by the Minneapolis Symphony Orchestra.

1914. American Symphony Orchestra organized in Chicago with Glenn Dillard Gunn as conductor.

1914. Great organ with 7000 pipes installed at the Pan-American Exposition in San Francisco, Cal.

1915. Jan. 4. F. Leoni's opera "L'Oracolo" presented at the Metropolitan Opera House, New York City, with Bori, Braslau, Scotti and Didur.

1915. Jan. 8. Theophile Ysaye's "Fantasia on a Popular Walloon Theme" given by the St. Louis Symphony Orchestra.

1915. Jan. 17. First public performance of Edmund Severn's Violin Concerto in D minor given by the Philharmonic Society, New York City, with Max Pilser as soloist.

1915. Jan. 25. Production of U. Giordano's opera "Madame Sans-Gêne" at the Metropolitan Opera House, New York City, with Geraldine Farrar, Leonora Sparkes, Amato, Martinelli, and Segurola. Toscanini conducting.

1915. Jan. 30. Notable revival of Beethoven's opera "Fidelio" at the Metropolitan Opera House, New York City, with Matzenauer and Urlus in the leading rôles.

1915. Jan. 31. Roger Ducasse's "La Jolie Jeu de Furet" given by the Symphony Society of New York City.

1915. Jan. 31. Production of Henry Burck's "Meditation" for strings; and Nicola Laucella's "Prelude and Temple Dance" given by the Philharmonic Society in New York City.

1915. Feb. 5. S. Stojowski's Suite for Orchestra in E flat major given by the Philharmonic Society, New York City.

1915. Feb. 13. S. E. Bortkiewitch's Pianoforte Concerto in B flat major given by the Russian Symphony Orchestra in New York City, with Margaret Volovy as soloist.

1915. Feb. 22. F. Cowen's oratorio "The Veil" given by the Apollo Musical Society in Chicago.

1915. Mar. 19. Production of John Alden Carpenter's orchestral suite "Adventures in a Perambulator" by the Chicago Symphony Orchestra.

1915. Mar. 19. Production of Scriabin's "Poem of Fire — Prometheus" by the Russian Symphony Orchestra in New York City. (Had been played in Chicago Mar. 5, but without effects of light.)

1915. Mar. 27. First of Reger's "Four Tone Poems" for orchestra (after Boecklin) given by the Boston Symphony Orchestra.

1915. April 3. F. Klose's Prelude and Double Fugue for Organ, with choral for trumpets and trombones, given by the Boston Symphony Orchestra.

1915. June 3. Production of G. W. Chadwick's ballade for orchestra "Tam O'Shanter" at the Litchfield County Choral Union Festival, Norfolk, Conn.

1915. June. Production of F. A. Stock's Violin Concerto, under direction of the composer, with Efrem Zimbalist as soloist, and C. V. Stanford's "Pianoforte Concerto in G major" (first time in America) with Harold Bauer as soloist, at the Litchfield County Choral Union Festival, Norfolk, Conn.

1915. Summer. Walter Damrosch's incidental music to the Greek play "Iphigenia in Aulis" produced at the Greek Theatre, Berkeley, Cal. (Was given in New York Dec. 15 the same year.)

1915. July 1. Production of H. W. Parker and Brian Hooker's opera "Fairyland" at Los Angeles, Cal. This opera won the prize offered by the Los Angeles Opera Association.

1915. Aug. 7. Production of Edward F. Schneider's opera "Apollo" at Bohemian Grove, Cal.

1915. Oct. 22. Further excerpts from Ravel's ballet "Daphnis and Chloe" given by the Symphony Society of New York City.

1915. Nov. 5. F. Delius's "A Dance Rhapsody" given by the Minneapolis Symphony Orchestra.

1915. Nov. 5. Arnold Schoenberg's "Kammer Symphonie" given by the Philadelphia Symphony Orchestra.

1915. Nov. 9. Production of Clarence Loomis's Pianoforte Concerto by the American Symphony Orchestra, Chicago, with Glenn Dillard Gunn as soloist.

1915. Nov. 9. Production of Carlo Minetti's Aria for tenor and orchestra, with George Hamlin as soloist, by the American Symphony Orchestra in Chicago. This work won a prize offered by George Hamlin.

1915. Nov. 18. Schoenberg's symphonic poem "Pelléas et Mélisande" given by the Philharmonic Society in New York City.

1915. Nov. 26. Delius's Pianoforte Concerto in C minor given by the Philharmonic Society in New York City, with Percy Grainger as soloist.

1915. Dec. 9. Saint-Saëns's opera "Dejanire" presented by the Chicago Opera Company with Carmen Melis, de Cisneros, and Muratore. Campanini conducting.

1915. Dec. 30. Borodin's opera "Prince Igor" given at the Metropolitan Opera House, New York City, with F. Alda, F. Perini, Amato, Segurola, and Didur. Polacco conducting.

1915. Dec. 31. Production of Edward B. Hill's symphonic poem "The Parting of Lancelot and Guinevere" by the St. Louis Symphony Orchestra.

1915. Dec. 31. Schelling's theme and variations for orchestra "Impressions, from an Artist's Life," given by the Boston Symphony Orchestra with the composer as soloist.

1915. The San Francisco Symphony Orchestra reorganized with Alfred Hertz as conductor.

1915. The Baltimore Symphony Orchestra organized with Gustav Strube as conductor.

1916. Jan. 7. Duka's dance poem "La Péri," given by the San Francisco Symphony Orchestra, A. Hertz conducting.

1916. Jan. 10. Massenet's opera "Cléopâtre" presented by the Chicago Opera Company at the Auditorium with M. Kuznetsof in the title rôle.

1916. Jan. 15. Stravinsky's "First Symphony" (E flat) given by the Russian Symphony Orchestra in New York City.

1916. Jan. 20. Fibich's idyll for orchestra "At Evening" given by the Philharmonic Society, New York City.

1916. Jan. 23. F. Schmitt's "Pupazzi" given by the Symphony Society of New York City.

1916. Jan. 28. Production of E. Granados's opera "Goyescas" at the Metropolitan Opera House, New York City, with Anna Fitziu, F. Perini, Martinelli, and de Luca. Bavagnoli conducting.

1916. Feb. 4. Production of F. Stahlberg's Suite for Orchestra (Op. 53) given by the Philharmonic Society of New York City.

1916. Feb. 5. Centennial anniversary performance of Rossini's opera "The Barber of Seville" at the Metropolitan Opera House, New York City, with Madame Barrientos as *Rosina*.

1916. Feb. 6. Production of Seth Bingham's Suite for Orchestra by the Philharmonic Society of New York City.

1916. Feb. 11. Production of Arthur Shepherd's overture "The Festival of Youth" by the St. Louis Symphony Orchestra.

1916. Feb. 17. Rimsky's-Korsakof's "Serbian Fantaisie" and G. Hüe's suite "Croquois d'Orient" given by the Symphony Society of New York City.

1916. Feb. 18. Production of Daniel Gregory Mason's First Symphony (C minor) by the Philadelphia Symphony Orchestra.

1916. Mar. 3. Gustav Mahler's "Giant Symphony (Eighth) given by the Philadelphia Symphony Orchestra with more than one thousand performers.

1916. Mar. 10. Production of J. A. Carpenter's "Concertino" by the Chicago Symphony Orchestra, with Percy Grainger as pianist.

1916. April 23. Victor Louis Saar's "Suite Rococo" given by the Cincinnati Symphony Orchestra.

1916. April 25. R. Strauss's "Alpine Symphony" given by the Cincinnati Symphony Orchestra.

1916. April 25. Production of Franz C. Bornscheim's cantata "Onawa" at the Tri-City Musical Festival at Paterson, N. J. (This work won the prize offered by the New Jersey Choral Society.)

1916. May 4. V. d'Indy's prize choral work "Le Chant de la Cloche" given by the Cecilia Society in Boston.

1916. June. Production by the Litchfield County Choral Union at Norfolk, Conn., of Percy Grainger's suite for orchestra "In a Nutshell" conducted by the composer; C. M. Loeffler's symphony "Hora Mystica" conducted by the composer.

1916. July 12–16. Production at the Seattle Festival of State Federation of Musical Clubs of C. W. Cadman's symphonic fantasy "To a Vanishing Race" and J. H. Howe's "Festival Overture."

1916. Oct. 16. Ernest Bloch's two poems, "Winter" and "Spring," played at the 44th St. Theatre, New York City. (They were given by the New Symphony Orchestra, New York City, on Nov. 5, 1919.)

1916. Oct. 20. Schelling's "Violin Concerto" produced by the Boston Symphony Orchestra with Fritz Kreisler as soloist.

1916. Oct. 26. J. M. Ravel's "Valses Nobles et Sentimentales" given by the Symphony Society, New York City.

1916. Oct. 29. C. S. Skilton's "Two Indian Dances," (1) "Deer Dance" (Rogue River, Ore.), and (2) "War Dance" (Cheyenne), produced by the Minneapolis Symphony Orchestra. (They had been played as a string quartet in January by the Zoellner Quartet."

1916. Nov. 13. Bizet's opera "Les Pêcheurs des Perles" presented entire at the Metropolitan Opera House, New York City. (Two acts were given in 1897.)

1916. Nov. 18. American début of Amelita Galli-Curci, as *Gilda* in "Rigoletto" with the Chicago Opera Company in Chicago. L. Campanini conducting.

1916. Nov. 24. Michael Dvorsky's Symphonic Duologue for pianoforte and orchestra, produced by the Cincinnati Symphony Orchestra with Josef Hofmann (M. Dvorsky) as soloist.

1916. Nov. 25. Gluck's opera "Iphigenia in Tauris" presented at the Metropolitan Opera House, New York City, with Melanie Kurt, Marie Rappold, L. Sparkes, Sembach, Weil.

1916. Nov. 26. Elgar's adagio "Sospiri," for strings, harps, and organ, given by the Symphony Society of New York City; also Sinigaglia's "Étude Caprice" for strings.

1916. Dec. 3. M. Ravel's "Introduction et Allegro" for harp, strings, quartet, flute and clarinet, given by the Symphony Society, New York City.

1916. Dec. 14. Gustav Mahler's "Lied von der Erde" given by the Philadelphia Symphony Orchestra.

1916. Dec. 22. Zandonai's opera "Francesca da Rimini" presented at the Metropolitan Opera House, New York City.

1917. Jan. 12. Sibelius's symphonic fantasy "Polyola's Daughter," and his symphonic poem "Night Ride and Sunrise" (Op. 53), given by the Boston Symphony Orchestra.

1917. Jan. 18. Leo Sowerby's "Come Autumn Time" produced at a concert in Orchestral Hall, Chicago, conducted by Eric De Lamarter.

1917. Jan. 19. Ballantine's symphonic poem "The Eve of St. Agnes" produced by the Boston Symphony Orchestra.

1917. Jan. 26. Percy Grainger's "The Warriors" given by the Symphony Society at Aeolian Hall, New York City, with the composer at the pianoforte.

1917. Feb. 2. Widor's Symphony No. 3 (in E minor) for organ and orchestra given by the Philharmonic Society, New York City, with Gilbert Spross as soloist.

1917. Mar. 8. Reginald de Koven's opera "The Canterbury Pilgrims" produced at the Metropolitan Opera House, New York City, with Ober, Althouse, Ruysdael, and Sembach.

1917. Mar. 23. The First of E. Bloch's "Trois poèms Juifs" (Op. 133), "Dance," "Rite," and "Cortège Funèbre," presented by the Boston Symphony Orchestra.

1917. Feb. 6. E. De Lamarter's "The Fable of the Hapless

Folktune " produced by the Chicago Symphony Orchestra.
1917. April 6. Philip Greeley Clapp's Symphony in E flat produced by the Boston Symphony Orchestra.
1917. April 13. Debussy's "Gigues" given by the Boston Symphony Orchestra.
1917. April 15. Adolf Brune's overture "A Twilight Picture" produced by the Cincinnati Symphony Orchestra.
1917. April 20. Noren's symphony "Vita" given by the Boston Symphony Orchestra.
1917. April 27. F. S. Converse's tone poem "Ave atque Vale" produced by the Boston Symphony Orchestra.
1917. May 3. Ernest Bloch's "Two Psalms," for soprano and orchestra, given in New York City.
1917. June. Production of the following works by the Litchfield County Choral Union at Norfolk, Conn.: Nicola Laucella's symphonic impressions "Whitehouse" under the direction of the composer. John Alden Carpenter's symphony "Sermons in Stones" conducted by F. Stock. Percy Grainger's "The Warriors" (Music to an Imaginary Ballet) conducted by the composer. First performance in America of C. Villiers Stanford's "Irish Rhapsody" No. 5 (dedicated to Lord Roberts).
1917. Oct. 7. First concert of the Chicago Philharmonic Orchestra, recently organized, under Arthur Dunham, conductor.
1917. Oct. 26. Mozart's operetta "Bastien et Bastienne" presented at the Empire Theatre, New York City, under Albert Reiss.
1917. Oct. 27. American début of Jascha Heifetz, Russian violinist, in a recital at Carnegie Hall, New York City.
1917. Nov. 12. Mascagni's opera "Isabeau" presented at the Auditorium, Chicago, by the Chicago Opera Association, with Rosa Raisa, Jeska Swartz, Crimi, Rimini, Maguenat, and Nicolay. Campanini conducting.
1917. Nov. 17. S. M. Liapounov's Second Concerto for pianoforte given by the Russian Symphony Orchestra, New York City, with Tamara Labinova (début) as soloist.
1917. Nov. 17. American début, as conductor, of Pierre Mon-

teux, at the Metropolitan Opera House, New York City, — a matinée performance of " Faust."

1917. Nov. 19. Operatic début of Anna Fitziu as *Tosca* with the Chicago Opera Association.

1917. Nov. 29. Début of May Peterson as *Michaela*, in " Carmen," at the Metropolitan Opera House, New York City.

1917. Nov. 30. S. Palmgren's Second Symphony given by the Chicago Symphony Orchestra.

1917. Nov. 30. Max Bruch's Concerto for Two Pianofortes and Orchestra given by the Philharmonic Society in New York City, with Rose and Ottilie Sutro as pianists. (First time in New York.)

1917. Dec. 1. Operatic début of Genevieve Vix as *Manon* with the Chicago Opera Association.

1917. Dec. 6. Liszt's " Twenty-third Psalm " given with chorus and orchestra by the Philharmonic Society, New York City, Vernon Stiles, soloist. J. Stransky, conductor.

1917. Dec. 6. Frederick Jacobi's orchestral suite " California " produced at the Cort Theatre, San Francisco, Cal., by the San Francisco Symphony Orchestra.

1917. Dec. 14. Widor's " Prelude " for organ, three trumpets, three trombones, and kettledrums, given by the Chicago Symphony Orchestra.

1917. Dec. 19. Henri Rabaud's opera " Marouf " presented by the Metropolitan Opera Company, New York City, with F. Alda, K. Howard, de Luca, Rothier, de Segurola, T. Chalmers, Rossi. P. Monteux conducting.

1917. Dec. 26. Arthur Hadley's opera " Azora " produced by the Chicago Opera Association, with Anna Fitziu, Cyrena van Gordon, and F. Lamont. Conducted by the composer.

1917. Dec. 28. Henry K. Hadley awarded the Hinshaw prize for an opera, " Bianca," for small orchestra, without chorus.

1917. A Symphony Orchestra organized in New Orleans, La.

1917. Dec. 27. Production of Percy Mackaye and Arthur Farwell's masque " The Evergreen Tree," by the MacDowell Club, assisted by the Manuscript Society and Prospect Heights (Brooklyn) Choral Society, in New York City.

1918. Jan. 3. Liszt's oratorio " St. Elizabeth " presented in operatic form at the Metropolitan Opera House, New York City, with Florence Easton, M. Matzenauer, Clarence Whitehill, Schlegel, Leonard and Ruysdael. Bodansky conducting.

1918. Jan. 5. World première of Arthur Nevin's one-act opera, " Daughter of the Forest," by the Chicago Opera Association, with Vix, Peralta, Lamont, and Godfrey. Conducted by the composer.

1918. Jan. 6. Hubay's Concerto for Violin and Orchestra given by the Symphony Society, New York City, at Aeolian Hall, with E. Zimbalist as soloist. Also, Kalikinnov's Second Symphony (in G minor).

1918. Jan. 10. E. Bloch's " Trois Poèmes Juifs "—" Danse," " Rite," and " Cortège Funèbre " — given by the Symphony Society, New York City.

1918. Jan. 12. Mascagni's opera " Lodoletta " presented at the Metropolitan Opera House, New York City, with G. Farrar, Lila Robeson, Caruso, de Segurola, Amato, Didur, and Cecil Arden. Moranzoni conducting.

1918. Jan. 12. American début of Max Rosen, violinist, in Goldmark's violin concerto in A minor, with the Philharmonic Society, New York City.

1918. Jan. 18. Glière's third symphony (B minor) " Ilia Mourometz " given by the Chicago Symphony Orchestra, F. Stock conducting.

1918. Jan. 19. World première of Sylvio Lazzari's opera, " Le Sauteriot," by the Chicago Opera Association, with G. Vix, Carolina Lazzari, Myrna Sharlow, M. Claessens, Dalmores, Dufranne.

1918. Jan. 19. Jurassorsky's symphonic poem " The Phantoms," Speniarov's legend, " The Sermon of Resia," Rachmaninov's " Veralize " (arranged for orchestra by M. Atshuler, Rimsky-Korsakov's four tableaux from " Le Coq d'Or," and Slavinski's " The Shepherdess and the Faun," given by the Russian Symphony Orchestra in New York City.

1918. Jan. 25. F. Borowski's " Peintures Portrait d'une Jeune Fille," " Le Jardin de Nuit," and " La Fête," produced by the Chicago Symphony Orchestra.

1918. Jan. 27. E. B. Hill's orchestral suite " Stevensoniana " produced by the Symphony Society, New York City. Walter Damrosch conducting.

1918. Jan. 31. American début of Hipolito Lazari, Spanish tenor, as *The Duke* in "Rigoletto," at the Metropolitan Opera House, New York City.

1918. Feb. 15. American début of Mayer Wadler, American violinist, in a miscellaneous program, at Aeolian Hall, New York City.

1918. Feb. 15. Production of Leo Sowerby's orchestral suite, "Set of Four," by the Chicago Symphony Orchestra.

1918. Feb. 17. A. Chiaffarelli's "Prelude and Fugue" produced by the Philharmonic Society, New York City.

1918. Feb. 21. Henri Verbrugghen, noted Belgian conductor, appeared with the Russian Symphony Orchestra in Carnegie Hall, New York City, conducting a Beethoven program.

1918. Mar. 2. Jeral's "Concerto for Violoncello," with W. Willeke as soloist, given by the Russian Symphony Orchestra, at Carnegie Hall, New York City.

1918. Mar. 6. Rimsky-Korsakov's opera "Le Coq d'Or" presented at the Metropolitan Opera House, New York City, with Marie Sundelius as *Le Coq*, Sophie Braslau, Didur, Diaz, Audisio, Ruysdael, and Reschigliani. Monteux conducting.

1918. Mar. 8. E. Bloch's Symphony in C sharp minor given by the Philharmonic Society, New York City, conducted by the composer.

1918. Mar. 15. F. Stock's "Overture to a Romantic Comedy" produced by the Chicago Symphony Orchestra, conducted by the composer.

1918. Mar. 23. Tscherepin's folklore "Fire Bird" and "Rhapsodie Negre," and John Powell's suite, "The Fair," with the composer at the piano, given by the Russian Symphony Orchestra, at Carnegie Hall, New York City.

1918. Mar. 23. Henry F. Gilbert's ballet pantomime "The Dance in Place Congo" produced at the Metropolitan Opera House, New York City. P. Monteux conducting.

1918. Mar. 23. Charles Wakefield Cadman's opera "Shanewis" produced at the Metropolitan Opera House, New York City, with Alice Gentle, Kathleen Howard, Marie Sundelius, Paul Althouse, and Chalmers. Moranzoni conducting.

1918. April. Eugene Ysaye, noted Belgian violinist, appointed conductor of the Cincinnati Symphony Orchestra.

1918. April 26. A. T. Davison's "Tragic Overture" produced by the Boston Symphony Orchestra. Ernest Schmidt conducting.

1918. May. 9. Eugene Ysaye's poem "Exil," for string orchestra without basses, produced at the Cincinnati May Festival, conducted by the composer.

1918. May 10. Edgar Stillman Kelley's choral work, "The Pilgrim's Progress," produced at the Cincinnati May Festival.

1918. May 30. David Stanley Smith's oratorio "Rhapsody of St. Bernard" produced at the North Shore Festival, Evanston, Ill., under the direction of Peter C. Lutkin.

1918. June. Ossip Gabrilovitsch, noted pianist, appointed conductor of the Detroit Symphony Orchestra.

1918. June 4. David Stanley Smith's Second Symphony (D major). (Played in New York by the Philharmonic Society Dec. 2.) Also G. W. Chadwick's "Land of Our Hearts" for chorus and orchestra, and Horatio Parker's cantata "Dream of Mary," with Mabel Garrison and Carl Formes as soloists, produced at Norfolk, Conn., by the Litchfield County Choral Association.

1918. June 6. C. Villiers Stanford's tone poem "Verdun" given at Norfolk, Conn. (and by the Philharmonic Society New York Dec. 2).

1918. Oct. 15. First concert in America of "Le Société des Concerts du Conservatoire de Paris," André Messager, conductor, at the Metropolitan Opera House, New York City.

1918. Oct. 18. A. Hadley's one-act opera "Bianca" produced at the Park Theatre, New York City, with Maggie Teyte, Henri Scott, Craig Campbell, Howard White, and Carl Formes. (This opera won a prize offered by Wm. Hinshaw.)

1918. Oct. 20. American début of Alfred Cortot, noted French pianist, at a concert of "Le Société des Concerts du Conservatoire de Paris" at the Metropolitan Opera House, New York City. He played the Fourth Concerto of Saint-Saëns.

M. Cortot's first recital was given at Aeolian Hall, Nov. 11.

1918. Nov. 3. American début of Thelma Given, violinist, at Carnegie Hall, New York City. The program included Conus's "Concerto in E minor," Kryjenovsky's "Russian Romance" (new), Achron's "Hebrew Lullaby," and Halverson's "Norwegian Dance" (new).

1918. Nov. 9. Paul Vidal's "Danses Tanagréennes" given by the New York Symphony Society, New York City.

1918. Nov. 11. American début of B. Cousinou, baritone, in "Samson et Delila" at the Metropolitan Opera House, New York City.

1918. Nov. 13. American début of G. Crimi, tenor, and Montesanto, baritone, in "Aïda" at the Metropolitan Opera House, New York City.

1918. Nov. 13. American début of Raoul Vidas, violinist, in a miscellaneous program at Carnegie Hall, New York City.

1918. Nov. 14. Production of Edgar Stillman Kelley's song "A California Idyll" by the Symphony Society of New York, with Mabel Garrison as soloist.

1918. Nov. 14. Roger-Ducasse's symphonic poem "Sarabande," for orchestra and invisible choir, given by the Philharmonic Society, New York City, with Mr. Koemmenich's chorus.

1918. Nov. 15. Operatic début of Rosa Ponselle, soprano, as *Donna Leonora* in "La Forza del Destino," at the Metropolitan Opera House, New York City.

1918. Nov. 16. Daniel Gregory Mason's "Four Songs — Russians," for baritone and orchestra, produced by the Chicago Symphony Orchestra, with R. Werrenrath as soloist.

1918. Nov. 17. David Stanley Smith's suite for orchestra, "Impressions," produced by the Minneapolis Symphony Orchestra, Emil Oberhoffer conducting.

1918. Nov. 30. Lekeu's "Symphonic Fantasia on Two Popular Angevin Tunes" given by the Symphony Society, New York City.

1918. Dec. 3. Leo Schulz's "American Rhapsody," for violoncello and orchestra, produced by the Philharmonic Society, New York City, with the composer as soloist.

1918. Dec. 6. S. Prokofieff's First Concerto (in D flat major)

for pianoforte and orchestra (with the composer as soloist), and his Scythian suite, "Ala and Lilli" (conducted by the composer), given by the Chicago Symphony Orchestra.
1918. Dec. 7. American début of Alexandro Dolci, Italian tenor, as *Enzo* in "La Gioconda," with the Chicago Opera Association, at the Auditorium, Chicago.
1918. Dec. 8. A. de Greef's "Four Old Flemish Folk Songs" for orchestra, given by the Symphony Society, New York City.
1918. Dec. 8. Vittore di Sabata's Symphonic Suite, given by the New York Symphony Society.
1918. Dec. 11. First appearance of Nicolai Sokolov as conductor of the Cleveland (O.) Symphony Orchestra.
1918. Dec. 14. World première of Puccini's three one-act operas, "Il Tabarro," "Gianni Schecchi," and "Suor Angelica," at the Metropolitan Opera House, New York City, with Farrar, Muzio, Easton, Crimi, de Luca, and Montesanto. Moranzoni conducting.
1918. Dec. 26. Lili Boulanger's cantata, "Faust et Hélène," given at a concert of the New York Symphony Society at Carnegie Hall, with Julia Claussen as *Hélène*, Craig Campbell as *Faust*, and Edgar Schofield as *Mephisto*. (Composed at the age of 19, and won Grand Prix de Rome. Composer died 1918.)
1919. Jan. 5 Felix Borowski's "Elégie Symphonique" given by the New York Symphony Society at Aeolian Hall, New York City.
1919. Jan. 14. World première of Fevrier's opera "Gismonda" by the Chicago Opera Association, with Mary Garden, E. Fontaine, Maguenat and Journet. Campanini conducting.
1919. Jan. 17. Catalani's opera "Loreley" presented by the Chicago Opera Association, with Anna Fitziu, Florence Macbeth, A. Dolci, V. Lazzari, and C. Rimini. Polacco conducting.
1919. Jan. 24. Xavier Leroux's opera "La Reine Fiamette" presented at the Metropolitan Opera House, New York City, with Farrar, Lazaro, Rothier and Didur. P. Monteux conducting.

1919. Jan. 25. Xavier Leroux's opera "Le Chemineau," presented at the Auditorium by the Chicago Opera Association, with Yvonne Gall, Desiré Defrere, Maguenat, Baklanov, and Huberdeau. Hasselmans conducting.

1919. Jan. 26. Humiston's Suite in F sharp minor produced by the Philharmonic Society, New York City, conducted by the composer.

1919. Jan. 28. American début of Leopold Auer, noted Russian violinist and teacher, at Aeolian Hall, New York City. He played Beethoven's violin sonatas in C minor (Op. 30), G major (Op. 30) and A major (Op. 47).

1919. Jan. 28. S. Rachmaninov's First Pianoforte Concerto given by the Russian Symphony Orchestra, New York City, with the composer as soloist. M. Altschuler conducting.

1919. Jan. 30. R. Goldmark's "Requiem" given by the Philharmonic Society, New York City.

1919. Jan. 30. Victor de Sabata's symphonic poem "Juventus" given by the Symphony Society, New York City.

1919. Jan. 31. American operatic début of Charles Hackett, American tenor, at the Metropolitan Opera House, New York City, as *Count Almaviva* in "Il Barbiere."

1919. Jan. 31. Chausson's Symphony in B flat major given by the Philadelphia Symphony Orchestra.

1919. Feb. 2. A. Casella's "Films — War Pictures" given by the Symphony Society, at Carnegie Hall, New York City:
  1. Belgium — "Heavy Artillery Passing."
  2. France — "Before the Ruins of a Cathedral."
  3. Alsatia — "The Wooden Cross."
  4. Italy — "Man-o'-war Cruising in the Adriatic."

1919. Feb. 9. G. W. Chadwick's symphonic poem "The Angel of Death" produced by the Symphony Society, New York City, at a concert given in memory of Theodore Roosevelt.

1919. Feb. 12. American début of Winifred Christie, noted English pianist, at Aeolian Hall, New York City.

1919. Feb. 13. O. Respighi's symphonic poem "Fontane di Roma" (Fountains of Rome) given by the Philharmonic Society, New York City.

1919. Feb. 14. Felix Borowski's suite from the ballet panto-

mine "Boudour" produced by the Chicago Symphony Orchestra with the composer conducting.
1919. Feb. 17. Stanley R. Avery's overture to "The Taming of the Shrew" produced by the Chicago Symphony Orchestra.
1919. Feb. 23. A. Weidig's Concert Overture (Op. 65) produced by the Minneapolis Symphony Orchestra, conducted by the composer.
1919. Feb. 28. F. Stock's "March and Hymn to Democracy" produced by the Chicago Symphony Orchestra.
1919. Mar. 2. Elgar's two songs, "Carillon" and "Le Drapeau Belge," for orchestra and narrator, given by the Philharmonic Society, New York City, with Carlo Liten as narrator.
1919. Mar. 6. Harold Morris's Tone Poem (from MS.) produced by the Philharmonic Society, New York City.
1919. Mar. 12. Joseph Breil's opera "The Legend" produced at the Metropolitan Opera House, New York City, with Rosa Ponselle, Kathleen Howard, Paul Althouse, and L. d'Angelo in the leading rôles; also J. A. Hugo's opera, "The Temple Dancer" with Florence Easton, Carl Schlegel and Morgan Kingston. Moranzoni conducting.
1919. Mar. 14. Rosseter G. Cole's "Pioneer" overture produced by the Chicago Symphony Orchestra, conducted by the composer.
1919. Mar. 17. Vincenzo Tommasini's "Moonlights"; two pieces, "Churches and Ruins" and "Serenade," given by the Chicago Symphony Orchestra.
1919. Mar. 24. Griffes's "Three Songs" for soprano and orchestra produced by the Philadelphia Symphony Orchestra, with Marcia van Dresser as soloist.
1919. Mar. 28. G. Faure's prelude to the opera "Pénélope" given by the Boston Symphony Orchestra.
1919. April 4. G. Francesco Malipieri's "Pause del Silenzio" (Pauses of Silence) given by the Boston Symphony Orchestra, Henri Rabaud conducting.
1919. April 9. Ildebrando Pizzetti's prelude to Act 1 of "Fédra" (d'Annunzio) given by the Philadelphia Symphony Orchestra.

1919. April 11. Alberic Magnard's "Hymn à la Justice" (Op. 14) given by the Boston Symphony Orchestra.

1919. April 11. First concert of the Musicians' New Symphony Orchestra of the New York Federation of Musicians, given at Carnegie Hall, New York City, Varese conducting. (Organized in February.)

1919. April 18. R. Laparra's poem on four popular verses, "Un Dimanche Basque," for orchestra with pianoforte, produced by the Boston Symphony Orchestra, with the composer as soloist. P. Monteux conducting.

1919. June. Charles T. Griffes's "The White Peacock" produced at the Rivoli Theatre, New York City.

1919. July 4. Arthur Farwell's "Chant of Victory" produced at the Greek Theatre, Berkeley, Cal.

1919. July 7. Samuel Gardner's tone poem, "New Russia," produced at a concert in the Stadium, New York City, conducted by the composer.

1919. Oct. 24. Vincent d'Indy's "Sinfonia Brevis de Bello Gallico" (No. 3. Op. 70) given by the Boston Symphony Orchestra, P. Monteux conducting.

1919. Oct. 31. V. d'Indy's descriptive symphony, "La Queste de Dieu" (The search for God), from the opera "La Légende de Saint-Christophe," given by the Chicago Symphony Orchestra.

1919. Nov. 7. Michael Dvorsky's tone poem, "Haunted Castle," given by the Philadelphia Symphony Orchestra.

1919. Nov. 13. Vitaslev Novak's symphonic poem, "In the Tatra Mountains" (Op. 26), given by the Philharmonic Society, New York City; also B. Roger's dirge, "To the Fallen."

1919. Nov. 13. Vincent d'Indy's Third Symphony; also Duparc's "Aux Etoiles," Debussy's "Berceuse Héroique," and J. Turina's "La Procession del Racio," given by the Symphony Society, New York City.

1919. Nov 16. C. T. Griffes's "Poem, for flute and orchestra," produced by the Symphony Society, New York City, with G. Barrère as soloist.

1919. Nov. 18. Montemezzi's opera "La Nave" presented

by the Chicago Opera Association, with Rosa Raisa, Lazzari, Dolci, and Rimini. The composer conducting.
1919. Nov. 19. E. DeLamarter's suite from "The Betrothed" (Maeterlinck) produced at the Schubert Theatre, New York City, Theodore Spiering conducting.
1919. Nov. 21. Dvořák's Third Symphony given by the Philharmonic Society, New York City.
1919. Nov. 28. Griffes's symphonic poem "The Pleasure-Dome of Kubla Khan" produced by the Boston Symphony Orchestra, P. Monteux conducting.
1919. Nov. 29. Percy Grainger's children's march, "Over the Hills and Far Away," given by the New York Symphony Society, with the composer at the Pianoforte. (First performance of the version for orchestra.)
1919. Nov. 29. American début of Benno Moisevitch, Russian pianist, in a recital at Carnegie Hall, New York City.
1919. Dec. 5. Albert Chiaffarelli's "Prelude to a Merry Play" produced (from MS.) by the Philharmonic Society, New York City.
1919. Dec. 10. American début of Madame Besanzoni, mezzo soprano, as *Delila*, at the Metropolitan Opera House, New York City.
1919. Dec. 11. Prokofieff's "Classical Symphony" produced by the Russian Symphony Orchestra (from MS.) at Carnegie Hall, New York City.
1919. Dec. 19. C. T. Griffes's "Notturno," "The White Peacock," "Clouds," and "Bacchanale" produced by the Philadelphia Symphony Orchestra. (N. B. "The White Peacock" had already been given at the Rivoli Theatre in June.)
1919. Dec. 19. Sylvio Lazzari's symphonic picture, "Impressions of Night," given by the Philharmonic Society, New York City.
1919. Dec. 23. John Alden Carpenter's ballet, "The Birthday of the Infanta," produced by the Chicago Opera Association.
1919. Dec. 27. Albert Wolff's opera "The Blue Bird" (Maeterlinck) presented at the Metropolitan Opera House, New York City, conducted by the composer. (Maeterlinck also present.)

1919. Dec. 28. American début of Madame Wurmser-Delcourt, harpist, at a concert of the Symphony Society, New York City. (She played, for the first time in America, the harp chromatique.)

1920. Jan. 2. Reginald de Koven's opera "Rip van Winkle" produced by the Chicago Opera Association, with E. Herbert, E. Darch, Baklanov, Dufranne, Cotreuil and Huberdeau. A. Smallens conducting.

1920. Jan. 2. Debussy's dance poem "Jeux" given by the Boston Symphony Orchestra.

1920. Jan. 2. Fibich's overture to the merry play, "A Night at Karluv-Tyn," given by the Philharmonic Society, New York City.

1920. Jan. 5. Ravel's opera "L'Heure Espagnol" presented by the Chicago Opera Association with Y. Gall, D. Defrere, Maguenat, Cotreuil and Warnery. Hasselmans conducting.

1920. Jan. 17. Leoncavallo's opera "Zaza" presented at the Metropolitan Opera House, New York City, with Farrar, K. Howard, Crimi and Amato.

1920. Jan. 19. André Messager's opera "Madame Chrysanthème" presented by the Chicago Opera Association with Miura, Fontaine, Dufranne and Warnery. Hasselmans conducting.

1920. Jan. 21. American début of Carlos Valderranea, Peruvian pianist, in a program of Inca music, at Carnegie Hall, New York City.

1920. Jan. 23. Kalinnikov's symphonic poem, "The Fir Tree and the Palm," given by the Philharmonic Society, New York City.

1920. Jan. 30. F. Converse's Symphony in C minor given by the Boston Symphony Orchestra, P. Monteux conducting.

1920. Jan. 31. Arthur Hadley's opera in two acts, "Cleopatra's Night," produced at the Metropolitan Opera House, New York City, with Frances Alda, Jeanne Gordon, Marie Tiffany, Orville Harold, V. Reschiglian, M. Picco and L. d'Angelo. Gennaro Papi conducting.

1920. Feb. 1. Louis Aubert's "Habañera" given by the New York Symphony Society at Aeolian Hall, New York City.

1920. Feb. 6. Hugo Riesenfeld's " Overture in Romantic Style " produced by the Philharmonic Society, New York City, conducted by the composer.

1920. Feb. 6. Rachmaninov's third symphony, " The Bells," for soprano, tenor, bass and chorus, with orchestra, given by the Philadelphia Symphony Orchestra with Florence Hinkle, Arthur Hackett, F. Patten, and a chorus trained by Stephen Townsend.

1920. Feb. 13. Elgar's variations, " Enigma," given by the Philadelphia Symphony Orchestra.

1920. Mar. 3. American début of Sascha Culbertson, violinist, at Carnegie Hall, New York City.

1920. Mar. 5. Leo Sowerby's Pianoforte Concerto in F major given by the Chicago Symphony Orchestra with the composer as soloist. (N. B. As originally arranged, for voice and orchestra, it was given at a concert at Orchestra Hall, Jan. 18, 1917.)

1920. Mar. 19. A. Brune's symphonic poem, " A Fairy Tale," produced by the Chicago Symphony Orchestra.

1920. April 2. Eric De Lamarter's Concerto in E major for organ, produced by the Chicago Symphony Orchestra, with the composer as soloist.

1920. April 16. Debussy's " Fantasy " for pianoforte and orchestra given by the Boston Symphony Orchestra, with Alfred Cortot as soloist.

1920. May 25. Felix Borowski's poème " Le Printemps Passionné " produced at the North Shore Festival, Evanston, Ill., conducted by the composer.

1920. Aug. 23. Charles Wakefield Cadman's Indian music-drama, " The Sunset Trail," produced by the California Theatre Ensemble at San Diego, Cal., under Dr. H. J. Stewart.

1920. Oct. 3. American début of Michel Piastro, Russian violinist, at Carnegie Hall, New York City.

1920. Oct. Production of Mortimer Wilson's overture " New Orleans " at the Rialto Theatre, New York City, conducted by the composer. (This work won a prize of $500 offered by Hugo Riesenfeld.)

1920. Oct. 16. American début of Josef Stopak, violinist, in a recital at Carnegie Hall, New York City.

1920. Oct. 22. G. Ropartz's "Divertissement" for orchestra given by the Boston Symphony Orchestra. P. Monteux conducting.

1920. Oct. 22. E. Goossens's "By the Tarn," for string orchestra and clarinet, given by the Chicago Symphony Orchestra.

1920. Oct. 25. American début of Michel Gusikov, Russian violinist, in a recital at Carnegie Hall, New York City.

1920. Oct. 29. A. Bax's "The Garden of Fand" produced by the Chicago Symphony Orchestra. F. Stock conducting.

1920. Oct. 29. E. B. Hill's poem for orchestra, "The Fall of the House of Usher," produced by the Boston Symphony Orchestra. P. Monteux conducting.

1920. Nov. 2. American début of Duci Karekjarto, Jugo-Slavian violinist, in a recital at Carnegie Hall, New York City.

1920. Nov. 5. American début of Cyril Scott, English composer and pianist, in a concert with the Philadelphia Orchestra. He played his "Concerto in C," and conducted his "Two Passacaglias."

1920. Nov. 5. Sabata's symphonic poem "Juventus" given by the Chicago Symphony Orchestra.

1920. Nov. 5. First performance of the orchestral version of Ernest Bloch's "Suite for Viola and Orchestra" (or pianoforte) given by the National Symphony Orchestra at Carnegie Hall, New York City, with Mr. Bailly as soloist. (This work was produced, with piano, at the Berkshire Festival of Chamber Music, Pittsfield, Mass., on Sept. 25, 1919.)

1920. Nov. 12. Gustav Strube's "Four Preludes for Orchestra" produced by the Boston Symphony Orchestra.

1920. Nov. 17. Première of Marinuzzi's opera "Jacquerie" by the Chicago Opera Association, with Yvonne Gall, Olga Carrara, L. Olivieri, Desiré Defrère, Vitto Trevisan, A. Paillard, S. Civai and T. Dentale. Conducted by the composer.

1920. Nov. 19. Albert Dupuis's symphonic fragments "Jean

Michel" given by the Cincinnati Symphony Orchestra.

1920. Nov. 21. J. Albeniz's rhapsody "A Night in Seville" given by the St. Louis Symphony Orchestra.

1920. Nov. 21. American début of the Hungarian pianist, Nyredghasi, in Chaikovsky's pianoforte concerto in B flat, with the National Symphony Orchestra, at the Lexington Theatre, New York City.

1920. Nov. 22. American début of Vasa Prihoda, Czecho-Slovak violinist, in a recital at Carnegie Hall, New York City.

1920. Nov. 26. Alfvén's Second Symphony given by the Philharmonic Society, New York City.

1920. Nov. 23. J. A. Carpenter's "A Pilgrim Vision," written to celebrate the tercentenary of the landing of the "Mayflower" Pilgrims, produced by the Philadelphia Symphony Orchestra.

1920. Nov. 29. American début of Daisy Kennedy (Mrs. Benno Moisevitch), Australian violinist, at Aeolian Hall, New York City.

1920. Dec. 2. Riccardo Pick-Mangialli's symphonic comedy "Il Carillon Magico" presented at the Metropolitan Opera House, New York City.

1920. Dec. 5. First concert of the newly organized Civic Music Students' Orchestra, in Orchestral Hall, Chicago, Ill.

1920. Dec. 5. Alfredo Casella's "The Venetian Convent" given by the New York Symphony Orchestra, at the Academy of Music, New York City.

1920. Dec. 12. Edward F. Kurtz's march "Victory" given at a popular concert by the Cincinnati Symphony Orchestra.

1920. Dec. 13. Leoncavallo's posthumous opera "Edipo Rè" produced by the Chicago Opera Association, with Titta Ruffo and Dorothy Francis in the leading parts. Marinuzzi conducting.

1920. Dec. 14. Samuel Gardner's Violin Concerto produced by the Boston Symphony Orchestra at Providence, R. I., with the composer as soloist.

1920. Dec. 23. Revival of Verdi's opera "Don Carlos" at the Metropolitan Opera House, New York City, with Rosa Ponselle, Matzenauer, Martinelli, de Luca, and Didur.

1920. Dec. 23. G. Francesco Malipiéro's "Impressioni dal Vero." Part 1, "Il Capinero" (The Blackcap), Part 2, "Il Picchio" (The Woodpecker), Part 3, "Il Chiù" (The Owl), given by the Boston Symphony Orchestra.

1920. Dec. 29. Revival of Gay's "The Beggar's Opera" (the first ballad opera performed in America) at the Greenwich Village Theatre, New York City, with Sylvia Nelis as *Polly Peachum*.

1920. Dec. 30. Ralph Vaughan Williams's "A London Symphony" given by the New York Symphony Society, when Albert Coates (noted English conductor) made his American début as conductor.

1920. Dec. 30. First Concert of Toscanini's "La Scala" Orchestra, at Carnegie Hall, New York City.

1920. Dec. 31. Gustav Holst's symphony, "The Planets," given by the Chicago Symphony Orchestra.

1920. Dec. Adolph Tandler appointed conductor of the Los Angeles (Cal.) Symphony Orchestra.

1921. Jan. 9. American début of Selma Kurtz, Viennese soprano, in a concert at the Hippodrome, New York City, in a miscellaneous program.

1921. Jan. 13. Mary Garden appointed artistic director of the Chicago Opera Association.

1921. Jan. 13. Production, from MS., of Josef Stransky's two songs for voice and orchestra, "Thy Fragrant Hair," and "Hymnus," by the Philharmonic Orchestra, New York City, with Margarete Matzenauer as soloist.

1921. Jan. 14. American début of Ignaz Friedman, pianist, in a recital at Aeolian Hall, New York City.

1921. Jan. 14. Francesco Malipiero's "Grottesco," for small orchestra, given by the National Symphony Orchestra, New York City. A. Bodansky conducting.

1921. Jan. 14. American début of Alexander Schmuller, Russian violinist, in a recital at Carnegie Hall, New York City.

1921. Jan. 17. American début of Izzy Mitnisky, Russian violinist, in a recital at Carnegie Hall, New York City.

1921. Jan. 19. American début of Daisy Jean, Belgian violoncellist, in a recital at Aeolian Hall, New York City.

1921. Jan. 19. Frank Bridge's Suite for String Orchestra, and Debussy's "Jet d'Eau" for voice and orchestra, given by the Boston Musical Association, in Jordan Hall.

1921. Feb. 2. National Symphony Orchestra of New York merged with the Philharmonic Orchestra, under Josef Stransky.

1921. Feb. 2. American début of Erika Morini, Austro-Italian violinist, in a recital at Carnegie Hall, New York City, supported by an orchestra under Bodansky. She played the Mendelssohn concerto and one by Vieuxtemps.

1921. Feb. 3. Respighi's "Suite of Four Songs and Dances of the Sixteenth Century" for the lute (transcribed for orchestra) given by the Symphony Society, New York City.

1921. Feb. 4. Granville Bantock's prelude to "Sappho" given by the Minneapolis Symphony Orchestra.

1921. Feb. 6. Pietro Yon's "Concerto Gregoriano" for organ and orchestra given by the Symphony Society, New York City. (Had been previously played by the composer as an organ piece at Wanamaker's, and in Chicago.)

1921. Feb. 12. R. Strauss's orchestral suite from "Der Bürger als Edelman" (opera based on Molière's play "Le Bourgeois Gentilhomme") given by the Boston Symphony Orchestra, with Alfred de Voto at the pianoforte.

1921. Feb. 14. American début of Paul Kochanski, Russian violinist, at Carnegie Hall, New York City, in Brahms's concerto in D. Walter Damrosch conducting.

1921. Feb. 16. A Bruneau's symphonic poem "Penthesilée," for voice and orchestra; V. Davico's "Impressionna Romana" from MS., and M. Ravel's "Alborada del Gracioso," also from MS., given by the Boston Musical Association in Jordan Hall. Georges Longy, conductor.

1921. Feb. 17. Debussy's Two Nocturnes for pianoforte and orchestra, and a "Fantasy," given by the Symphony Society, New York City, with Alfred Cortot at the pianoforte.

1921. Feb. 22. American début of Carlo Sabatini at Carnegie Hall, New York City, in a miscellaneous program including the Bruch concerto in G minor and Beethoven's "Kreutzer Sonata,"

1921. Mar. 4. Production of H. F. Gilbert's orchestral suite "Indian Sketches" by the Boston Symphony Orchestra. P. Monteux conducting.

1921. Mar. 4. Daniel Gregory Mason's Prelude and Fugue for pianoforte and orchestra given by the Chicago Symphony Orchestra with John Powell, pianist.

1921. Mar. 4. Victor Vreuil's symphonic poem "Jour de Fête" given by the Cincinnati Symphony Orchestra, E. Ysaye conducting.

1921. Mar. 4. Production from MS. of Reginald Sweet's overture to the one-act opera "Riders to the Sea" by the Philharmonic Orchestra, New York City.

1921. Mar. 5. Emanuel Moór's Concerto for string quartet and orchestra given by the Chicago Symphony Orchestra.

1921. Mar. 9. Karl Weiss's opera "The Polish Jew" presented at the Metropolitan Opera House, New York City, with Emile Capoulican, Kathleen Howard, Raymonde Delaunais, Mario Chamlee, Angelo Bada, R. Leonhardt, William Gustafson, L. d'Angelo and Paolo Ananian. Conducted by A. Bodansky.

1921. Mar. 11. Kurt Atterbury's First Symphony (F major) given by the Minneapolis Symphony Orchestra.

1921. April 27. Florent Schmitt's "Chant de Guerre" given for the first time in America with orchestra, by the Boston Musical Association, assisted by the Harvard Glee Club; also Charles Bordes's "Rhapsodie Basque" for pianoforte and orchestra, with Miss Marion Carley, pianist.

1921. May 26. F. Stock's choral work, "A Psalmodic Rhapsody," produced at the North Shore Festival, Evanston, Ill., conducted by the composer.

1921. June 7. Production of Paolo Gallico's prize oratorio, "The Apocalypse," in the gymnasium of Augustana College, Rock Island, Ill., at the Biennial Convention of the National Federation of Music Clubs.

1921. July 20. Production of music by Edgar Stillman Kelley, F. S. Converse, George W. Chadwick, Arthur Foote, John Powell, E. B. Hill, Leo Sowerby, Chalmers Clifton, and Henry F. Gilbert, at the pageant given at Plymouth, Mass., to celebrate the tercentenary of the Pilgrims' landing.

1921. Oct. 14. Walter Braunfels's "Fantastic Variations on a Theme of Berlioz," given by the Philadelphia Symphony Orchestra.

1921. Oct. 14. American début of Emil Telmanyi, Hungarian violinist, in Lalo's "Symphony Espagnole," with the Philadelphia Orchestra.

1921. Oct. 15. American début of Elly Ney, noted French pianist, in a recital of Beethoven's works at Carnegie Hall, New York City. She appeared with the Philharmonic Orchestra Nov. 26, and played Chaikovsky's "First Concerto."

1921. Oct. 21. César Franck's Organ Chorale No. 2, B. minor, arranged for orchestra and organ by Wallace Goodrich, given by the Boston Symphony Orchestra with Wallace Goodrich as soloist.

1921. Oct. 21. Jan Sibelius's "Fifth Symphony" (E flat) given by the Philadelphia Symphony Orchestra.

1921. Oct. 23. Production of Louis T. Gruenberg's symphonic poem "The Hill of Dreams" by the Symphony Society, New York City, at Aeolian Hall. (This work won the prize offered in 1920 by Harry Harkins Flagler.)

1921. Oct. 28. Ravel's "La Valse" given by the San Francisco Symphony Orchestra, under Alfred Hertz.

1921. Nov. 4. Gregor Fitelberg's "Polish Rhapsody" given by the Philadelphia Symphony Orchestra. (This work in its original form, won the $1000 prize offered by Mrs. F. S. Coolidge in 1919, and was played at the Berkshire Festival of Chamber Music at Pittsfield, Mass., in September of that year.)

1921. Nov. 6. Rudolf Ganz formally welcomed as conductor of the St. Louis Symphony Orchestra.

1921. Nov. 13. H. H. Wetzler's overture to "As You Like It," given by the San Francisco Symphony Orchestra.

1921. Nov. 14. American début of Beniami Gigli, Italian tenor, as *Alfredo* in "La Traviata," at the Metropolitan Opera House, New York City.

1921. Nov. 15. American début of Tino Pattiera, Italian tenor, as *Mario* in "La Tosca" with the Chicago Opera Association.

1921. Nov. 16. Operatic début of Edith Mason as *Cio-Cio-San* in "Madama Butterfly," with the Chicago Opera Assocation.

1921. Nov. 17. Production of H. K. Hadley's tone poem "The Ocean" by the Philharmonic Orchestra, New York City, conducted by the composer.

1921. Nov. 19. Erich W. Korngold's opera, "Die Tote Stadt," presented at the Metropolitan Opera House, New York City, on which occasion Marie Jeritza, noted Moravian soprano, made her American début. Bodansky conducting.

1921. Nov. 28. American début (as pianist) of Alfredo Casella, noted Italian composer, at a recital in the Town Hall, New York City.

1921. Nov. 29. American operatic début of Claire Dux, soprano, as *Mimi* in "La Bohème," with the Chicago Opera Association.

1921. Dec. 16. Production of Serge Prokofiev's "Classical Symphony" (D major) by the Chicago Symphony Orchestra with the composer as pianist.

1921. Dec. 23. Production of the music of John Alden Carpenter's jazz pantomime, "Krazy Kat," by the Chicago Symphony Orchestra.

1921. Dec. 25. American début of Artur Schnabel, German pianist, in a recital at Carnegie Hall, New York City.

1921. Dec. 30. Production of S. Prokofiev's satirical opera, "Love for Three Oranges," by the Chicago Opera Association.

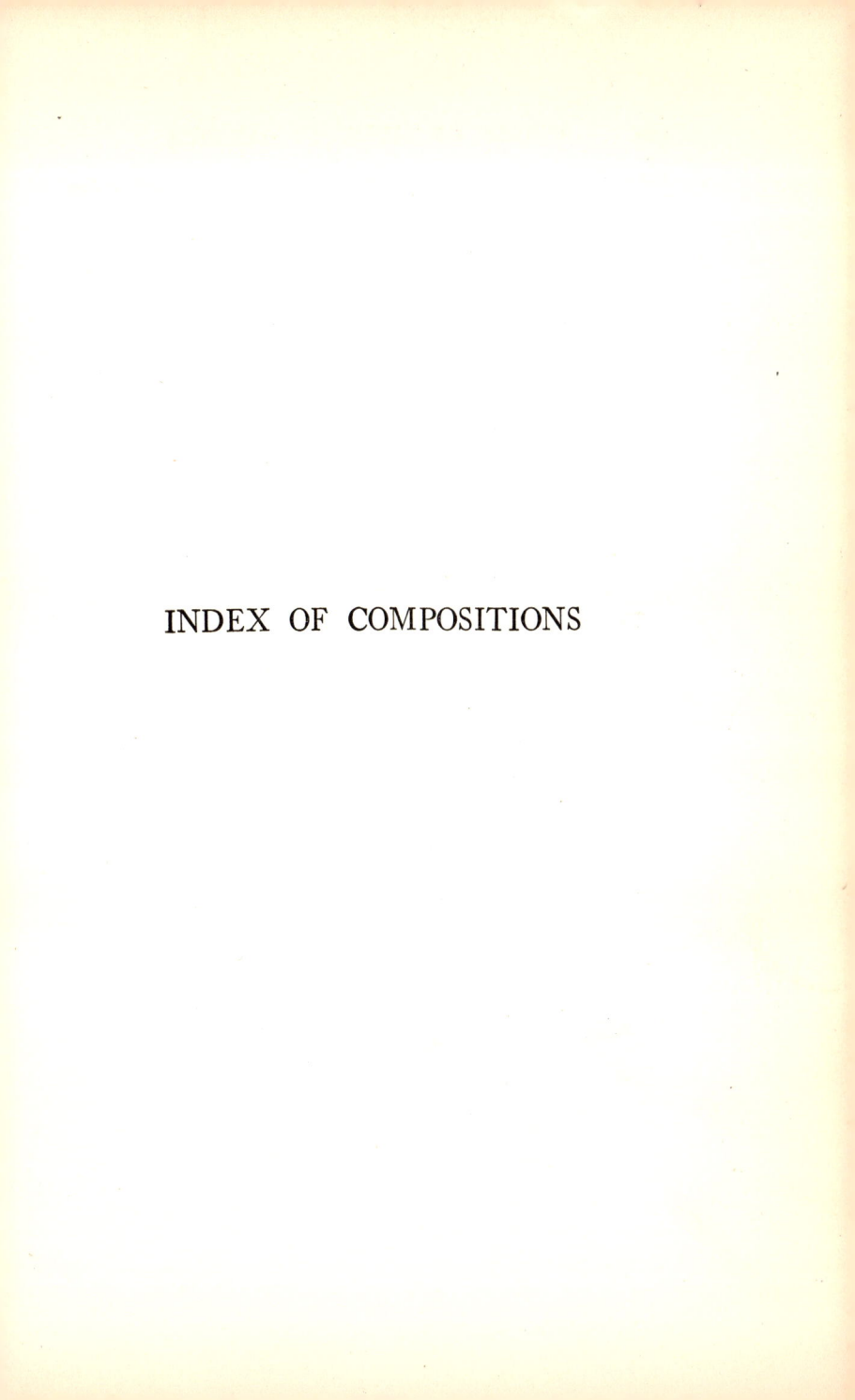

INDEX OF COMPOSITIONS

INDEX OF COMPOSITIONS

ABERT, J. J.
   1866. Oct. 27. First Symphony. New York, N. Y.

ADAM, A. C.
   1839. "Le Postillon de Longjumeau," opera. New York, N. Y.
   1858–9. "Chalet." New Orleans, La.
   1858–9. "Si j'étais Roi." New Orleans, La.

AKIMENKO, TH.
   1904. Feb. 27. Lyric Poem. Boston, Mass.

ALBENIZ, P.
   1920. Nov. 21. "A Night in Seville," rhapsody. St. Louis, Mo.

ALFVÉN, H.
   1914. Nov. 6. Third Symphony (E minor). Minneapolis, Minn.
   1914. Dec. 13. Festspel Polonaise. Minneapolis, Minn.
   1920. Nov. 26. Second Symphony (D). New York, N. Y.

d'AMBROSIO.
   1905. Jan. 7. Quatre Pièces d'Orchestre. Boston, Mass.
   1907. Dec. 21. Violin Concerto (B minor). Boston, Mass.

ARBOS, E. F.
   1903. Oct. 24. "Tango," Morceau de Concert. Boston, Mass.
   1913. Nov. 28. "Guajiras" for violin and orchestra. Philadelphia, Pa.

ARENS, F. X.
   1900. Dec. 10. "Salve Regina." New York, N. Y.

ARENSKY, A. S.
   1899. Oct. 14. Pianoforte Concerto (F minor). Boston, Mass.

1903. Jan. 4. Introduction to "Nala and Damayanti." Boston, Mass.

1904. Mar. 3. Variations on an Original Theme. New York, N. Y.

1905. Feb. 25. "Silhouettes," suite. New York, N. Y.

1905. Dec. 30. Violin Concerto (Op. 54). New York, N. Y.

1907. Dec. 20. First Symphony. New York, N. Y.

1909. Nov. 18. Variations for Strings. New York, N. Y.

1913. Jan. 16. Serenade. New York, N. Y.

ARNE, DR. T. A.

1757. Masque of Alfred. Philadelphia, Pa.

ARNOLD, M.

1895. Feb. 28. American Plantation Dances. New York, N. Y.

TTERBURY, K.

1921. Mar. 11. First Symphony (F Major). Minneapolis, Minn.

AUBER, D. F. E.

1829. Nov. 7. "Masaniello," opera. New York, N. Y.

1833. June 20. "Fra Diavolo," opera. New York, N. Y.

1843. May 25. "L'Ambassadrice," opera. New York, N. Y.

1843. June 17. "Le Domino Noir," opera. New York, N. Y.

1843. July 5. "Pré aux Clerc," opera. New York, N. Y.

1858–9. "Diamans de Couronne," opera. New Orleans, La.

1862. Sept. 18. Grand Inauguration March. New York, N. Y.

1895. April 13. "L'Enfant Prodigue," overture. Boston, Mass.

AUBERT, L.

1913. Mar. 8. "La Forêt Bleue," opera. Boston, Mass.

1920. Feb. 1. "Habañera" opera. New York, N. Y.

AVERY, S. R.

1919. Feb. 17. "Taming of the Shrew," overture. Chicago, Ill.

BACH, C. P. E.
- 1862. Sept. 18. Symphony in D major. New York, N. Y.
- 1866. Jan. 13. Symphony in C. New York, N. Y.
- 1908. April 11. Symphony in E flat. Boston, Mass.

BACH, J. S.
- 1865. Jan. 13. Toccata in F. New York, N. Y.
- 1865. April 8. Passacaglia. New York, N. Y.
- 1867. Oct. 7. Third Suite (in D). New York, N. Y.
- 1874. May 8. St. Matthew Passion, in part. Boston, Mass.
- 1874. Nov. 27. Suite in B minor. New York, N. Y.
- 1874. Dec. 12. Ciaconna in D minor. New York, N. Y.
- 1876. Nov. 25. Suite in C. New York, N. Y.
- 1877. Dec. 23. Christmas Oratorio (Parts I and II). Boston, Mass.
- 1879. April 11. St. Matthew Passion (complete). Boston, Mass.
- 1883. April 2. Christmas Oratorio (Part VI). Boston, Mass.
- 1884. Nov. 22. Christmas Oratorio (Pastoral). Boston, Mass.
- 1885. Jan. 31. Three Sonata Movements for Orchestra. Boston, Mass.
- 1900. Mass in B minor. Bethlehem, Pa.
- 1901. Dec. 28. Concerto (F major). Boston, Mass.
- 1902. Dec. 6. Concerto for Violin (A minor). Boston, Mass.
- 1904. Dec. 3. Second Violin Concerto (E major). Boston, Mass.
- 1907. Mar. 9. Brandenburg Concerto (G). Boston, Mass.

BALAKIREF, M. A.
- 1891. April 29. "Islamay," orchestral fantasia. Boston, Mass.
- 1893. June 6. Overture on Russian Themes. Chicago, Ill.
- 1896. Oct. 23. "Tamara," symphonic poem. Chicago, Ill.
- 1908. Jan. 21. "En Bohème," symphonic poem. Boston, Mass.
- 1908. Mar. 14. Symphony in C major. Boston, Mass.
- 1910. April 19. Overture. Boston, Mass.
- 1911. Nov. 25. Overture on Theme of a Spanish March. Boston, Mass.

BALFE, M. W.
- 1844. Nov. 25. "The Bohemian Girl," opera. New York, N. Y.

BALLANTINE, E.
- 1917. Jan. 19. "The Eve of St. Agnes," symphonic poem. Boston, Mass.

BANTOCK, G.
- 1909. Oct. 23. "The Pierrot of the Minute." Boston, Mass.
- 1910. Mar. 6. "Fine Old English Tunes." New York, N. Y.
- 1910. Sept. 29. "Omar Khayyàm" (first part). Worcester, Mass.
- 1910. Dec. 1. "Omar Khayyàm" (complete). Boston, Mass.
- 1911. Oct. 28. "Dante and Beatrice" symphonic poem. Boston, Mass.
- 1913. April 17. "Atalanta" symphonic poem. New York, N. Y.
- 1921. Feb. 4. "Sappho," prelude to. Minneapolis, Minn.

BARGIEL, W.
- 1866. Jan. 13. Symphony in C. New York, N. Y.

BARNARD, F.
- 1886. Jan. 9. Violin Concerto (G major). Boston, Mass.

BARNETT, J. F.
- 1869. Feb. 11. "The Ancient Mariner" cantata. Roxbury, Mass.

BASSI
- 1907. Dec. 21. Goldonian Intermezzo from Suite Variée (Op. 27). Boston, Mass.

BAYER, J.
- 1890. Jan. 4. "Die Puppensee" ballet. New York, N. Y.

BAX, A.
- 1920. Oct. 29. "The Garden of Fand." Chicago, Ill.

BEACH, MRS. H. H. A.
- 1896. April 7. Pianoforte Concerto (C sharp minor). Boston, Mass.

1896. Oct. 31. "Gallic Symphony" (E minor). Boston, Mass.

BECHER, WM.
   1912. Nov. 8. Pianoforte Concerto. New York, N. Y.

BECKER, G.
   1900. April 27. "Scènes Luxembourgeoises." Boston, Mass.

BEETHOVEN, L. van
   1821. April 24. First Symphony (C). Philadelphia, Pa.
   1839. Sept. 9. "Fidelio" opera (in English). New York, N. Y.
   1840. Fifth Symphony. Philadelphia, Pa.
   1842. Jan. 15. Sixth Symphony "Pastoral" (F). Boston, Mass.
   1842. Nov. 12. Second Symphony (D). Boston, Mass.
   1843. Feb. 15. Third Symphony "Eroica" (E flat). New York, N. Y.
   1844. Nov. 16. Eighth Symphony (F). New York, N. Y.
   1844. Nov. 16. "Egmont" overture. Boston, Mass.
   1844. Dec. 14. "Wellington Symphony." New York, N. Y.
   1846. May 20. Ninth Symphony "Choral" (D minor). New York, N. Y.
   1848. Jan. 8. Seventh Symphony. Boston, Mass.
   1849. Nov. 24. Fourth Symphony (B flat). New York, N. Y.
   1850. Jan. 19. Third Pianoforte Concerto (C minor). Boston, Mass.
   1850. Dec. 7. "Leonore" overture. Boston, Mass.
   1853. Nov. 22. Violin Concerto (first movement). Boston, Mass.
   1854. Feb. 4. Fourth Pianoforte Concerto (G). Boston, Mass.
   1854. Mar. 4. Fifth Pianoforte Concerto (E flat). Boston, Mass.
   1856. Dec. 29. "Fidelio" opera (in German). New York, N. Y.
   1859. Mar. 26. "Egmont" music. Boston, Mass.
   1865. Feb. 18. Second Pianoforte Concerto (B flat). New York, N. Y.

1865. Feb. 18. Triple Concerto. New York, N. Y.
1866. Jan. 13. Choral Fantasia. New York, N. Y.
1866. Dec. 2. Overture in C. New York, N. Y.
1867. Dec. 15. "Prometheus" music. New York, N. Y.
1869–1874. Mass in D. New York, N. Y.
1884. April 4. Grand Quatuor. New York, N. Y.
1908. Jan. 15. Twelve Dances. New York, N. Y.
1912. Dec. 29. "Jena Symphony." Boston, Mass.
1915. Jan. 30. "Fidelio" (revival). New York, N. Y.

BELLINI, V.
1832. Dec. 5. "Il Pirata" opera. New York, N. Y.
1833–4. "La Straniera" opera. New York, N. Y.
1835. Nov. 13. "La Sonnambula" (in English). New York, N. Y.
1840. "Norma" opera. Philadelphia, Pa.
1844. Feb. 2. "I Puritani" opera. New York, N. Y.
1844. Mar. 18. "Beatrice di Finda" opera. New York, N. Y.
1848. Feb. 1. "I Capuletti e Montecchi" opera. New York, N. Y.

BEMBERG, H.
1894. Dec. 17. "Elaine" opera. New York, N. Y.

BENDIX, V.
1907. April 27. Fourth Symphony (D minor). Boston, Mass.

BENNETT, W. S.
1845. Mar. 1. "The Naiads" (Die Nadajen), overture. New York, N. Y.
1848. Dec. 2. "The Woodnymph" (Die Waldnymphe), overture. New York, N. Y.
1873. Nov. 6. Concerto in E. Boston, Mass.
1875. April 24. "Paradise and the Peri" overture. New York, N. Y.
1875. Sept. 7. Symphony in G minor. New York, N. Y.

BENOIT, P.
1894. Nov. 17. Symphonic Poem. Boston, Mass.

BERGER, W.
 1899. Nov. 4. Symphony in B flat major. Boston, Mass.

BERLIOZ, H.
 1846. Nov. 21. "King Lear" overture. New York, N. Y.
 1857. Jan. 24. "Roman Carnival" overture. Boston, Mass.
 1863. Mar. 7. "Corsair" overture. New York, N. Y.
 1863. May 9. "Harold in Italy" symphony. New York, N. Y.
 1864. Dec. 3. "Romeo et Juliette" (second part) dramatic symphony. New York, N. Y.
 1866. Jan. 27. "Fantastic Symphony." New York, N. Y.
 1867. Jan. 19. "Romeo et Juliette" overture. Brooklyn, N. Y.
 1867. Nov. 9. "Benvenuto Cellini" overture. Brooklyn, N. Y.
 1880. Feb. 12. "Damnation de Faust." New York, N. Y.
 1882. April 6. "Requiem." New York, N. Y.
 1882. May 6. "Les Troyens" (second act). New York, N. Y.
 1884. Mar. 7. "The Childhood of Christ" (selections). New York, N. Y.
 1885. Feb. 5. "Tristia." New York, N. Y.
 1887. Feb. 26. "Les Troyens" (complete). New York, N. Y.
 1891. May 5. "Te Deum." New York, N. Y.
 1891. Nov. 29. "The Fifth of May." Boston, Mass.
 1900. Nov. 2. "Rob Roy" overture. Chicago, Ill.
 1902. Dec. 6. "Les Francs Juges" overture. Boston, Mass.
 1903. April 15. "Marche Funèbre" from "Hamlet." Boston, Mass.

BERNARD, E.
 1886. Jan. 9. Violin Concerto in G major. Boston, Mass.

BERWALD, W.
 1910. Jan. 14. Dramatic Overture. Syracuse, N. Y.
 1912. May 16. "Walthari" overture. Syracuse, N. Y.
 1914. April 5. "The Seven Last Words of Christ" cantata. New York, N. Y.

BINGHAM, S.
   1916. Feb. 6. Suite for Orchestra. New York, N. Y.
BIRD, A.
   1886. Nov. 5. First Symphony (A). New York, N. Y.
   1887. April 23. Carnival Scene. New York, N. Y.
   1893. June 12. Third Suite. Chicago, Ill.
BISCHOFF, H.
   1908. Jan. 14. Symphony (E major). Boston, Mass.
BISHOP, SIR H.
   1823. "Clari" ballad opera. New York, N. Y.
BIZET, G.
   1878. Oct. 23. "Carmen" opera. New York, N. Y.
   1881. April 2. "Arlesienne" suite. Boston, Mass.
   1882. Feb. 18. "La Patrie" overture. Boston, Mass.
   1884. Feb. 9. "Roma" third suite. Boston, Mass.
   1893. Aug. "The Pearl Fishers" (in English). Philadelphia, Pa.
   1896. Jan. 11. "Les Pêcheurs des Perles" (2 acts). New York, N. Y.
   1916. Nov. 13. "Les Pêcheurs des Perles" opera (complete). New York, N. Y.
BLECH, L.
   1911. Jan. 20. "Versiegelt" opera. New York, N. Y.
BLOCH, E.
   1916. Oct. 16. Two poems, "Winter" and "Spring." New York, N. Y.
   1917. Mar. 23. The first of "Trois Poêmes Juifs." Boston, Mass.
   1917. May 3. "Two Psalms." New York, N. Y.
   1918. Jan. 10. "Trois Poêmes Juifs" (complete). New York, N. Y.
   1918. Mar. 8. Symphony in C sharp minor. New York, N. Y.
   1920. Nov. 5. Suite for Viola and Orchestra. New York, N. Y.
BLOCKX, J.
   1903. Jan. 7. "Danse Flamande." Boston, Mass.

1909. Mar. 10. "Princesse Auberge" opera. New York, N. Y.

BOEHE, E.
  1904. Nov. 11. "Wanderings of Odysseus." Philadelphia, Pa.
  1906. Mar. 3. First four "Episodes." Boston, Mass.
  1907. Nov. 30. "Taormina" symphonic poem. Boston, Mass.

BOËLLMAN, L.
  1902. Nov. 14. Variations Symphoniques. Chicago, Ill.

BOITO, A.
  1880. Oct. 24. "Mefistofele" opera. New York, N. Y.

BOIELDIEU, F. A.
  1827. Sept. 28. "Jean de Paris" opera. New York, N. Y.
  1827. Oct. "The Caliph of Bagdad" opera. New York, N. Y.
  1831. May. "La Dame Blanche" opera. New York, N. Y.

BORDES, CHARLES
  1921. April 27. "Rhapsodie Basque." Boston, Mass.

BORDIER, J.
  1905. Jan. 4. Meditation. Boston, Mass.

BORNSCHEIN, F. C.
  1916. April 25. "Onawa" cantata. Paterson, N. J.

BORODIN, A.
  1886. Mar. 23. "On the Steppes of Central Asia." Brooklyn, N. Y.
  1890. Jan. 4. First Symphony (A flat). Boston, Mass.
  1892. Feb. 27. "A Prairie Scene." Boston, Mass.
  1912. Dec. 14. Second Symphony (D minor). Boston, Mass.
  1915. Dec. 30. "Prince Igor" opera. New York, N. Y.

BOROWSKI, F.
  1918. Jan. 25. "Peintures Portrait d'une Jeune Fille." Chicago, Ill.
  1919. Jan. 5. "Elégie Symphonique." New York, N. Y.
  1919. Feb. 14. Suite from "Boudour." Chicago, Ill.
  1920. May 25. "Le Printemps Passionné." Evanston, Ill.

BORTKIEVITCH, S. E.
  1915. Feb. 13. Pianoforte Concerto in B flat. New York, N. Y.
BOSSI, E.
  1910. Mar. 27. "Paradise Lost" oratorio. Boston, Mass.
BOULANGER, L.
  1918. Dec. 26. "Faust et Hélène" cantata. New York, N. Y.
BOURGAULT–DUCOUDRAY, L. A.
  1896. Oct. 17. "L'Interrement d'Ophelie." Boston, Mass.
  1906. April 17. "Rhapsodie Cambogienne." Boston, Mass.
BOYLE, G. F.
  1912. Feb. 2. Pianoforte Concerto (D minor). New York N. Y.
BRAHMS, J.
  1873. May 29. Serenade in D. New York, N. Y.
  1875. Jan. 16. Hungarian Dances. Brooklyn, N. Y.
  1877. Mar. 15. A German Requiem. New York, N. Y.
  1877. Dec. 17. First Symphony (C minor). New York, N. Y.
  1878. Oct. 3. Second Symphony (D major). New York, N. Y.
  1881. Oct. 14. "Academic Overture." Boston, Mass.
  1881. Oct. 29. "Tragic Overture." Boston, Mass.
  1882. Feb. 11. Rhapsody (voices and orchestra). Boston, Mass.
  1882. Dec. 9. Pianoforte Concerto (B flat). New York, N. Y.
  1884. Oct. 24. Third Symphony (F). New York, N. Y.
  1886. Nov. 6. Serenade for Strings (A major). Boston, Mass.
  1886. Dec. 11. Fourth Symphony (E minor). New York, N. Y.
  1889. April 4. Waltzes. Boston, Mass.
  1889. Dec. 7. Violin Concerto (D). Boston, Mass.
  1890. Jan. 31. "Liebeslieder Waltzes." New York, N. Y.
  1896. Mar. 28. Three Hungarian Dances. Boston, Mass.

1900. Dec. 1. First Pianoforte Concerto (D minor). Boston, Mass.
1912. Mar. 25. "Song of Triumph." New York, N. Y.

BRAUNFELS, W.
1921. Oct. 14. Fantastic Variations. Philadelphia, Pa.

BREIL, J.
1919. Mar. 12. "The Legend" opera. New York, N. Y.

BRIDGE, FRANK.
1921. Jan. 19. Suite. Boston, Mass.

BRIDGE, J. F.
1891. Sept. 23. "The Repentance of Nineveh." Worcester, Mass.
1902. Mar. 27. "The Forging of the Anchor." Brooklyn, N. Y.

BRISTOW, G. F.
1847. Nov. 14. Two Concert Overtures (Opus 3). New York, N. Y.
1855. Sept. 27. "Rip van Winkle" opera. New York, N. Y.
1866. Nov. 17. "Columbus Overture." New York, N. Y.
1874. Feb. 14. "Arcadian Symphony." New York, N. Y.
1879. May 10. "Great Republic" overture. Brooklyn, N. Y.
1889. Mar. 6. "The Jibbenainosay" overture. New York, N. Y.

BROCKWAY, H.
1901. April 6. "Sylvan Suite." Boston, Mass.
1907. April 6. Symphony (D major). Boston, Mass.

BRONSART, HANS VON
1881. Jan. 6. Spring Fantaisie. New York, N. Y.

BRUCH, M.
1868. First Violin Concerto (G minor). New York, N. Y.
1869. Mar. 13. Symphony in E flat. New York, N. Y.
1873. Nov. 15. Introduction to "Loreley." New York, N. Y.
1882. Dec. 15. Third Symphony. New York, N. Y.
1883. May 4. "Arminius" oratorio. Boston, Mass.

1888. Nov. 24. Fantaisie for violin and orchestra. Boston, Mass.

1889. Nov. 16. "Kol Nidrei" for cello and orchestra. Boston, Mass.

1892. Feb. 5. Second Violin Concerto (D minor). New York, N. Y.

1894. Feb. 7. "Romanza" (Op. 42). Boston, Mass.

1905. Feb. 11. Serenade for violin and orchestra. Boston, Mass.

1917. Nov. 30. Concerto for Two Pianofortes. New York, N. Y.

BRUCKNER, A.

1886. July 29. Seventh Symphony (E major). Chicago, Ill.

1888. Mar. 16. Fourth Symphony (Romantic). New York, N. Y.

1901. Mar. 9. Third Symphony (D minor). Boston, Mass.

1901. Dec. 28. Fifth Symphony (D flat major). Boston, Mass.

1904. Feb. 20. Ninth Symphony (unfinished). Chicago, Ill.

1909. Mar. 12. Eighth Symphony (C minor). Boston, Mass.

1912. Nov. 21. Sixth Symphony (A major), New York, N. Y.

BRÜLL, I.

1886. Nov. 9. "Das Golden Kreutz" opera. New York, N. Y.

1901. Feb. 2. Overture to "Macbeth." Boston, Mass.

BRUNE, A.

1917. April 13. "A Twilight Picture" overture. Cincinnati, O.

1920. Mar. 19. "A Fairy Tale" symphonic poem. Chicago, Ill.

BRUNEAU, A.

1903. Oct. 17. "Messidor" entr'acte symphonique. Boston, Mass.

1903. Nov. 7. "La Belle aux Bois Dormant." Chicago, Ill.

1906. Jan. 2. "Préludes de l'Ouragan." Boston, Mass.
1910. Feb. 8. "L'Attaque du Moulin." Harlem, N. Y.
1921. Feb. 16. "Penthesilée" symphonic poem. Boston, Mass.

BUCK, D.
1876. May 11. Centennial Meditation. Philadelphia, Pa.
1880. May 20. "Golden Legend" cantata. Cincinnati, O.
1885. Mar. 31. "Marmion" overture. New York, N. Y.
1888. "The Light of Asia" cantata. Newark, N. J.
1891. Feb. 23. "Romance" for four horns and orchestra. New York, N. Y.
1891. April 10. "The Star-Spangled Banner" overture. New York, N. Y.

BÜLOW, HANS von
1887. Feb. 10. "The Minstrel's Curse," symphonic poem. New York, N. Y.
1894. April 7. "Funerale." Boston, Mass.

BUNGERT, A.
1888. Feb. 28. "Auf der Wartling," symphonic poem. New York, N. Y.

BURCK, H.
1915. Jan. 31. "Meditation." New York, N. Y.

BURMEISTER, R.
1890. Dec. 12. Pianoforte Concerto in D. New York, N. Y.
1902. Jan. 10. "The Sisters" tone poem. New York, N. Y.

BUSCH, C.
1903. Nov. 30. "King Olaf" cantata. Chicago, Ill.

BUSONI, F.
1892. Feb. 20. Symphonic Suite (Op. 23). Boston, Mass.
1893. April 15. Symphonic Tone Poem. Boston, Mass.
1905. Nov. 18. Comedy Overture (C major). Boston, Mass.
1906. Mar. 31. "Geharnischte" suite. Boston, Mass.
1910. Mar 11. "Turandot" suite. New York, N. Y.

CADMAN, C. W.
1916. July. "To a Vanishing Race." Seattle, Wash.

1918. Mar. 23. "Shanewis" opera. New York, N. Y.
1920. Aug. 23. "The Sunset Trail." San Diego, Cal.

CAETANI.
1902. Nov. 15. Symphonic Prelude (A minor). New York, N. Y.

CAPLET, A.
1906. April 17. "Impressions d'Automne." Boston, Mass.

CARPENTER, J. A.
1915. Mar. 19. "Adventures in a Perambulator." Chicago, Ill.
1916. Mar. 10. Concertino. Chicago, Ill.
1917. June 5. Symphony. Norfolk, Conn.
1919. Dec. 23. "The Birthday of the Infanta." Chicago, Ill.
1920. Nov. 26. "A Pilgrim Vision." Philadelphia, Pa.

CARR, B.
1796. "The Archers of Switzerland." New York, N. Y.

CASELLA, A.
1919. Feb. 2. "Films — War Pictures." New York, N. Y.
1920. Dec. 5. "The Venetian Convent." New York, N. Y.

CATALANI, A.
1909. Jan. 6. "Le Wally" opera. New York, N. Y.
1919. Jan. 17. "Loreley" opera. Chicago, Ill.

CATEL, C. S.
1869. Jan. 9. Overture to "Semiramis." New York, N. Y.

CAUFFMAN, F. G.
1903. Nov. 27. "Salammbo" tone poem. Philadelphia, Pa.

CHABRIER, E.
1884. Dec. 6. "España" rhapsody. New York, N. Y.
1896. Oct. 24. "Gwendoline" overture. Boston, Mass.
1899. Mar. 4. Bourrée Fantastique." Boston, Mass.
1905. Jan. 4. "Danse Slave." Boston, Mass.
1911. Jan. 6. "Ode à la Musique." New York, N. Y.
1911. Mar. 3. "Briseis" opera. New York, N. Y.

CHADWICK, G. W.
1879. Dec. 11 "Rip van Winkle" overture. Boston, Mass.

1883. Jan. 13.   "Thalia" overture. Boston, Mass.
1884. Mar. 8.   Scherzo in F. Boston, Mass.
1886. Dec. 11. Second Symphony (B flat). Boston, Mass.
1887. Dec. 24. "Melpomene" overture. Boston, Mass.
1891. April 2. "The Pilgrims" cantata. Boston, Mass.
1892. Jan. 10. "A Pastoral Prelude." Boston, Mass.
1892. May 5.   "Phoenix Expirans." Springfield, Mass.
1892. Oct. 22. "Columbian Ode." Chicago, Ill.
1894. Oct. 20. Third Symphony (F major). Boston, Mass.
1900. Feb. 3.   "Elegiac" overture. Boston, Mass.
1901. Sept. 26. "Judith" oratorio. Worcester, Mass.
1904. April 23. "Euterpe" overture. Boston, Mass.
1905. Sept. 29. "Cleopatra" symphonic poem. Worcester, Mass.
1908. Feb. 22. Symphonic Sketches. Boston, Mass.
1909. June.   "Noël" Christmas pastoral. Norfolk, Conn.
1910. Feb. 12. Sinfonietta in D major. Boston, Mass.
1911. April 15. Suite Symphonique. Boston, Mass.
1912. June 4. "Aphrodite" symphonic fantasie. Norfolk, Conn.
1915. June 3. "Tam o' Shanter" ballad. Norfolk, Conn.
1918. June 4. "Land of our Hearts." Norfolk, Conn.
1919. Feb. 2. "The Angel of Death." New York, N. Y.

CHAIKOVSKY, P. I.
1875. Oct. 25. Pianoforte Concerto (B flat minor). Boston, Mass.
1876. April 22. "Romeo et Juliette" overture. New York, N. Y.
1879. Feb. 8. Third Symphony (D). New York, N. Y.
1880. Jan. 17. Suite for Giant Orchestra. New York, N. Y.
1883. Feb. 24. "Marche Slave." Boston, Mass.
1883. Dec. 7. Second Symphony (C). New York, N. Y.
1885. Jan. 23. Serenade for Strings. New York, N. Y.
1885. Nov. 24. Third Suite (Op. 55). New York, N. Y.
1886. Nov. 1. Italian Caprice. New York, N. Y.
1886. Dec. 4. "Manfred" symphony. New York, N. Y.
1888. Feb. 4. "Mozartiana" suite (Op. 61). New York,
1889. Jan. 19. Violin Concerto. New York, N. Y.

1889. Jan. 24.   Introduction and Fugue.   New York, N. Y.
1889. Mar. 5.   Fifth Symphony (E minor).   New York, N. Y.
1889. Mar. 15.   First Suite (Op. 43).   Brooklyn, N. Y.
1890. Feb. 1.   Fourth Symphony (F minor).   New York, N. Y.
1891. Feb. 4.   "Hamlet" overture.   Brooklyn, N. Y.
1891. May. 6.   Legende and Paternoster.   New York, N. Y.
1891. Dec. 31.   "Francesca da Rimini" fantasia.   Boston, Mass.
1892. Oct. 22.   "Caisse Noisette" suite.   Chicago, Ill.
1893. Dec. 30.   Overture — "1812."   Boston, Mass.
1894. Mar. 16.   Sixth Symphony (B minor).   New York, N. Y.
1896. Feb. 7.   First Symphony (G minor).   New York, N. Y.
1897. Nov 26.   "Voyvode" symphonic ballad.   New York, N. Y.
1898. Feb. 5.   Second Pianoforte Concerto (G).   Boston, Mass.
1900. Oct. 19.   "La Belle au Bois Dormant" suite.   Chicago, Ill.
1904. Dec. 24.   "The Battle of Poltava."   New York, N. Y.
1904. Dec. 24.   Hopak from "Mazeppa."   New York, N. Y.
1905. April 1.   "Night" fantasia.   New York, N. Y.
1908. Feb. 2.   "Eugene Onegin" (Yevgeni Onyegin) opera (in concert form).   New York, N. Y.
1908. Oct. 31.   Variations on a Rococo Theme.   Boston, Mass.
1910. Mar. 5.   "Pique Dame" opera.   New York, N. Y.
1910. Nov. 20.   Excerpts from "Jeanne d'Arc."   New York, N. Y.

CHAMINADE, C.
1895. Feb. 5.   Concertstück for Orchestra.   Chicago, Ill.
1897. Dec. 13. "Callirhoe" ballet.   New York, N. Y.

CHARPENTIER, G.
1893. Nov. 24. "Impressions of Italy" suite.   Chicago, Ill.

1905. April 4. " La Vie du Poëte " symphonic drama. Boston, Mass.
1908. Jan. 3. " Louise " opera. New York, N. Y.
1914. Feb. 26. " Julien " opera. New York, N. Y.

CHAUSSON, E.
1898. Oct. 22. " Viviani " symphonic poem. Chicago, Ill.
1904. Nov. 18. Poème for violin and orchestra. New York, N. Y.
1905. April 18. " Hymne Védique." Boston, Mass.
1906. Jan. 20. Symphony (A flat major). Boston, Mass.
1908. Jan. 21. " Poème d'Armour et de la Mer." Boston, Mass.
1919. Jan. 31. Symphony (B flat major). Philadelphia, Pa.

CHAUVET, C. A.
1902. Jan. 7. " Feuillets d'Album " suite. Boston, Mass.

CHERUBINI, L.
1842. Jan. 15. Overture to " Les deux Journées." Boston, Mass.
1866. Feb. 28. Overture to " Anacreon." Boston, Mass.
1867. Nov. 21. Overture to " Medea." Boston, Mass.
1872. Feb. " Les deux Journées " (The Water Carrier). New York, N. Y.
1873. Jan. 9. " Ali Baba " overture. Boston, Mass.
1876. Feb. 19. " Faniska " overture. Boston, Mass.
1883. May 2. Mass in D minor. Boston, Mass.
1892. Dec. 2. Overture. New York, N. Y.

CHEVILLARD, C.
1903. Jan. 7. " Le Chêne et le Roseau." Boston, Mass.

CHIAFFARELLI, A.
1918. Feb. 17. Prelude and Fugue. New York, N. Y.
1919. Dec. 5. Prelude to a Merry Play. New York, N. Y.

CHOPIN, F.
1861. Nov. 9. Second Pianoforte Concerto. New York, N. Y.

CILEA, F.
1907. Nov. 18. " Adrienne Lecouvreur " opera. New York, N. Y.

CIMAROSA, D.
   1833–4. "Il Matrimonio Segreto" opera. New York, N. Y.

CLAPP, P. G.
   1909. April 29. "Norge" tone poem. Cambridge, Mass.
   1912. Jan. 16. "In Summer" prelude. St. Louis, Mo.
   1912. April 14. Dramatic Poem. New York, N. Y.
   1914. April 11. Symphony in E minor. Boston, Mass.
   1917. April 6. Symphony in E flat. Boston, Mass.

COLE, R. E.
   1919. Mar. 14. "Pioneer Overture." Chicago, Ill.

CONVERSE, C. C.
   1868. Jan. 25. "Festival Overture." Brooklyn, N. Y.

CONVERSE, F. S.
   1899. Jan. 14. Symphony (D minor — first movement). Boston, Mass.
   1900. Dec. 22. "Festival of Pan." Boston, Mass.
   1903. April 11. "Endymion's Narrative." Boston, Mass.
   1905. Jan. 21. "Night" and "Day" tone poems. Boston, Mass.
   1905. Mar. 3. "The Mystic Trumpeter." Philadelphia, Pa.
   1906. Jan. 31. "The Pipe of Desire" opera. Boston, Mass.
   1906. Mar. 3. "La Belle Dame Sans Merci." Providence, R. I.
   1906. Oct. 15. "Jeanne d'Arc" incidental music. Philadelphia, Pa.
   1907. Oct. 2. "Job" dramatic poem. Worcester, Mass.
   1910. Nov. 16. "The Sacrifice" opera. Boston, Mass.
   1911. Jan. 27. Orchestral Fantasy. St. Louis, Mo.
   1912. Jan. 26. "Ormazd" tone poem. St. Louis, Mo.
   1914. May 28. "Cahokia" masque. St. Louis, Mo.
   1917. April 27. "Ave atque Vale" tone poem. Boston, Mass.
   1920. Jan. 30. Symphony in C minor. Boston, Mass.

COPPOLA, P. A.
   1847. Jan. 3. "Nina Pazza per Amore" opera. New York, N. Y.

CORNELIUS, P.
- 1888. Oct. 27. "Il Barbiere von Bagdad" overture. Boston, Mass.
- 1890. Jan. 4. "Il Barbiere von Bagdad" opera. New York, N. Y.

COWEN, F.
- 1882. Nov. 11. Third Symphony "Scandinavian." New York, N. Y.
- 1883. Jan. 27. First Symphony (in C). Boston, Mass.
- 1883. Nov. 21. "St. Ursula" cantata. New York, N. Y.
- 1885. April 11. Fourth Symphony (B minor) "Welsh." New York, N. Y.
- 1888. Feb. 28. Fifth Symphony (F). New York, N. Y.
- 1890. Nov. 24. Sixth Symphony (E major) "Idyllic." Boston, Mass.
- 1902. Oct. 28. "The Butterfly's Ball" overture. Chicago, Ill.
- 1903. Dec. 18. "Indian Rhapsody." Pittsburgh, Pa.
- 1915. Feb. 22. "The Veil" oratorio. Chicago, Ill.

CUI, C.
- 1886. Oct. 28. Tarantella. New York, N. Y.
- 1906. Mar. 17. Waltz. New York, N. Y.

CURRY, A.
- 1911. April 22. "Attala" symphonic poem. Boston, Mass.

DALYRAC
- 1790–1800. "Nina" opera. New Orleans, La.
- 1790–1800. "L'Amant Statue" opera. New Orleans, La.

d'ALBERT, E.
- 1887. Nov. 25. First Symphony (F). New York, N. Y.
- 1894. Feb. 2. "Esther" overture. Boston, Mass.
- 1895. Nov. 30. "Der Rubin" prelude. Boston, Mass.
- 1897. Dec. 3. "Gernot" introduction to Act II. Pittsburgh, Pa.
- 1901. Oct. 14. "Der Improvisatore" overture. Chicago,
- 1905. Feb. 4. Second Pianoforte Concerto (E major). Boston, Mass.
- 1908. Feb. 23. "Tiefland" opera. New York, N. Y.

DALCROZE, J.
   1906. Mar. 10.   Violin Concerto (C minor). Boston, Mass.

DAMROSCH, L.
   1875. Feb. 22.   "Ruth and Naomi" cantata. New York, N. Y.
   1882. April 20.   "Sulamith" cantata. New York, N. Y.
   1907. Dec. 1.   "Silver Wedding." New York, N. Y.

DAMROSCH, W.
   1896. Feb. 11.   "The Scarlet Letter" opera. Boston, Mass.
   1898. Dec. 3.   "Manilla Te Deum." New York, N. Y.
   1913. Feb. 27.   "Cyrano de Bergerac" opera. New York, N. Y.
   1915. Summer.   "Iphigenia in Aulis" incidental music, Berkeley, Cal.

DANIELS, MABEL
   1914. Feb. 19.   "The Guests of Sleep." Boston, Mass.

DARGOMYZHKY, A. S.
   1870. May 26.   "Kazachok" orchestral sketch. New York, N. Y.

DARLEY, F. T. S.
   1855. Dec. 8.   "The Cities of the Plains" oratorio. Philadelphia, Pa.

DAVICO, V.
   1921. Feb. 16.   "Impressionna Romana." Boston, Mass.

DAVID, F.
   1874. July 30.   Festival March. New York City.

DAVIDOFF, K.
   1907. Mar. 14.   Violoncello Concerto. New York, N. Y.

DAVISON, A. T.
   1918. April 28.   Tragic Overture. Boston, Mass.

DEBUSSY, C.
   1902. April 1.   "Aprèsmidi d'un Faun," symphonic poem. Boston, Mass.
   1903. Dec. 10.   "The Blessed Damosel." Boston, Mass.
   1904. Feb. 10.   Three Nocturnes. Boston, Mass.
   1907. Mar. 2.   "Le Mer." Boston, Mass.

1908. Feb. 19. "Pelléas et Mélisande" opera. New York, N. Y.
1909. Nov. 15. "Rondes de Printemps." New York, N. Y.
1910. Jan. 26. "March Ecossais." Boston, Mass.
1910. Nov. 16. "L'Enfant Prodigue" opera. New York, N. Y.
1911. Jan. 3. "Iberia" symphonic poem. New York, N. Y.
1912. Feb. 12. "Le Martyre de St. Sebastian." New York, N. Y.
1917. April 13. "Gigues." New York, N. Y.
1919. Nov. 13. "Berceuse Héroique." New York, N. Y.
1920. Jan. 2. "Jeux." Boston, Mass.
1920. April 16. Fantasy for Pianoforte and Orchestra. Boston, Mass.
1921. Jan. 19. "Le Jet d'Eau." Boston, Mass.
1921. Feb. 17. Two Nocturnes and Fantasy. New York, N. Y.

DE KOVEN, R.
1917. Mar. 8. "The Canterbury Pilgrims" opera. New York, N Y.

DELAMATER, E.
1917. April 6. "The Fable of the Hapless Folk-Tune." Chicago, Ill.
1919. Nov. 19. Suite from "The Betrothed." New York, N. Y.
1920. April 2. Concerto for organ and orchestra (E major). Chicago, Ill.

DE LARA, I.
1902. Jan. 22. "Messaline" opera. New York, N. Y.

DELIUS, F.
1909. Nov. 27. "Paris" symphonic poem. Boston, Mass.
1910. Oct. 28. "Brigg Fair" rhapsodie. New York, N. Y.
1911. Feb. Symphony. New York, N. Y.
1912. Jan. 26. "In a Summer Garden," tone poem. New York, N. Y.
1912. Nov. 7. "Life's Dance." Chicago, Ill.

1915. Nov. 5. "A Dance Rhapsody." Minneapolis, Minn.
1915. Nov. 26. Pianoforte Concerto (C minor). New York, N. Y.

DITTERSDORF, K.
1897. Jan. 16. Symphony (C major). Boston, Mass.

DOHNANYI, E.
1903. Nov. 28. Symphony (D minor). Boston, Mass.
1908. Jan. 29. Violoncello Concerto (D). Indianapolis, Ind.
1908. Feb. 29. Concert Piece in D major. Boston, Mass.
1914. Oct. 22. Suite No. 19. Minneapolis, Minn.

DONIZETTI, G.
1838. June 18. "L'Elisir d'Amore" opera. New York, N. Y.
1841. Dec. 28. "Lucia di Lammermoor" opera. New Orleans, La.
1843. Feb. 9. "La Favorita" opera. New Orleans, La.
1843. Mar. 6. "La Fille du Regiment" opera. New Orleans, La.
1843. Oct. 3. "Gemma di Vergi" opera. New York, N. Y.
1843. Dec. 15. "Marino Faliero" opera. New York, N. Y.
1844. April 27. "Lucrezia Borgia" opera. New Orleans, La.
1844. May 6. "Anne Boleyn" opera. New York, N. Y.
1844. Nov. 28. "Belisario" opera. New York, N. Y.
1846. Mar. 9. "Don Pasquale" opera. New York, N. Y.
1847. Jan. 4. "Linda di Chamounix" opera. New Orleans, La.
1848. "Robert Devereux" opera. New Orleans, La.
1849. Dec. 10. "Marie de Rohan" opera. New Orleans, La.
1849. Dec. 16. "The Martyrs" ("Il Poliuto" in oratorio form). Boston, Mass.
1850. Nov. 22. "Parisina" opera. New Orleans, La.
1852. Oct. 27. "Betley" opera. Philadelphia, Pa.
1853. "Torquato Tasso" opera. New Orleans, La.

1859. May 25. "Il Poliuto" opera. New York, N. Y.
1864. Nov. 25. "Don Sebastian" opera. New York, N. Y.

DOPPER, C.
   1912. Dec. 3. "Rembrandt" 3rd symphony (C minor). St. Paul, Minn.

DRAESEKE, F.
   1888. Nov. 22. "Serenata." New York, N. Y.
   1899. Dec. 9. "Jubel" overture. Boston, Mass.

DUBOIS, TH.
   1898. Jan. 27. Violin Concerto (D minor). Pittsburgh, Pa.
   1900. Feb. 11. "Marche de Batteurs." Boston, Mass.
   1900. April 27. Rigaudon and Danses Cénémoles. Boston, Mass.
   1903. Feb. 8. "Paradise Lost" oratorio. Boston, Mass.
   1904. Feb. 6. "Frithjof" overture. Boston, Mass.

DUCASSE, R.
   1910. April 16. "Française," suite (D minor). Boston, Mass.
   1910. April 19. "Variations Plaisantes." Boston, Mass.
   1912. Mar. 11. "Petit Suite." Boston, Mass.
   1915. Jan. 31. "La Joli Jeu de Furet." New York, N. Y.
   1918. Nov. 14. "Sarabande" symphonic poem. New York, N. Y.

DUKAS, P.
   1904. Oct. 22. "The Sorcerer's Apprentice." Boston, Mass.
   1910. Jan. 26. "Ariana et Barbe Bleue" excerpts. Boston, Mass.
   1911. Jan. 25. "Polyeucte" overture. Boston, Mass.
   1911. Feb. 3. "Ariana et Barbe Bleue" opera. New York, N. Y.
   1911. Feb. 5. Symphony in C. New York, N. Y.
   1916. Jan. 7. "Le Peri" dance poem. San Francisco, Cal.

DUPARC, M. E. H.
   1896. Nov. 13. "Lenore" symphonic poem. Chicago, Ill.
   1919. Nov. 13. "Aux Etoiles" symphonic poem. New York, N. Y.

DUPUIS, A.
  1920. Nov. 19. "Jean Michel" symphonic fragments. Cincinnati, O.

DURANTE, F.
  1870. Jan. 20. Magnificat in B. Boston, Mass.

DVOŘÁK, A.
  1879. Dec. 5. Slavonic Dances (No. 7 and 8). Boston, Mass.
  1880. Feb. 4. Slavonic Rhapsodie No. 3. Cincinnati, O.
  1880. Mar. 11. Slavonic Rhapsodie No. 2. New York, N. Y.
  1883. Jan. 6. First Symphony (D). New York, N. Y.
  1884. Oct. 24. "Husitska" overture. New York, N. Y.
  1884. Nov. 8. Scherzo Capriccioso. Brooklyn, N. Y.
  1886. Jan. 9. Second Symphony (D minor). New York, N. Y.
  1886. Mar. 20. "The Spectre Bride" cantata. Brooklyn, N. Y.
  1886. Nov. 6. "Legends" (Op. 59. 1st Collection). Boston, Mass.
  1886. Dec. 23. Slavonic Rhapsody No. 1. Boston, Mass.
  1887. Mar. 1. Legende. New York, N. Y.
  1887. Mar. 31. Suite (Op. 39). New York, N. Y.
  1887. Oct. 22. Suite in D. Boston, Mass.
  1887. Nov. 12. Slavonic Dances, second series. New York, N. Y.
  1888. July 19. Symphonic Variations (Op. 78). Chicago, Ill.
  1888. Nov. 17. Slavonic Dances (3rd and 4th series). Boston, Mass.
  1890. Mar. 23. Pianoforte Concerto (G minor. Op. 33). Boston, Mass.
  1892. Feb. 27. Fourth Symphony (G major). Boston, Mass.
  1892. Oct. 21. "Carnival Overture" and "Otello." New York, N. Y.
  1893. Dec. 15. Fifth Symphony (From the New World). New York, N. Y.
  1894. Jan. 5. Violin Concerto (A. Op. 53). New York, N. Y.

ANNALS OF MUSIC IN AMERICA

1896. Dec. 19. Violoncello Concerto (B minor). Boston, Mass.
1897. Jan. 1. "The Golden Spinning Wheel." Chicago, Ill.
1897. Feb. 4. "The Water Fay" symphonic poem. Brooklyn, N. Y.
1897. April 3. Rondo for Violoncello (Op. 94). Boston, Mass.
1899. Oct. 20. "The Wild Dove" tone poem. Chicago, Ill.
1899. Nov. 18. "Pisen Bohatýrské," symphonic poem. Boston, Mass.
1901. Nov. 15. "Mein Heim" overture. Chicago, Ill.
1910. Dec. 4. "In the Spinning Room." New York, N. Y.
1911. Feb. 15. Symphony (Posthumous). New York, N. Y.
1919. Nov. 21. Third Symphony (F major). New York, N. Y.

DVORSKY, M. (JOSEF HOFMANN).
1916. Nov. 24. Symphonic Duologue. Cincinnati, O.
1919. Nov. 7. "The Haunted Castle" tone poem. Philadelphia, Pa.

ECKER, K.
1885. Oct. 31. Concert Overture. Boston, Mass.

ECKERT, K. A. F.
1889. Nov. 16. Violoncello Concerto (A minor). Boston, Mass.

ELGAR, E.
1901. Mar. 15. "Cockaigne" overture. Chicago, Ill.
1901. Mar. 15. "In London Town." Chicago, Ill.
1902. Jan. 3. Variations on an Original Theme. Chicago, Ill.
1902. Nov. 28. "Pomp" and "Circumstance" marches. Chicago, Ill.
1903. Mar. 23. "Dream of Gerontius" oratorio. Chicago, Ill.
1903. Nov. 7. "Grania and Diamid" incidental music. Chicago, Ill.
1904. Feb. 9. "The Apostles" oratorio. New York, N. Y.

1904. Nov. 5. "In the South" overture. Chicago, Ill.
1904. Nov. 6. Fourth Symphony. New York, N. Y.
1905. Jan. 20. "Froissart" overture. Chicago, Ill.
1905. Feb. 8. "Benedictus." New York, N. Y.
1906. Nov. 27. "The Banner of St. George." New York, N. Y.
1907. Feb. 7. "Romance." New York, N. Y.
1907. Mar. 26. "The Kingdom" oratorio. New York, N. Y.
1909. Jan. 3. First Symphony (A flat). New York, N. Y.
1911. Nov. 24. Second Symphony (E flat). Cincinnati, O.
1913. Dec. 12. "Falstaff" (Opus 68). New York, N. Y.
1916. Nov. 26. "Sospire." New York, N. Y.
1919. Mar. 2. "Carillon" and "Le Drapeau Belge." New York, N. Y.
1920. Feb. 13. "Enigma" variations. Philadelphia, Pa.

ENESCO, G.
1902. Jan. 7. "Poème Roumain." Boston, Mass.
1911. Jan. 3. Suite (Op. 9). New York, N. Y.
1911. Feb. 17. Symphony (A flat major). New York, N. Y.

ERNST, H. W.
1878. Nov. 23. Violin Concerto (Pathetique). New York, N. Y.

ERTEL, J. P.
1908. April 16. "The Midnight Review" symphonic poem. Boston, Mass.

FANELLI, E.
1912. Nov. 16. "Thebes" symphonic poem. New York, N. Y.

FARWELL, A.
1917. Dec. 26. "The Evergreen Tree" masque. New York, N. Y.
1919. July 4. "Chant of Victory." Berkeley, Cal.

FAURÉ, G.
1906. Jan. 2. "Pavane." Boston, Mass.
1919. Mar. 28. "Penelope" prelude. Boston, Mass.

ANNALS OF MUSIC IN AMERICA

FÉVRIER
   1913. Dec. 5. "Mona Vanna" opera. New York, N. Y.
   1919. Jan. 14. "Gismonda" opera. Chicago, Ill.

FIBICH, Z.
   1903. Jan. 31. "A Night at Karlstein" overture. Boston, Mass.
   1916. Jan. 20. "At Evening" idyll. New York, N. Y.
   1920. Jan. 2. Overture to a Merry Play. New York, N. Y.

FITELBERG, G.
   1912. Dec. 6. "Das Lied vom Falcon" tone poem. St. Louis, Mo.
   1921. Nov. 4. Polish Rhapsody. Philadelphia, Pa.

FLOERSHEIM, O.
   1888. Jan. 28. "Elevation" for organ and orchestra. Boston, Mass.

FLORIDIA, P.
   1907. Mar. 22. Symphony (D minor). Cincinnati, O.
   1910. Aug. 29. "Paoletta" opera. Cincinnati, O.

FLOTOW, F.
   1852. Nov. 1. "Martha" opera. New York, N. Y.
   1856. Oct. 28. "Stradella" opera. New York, N. Y.

FOOTE, A.
   1887. Feb. 5. "In the Mountains" overture. Boston, Mass.
   1888. Jan. 26. "The Wreck of the Hesperus" cantata. Boston, Mass.
   1889. Nov. 23. Suite for Strings (D major). Boston, Mass.
   1891. Jan. 24. "Francesca da Rimini" symphonic prologue. Boston, Mass.
   1893. Feb. 4. "The Skeleton in Armor" ballad. Boston, Mass.
   1907. Jan. 20. Four Character Pieces. Chicago, Ill.
   1909. April 17. Suite (E major). Boston, Mass.
   1911. Jan. 27. Serenade (E major). St. Louis, Mo.

FORSYTH, C.
   1905. Jan. 4. Concerto in G minor (1st movement). Boston, Mass.

FRANCHETTI, A.
- 1890. Nov. 26. "Asrael" opera. New York, N. Y.
- 1910. Jan. 22. "Germania" opera. New York, N. Y.
- 1913. Nov. 20. "Cristoforo Colombo" opera. Philadelphia, Pa.

FRANCK, C.
- 1895. Nov. 8. "Les Sylphides" symphonic poem. Chicago, Ill.
- 1898. Jan. 29. "The Wild Huntsman" symphonic poem. Cincinnati, O.
- 1898. Mar. 7. Variations Symphoniques. Chicago, Ill.
- 1899. April 15. Symphony (D minor). Boston, Mass.
- 1900. Feb. 17. "Les Éolides" symphonic poem. Boston, Mass.
- 1900. Mar. 25. "The Beatitudes" oratorio. New York, N. Y.
- 1905. Dec. 2. "Psyche and Cupid" symphonic poem. Boston, Mass.
- 1906. Dec. 15. "Morceau Symphonique" (Redemption). New York, N. Y.
- 1910. April 19. Variations Plaisantes. Boston, Mass.
- 1914. Jan. 16. Prelude, Chorale, and Fugue. New York, N. Y.
- 1921. Oct. 21. Organ Chorale No. 2. Boston, Mass.

FRIED, O.
- 1907. Mar. 30. Prelude and Double Fugue for Strings. Boston, Mass.

FRY, WM. H.
- 1845. June 4. "Leonora" opera. Philadelphia, Pa.
- 1853. Four Symphonies, "Christmas, or Santa Claus," "The Breaking Heart," "Childe Harold," "A Day in the Country." New York, N. Y.
- 1863. April. "Notre Dame de Paris" opera. Philadelphia, Pa.

FUCHS, R.
- 1882. Mar. 9. Serenade in D. Boston, Mass.
- 1885. Oct. 31. Symphony in C major. Boston, Mass.

1893. Feb. 3.   Serenade (strings and two horns).   New York, N. Y.

GADSBY, H. R.
   1886. Oct. 26.   " The Forest of Arden " orchestral scene. New York, N. Y.

GADE, N. W.
   1852. Nov. 13.   " Ossian " overture. New York, N. Y.
   1852. Dec. 12.   First Symphony (C minor).   New York, N. Y.
   1868. April 13.   " The Crusaders " cantata. Boston, Mass.
   1868. Nov. 28.   " Hamlet " overture. New York, N. Y.
   1869. Jan. 16.   " Spring " fantasia. New York, N Y.
   1869. Feb. 18.   Second Symphony (E). Boston, Mass.
   1871. Feb. 23.   Third Symphony (A minor). Boston, Mass.
   1872. Feb. 23.   Third Concert Overture. Boston, Mass.
   1872. Dec. 5.   Fifth Symphony (D minor). Boston, Mass.
   1873. Feb. 15.   Eighth Symphony (B minor). Boston, Mass.
   1874. Feb. 14.   " Michael Angelo " overture. New York, N. Y.
   1877. Jan. 16.   " Noveletten." New York, N. Y.

GALLICO, P.
   1921. June 7.   " The Apocalypse " oratorio. Rock Island, Ill.

GARCIA, M.
   1825-6.   " L'Amante Astuto " opera. New York, N. Y.
   1825-6.   " La Figlia del Aria." New York, N. Y.

GARDNER, S.
   1919. July 7.   " New Russia." New York, N. Y.
   1920. Dec. 14.   Violin Concerto. Providence, R. I.

GAERTNER, L. von
   1903. Feb. 5.   " Macbeth " tone poem. New York, N. Y.

GAUBERT, P.
   1912. Mar. 11.   " Poéme Elegiaque." Boston, Mass.

GEORGES, A.
   1905. Jan. 4.   " Prélude d'Axël." Boston, Mass.

GERICKE, W.

1886. Jan. 16. "Chorus of Homage." Boston, Mass.
1886. Mar. 13. Three Movements from Serenade. Boston, Mass.

GERMAN, E.

1895. Oct. 25. Three Dances. Chicago, Ill.
1907. Nov. 17. Welsh Rhapsody. New York, N. Y.

GERNSHEIM, F.

1882. Dec. 9. Symphony (E flat). Boston, Mass.
1866. Mar. 23. Tarantella (from Symphony in F). Brooklyn, N. Y.
1897. Oct. 23. Violin Concerto (D major). Boston, Mass.
1911. Jan. 28. "To a Drama" tone poem. Boston, Mass.

GILBERT, H. F.

1906. Mar. 10. "Salammbo's Invocation." New York, N. Y.
1910. Aug. 17. Comedy Overture on Negro Themes. New York, N. Y.
1912. June 5. Negro Rhapsody. Norfolk, Conn.
1914. Sept. "Riders to the Sea." Peterboro, N. H.
1921. Mar. 4. "Indian Sketches" suite. Boston, Mass.

GILCHRIST, W. W.

1909. April 1. "The Lamb of God" oratorio. New York, N. Y.

GILSON, P.

1892. Dec. 17. "La Mer" symphony. New York, N. Y.

GIORDANO, U.

1896. Nov. 13. "Andrea Chenier" opera. New York, N. Y.
1906. Jan. 31. "Siberia" opera. New Orleans, La.
1906. Dec. 5. "Fedora" opera. New York, N. Y.
1915. Jan. 25. Madame Sans-Gêne" opera. New York, N. Y.

GLAZUNOF, A.

1893. June 7. Triumphal March. Chicago, Ill.
1896. Nov. 13. Oriental Rhapsody. Chicago, Ill.

1897. Oct. 16. " Poème Lyrique " (Op. 42). Boston, Mass.
1897. Oct. 29. Second Concert Waltz. Chicago, Ill.
1897. Nov. 4. " Printemps." Chicago, Ill.
1898. Mar. 5. Fifth Symphony (B flat major). New York, N. Y.
1899. Oct. 21. Sixth Symphony (C minor). Boston, Mass.
1901. Mar. 15. " Ruses d'Amor." Chicago, Ill.
1901. Dec. 7. Overture Solennelle. Chicago, Ill.
1902. Jan. 25. Suite from " Raymonda " ballet. Boston, Mass.
1903. Oct. 24. Fourth Symphony (E flat). Boston, Mass.
1903. Nov. 20. Seventh Symphony (F). Pittsburgh, Pa.
1904. Jan. 23. " Moyen Age " suite. Chicago, Ill.
1904. April 9. " Carnaval " overture. Boston, Mass.
1904. Dec. 24. " Stenka Razin " symphonic poem. New York, N. Y.
1906. Jan. 27. " The Kremlin " symphonic picture. Boston, Mass.
1906. Nov. 15. Scène Dansante. New York, N. Y.
1906. Dec. 20. Third Symphony (D). Opus 33. New York, N. Y.
1907. Nov. 14. Eighth Symphony (E flat). New York, N. Y.
1908. Feb. 13. " Winter " from ballet " The Seasons." New York, N. Y.
1910. Mar. 4. Violin Concerto. New York, N. Y.

GLEASON, F. G.
1904. April 17. " Edris " symphonic poem. Chicago, Ill.

GLIÈRE, R. M.
1906. Mar 17. First Symphony (E flat). New York, N. Y.
1918. Jan. 18. Third Symphony " Ilia Murometz." Chicago, Ill.

GLINKA, M. I.
1870. July 14. " Jota Aragonese." New York, N. Y.
1870. Aug. 25. " Kamarinskaya." New York, N. Y.
1873. July 10. " Rouslane et Ludmilla " overture. New York, N. Y.

GLOVER, J. W.

1897. Mar. 17. "St. Patrick at Tara" cantata. New York, N. Y.

GLUCK, C. W.

1796. July. "Iphegénie en Aulide" overture. Charleston, S. C.

1875. Jan. 8. "Paris and Helen" overture. New York, N. Y.

1896. Dec. 26. "Don Juan" selections from. Boston, Mass.

1903. Jan. 27. Symphony (A major). New York, N. Y.

1909. Dec. 25. "Orfeo ed Eurydice" opera. New York, N. Y.

1910. Nov. 14. "Armide" opera. New York, N. Y.

1916. Nov. 25. "Iphigenia in Tauris" opera. New York, N. Y.

GNECCHI, V.

1914. Feb. 26. "Cassandra" opera. Philadelphia, Pa.

GODARD, B.

1883. Nov. 17. Violin Concerto "Romantique." Boston, Mass.

GOETZ, H.

1880. Jan. 8. Symphony (F major). Cambridge, Mass.

1882. April 15. Violin Concerto (B flat). New York, N. Y.

1886. Jan. 4. "The Taming of the Shrew" opera. New York, N. Y.

1895. Mar. 30. "Spring" overture. Boston, Mass.

GOLDMARK, K.

1871. Jan. 5. "Sakuntala" overture. Boston, Mass.

1877. Jan. 13. "Ländliche Hochzeit" symphony. New York, N. Y.

1878. Feb. 16. Wedding March and Variations. Brooklyn, N. Y.

1879. Dec. 3. "Penthesilea" overture. Cincinnati, O.

1885. Dec. 2. "Die Koenigen von Saba" opera. New York, N. Y.

1887. Jan. 3. "Merlin" opera. New York, N. Y.

1888. April 7. Second Symphony (E flat major). Boston, Mass.
1889. Dec. 4. " In the Spring " overture. New York, N. Y.
1890. Nov. 1. " Prometheus " overture. Boston, Mass.
1890. Dec. 6. Violin Concerto (A minor). Boston, Mass.
1894. May 23. " Sappho " overture. Cincinnati, O.
1894. Dec. 28. Scherzo (A major. Op. 45). Chicago, Ill.
1896. Nov. 21. " Das Heimchen am Herd " intermezzo from. Chicago, Ill.
1904. Dec. 3. " In Italy " overture. Chicago, Ill
1912. Nov. 7. " Das Heimchen am Herd " opera. Philadelphia, Pa.

GOLDMARK, R.
1900. Jan. 13. " Hiawatha " overture. Boston, Mass.
1914. Mar. 14. " Samson " tone poem. Boston, Mass.

GOMEZ, A. C.
1884. Dec. " Il Guarany " opera. New York, N. Y.

GOOSSENS, E.
1920. Oct. 22. " By the Tarn " sketch. Chicago, Ill.

GOSSINEC
1790. Oct. 7. " Le Tonnelier " musical play. New York, N. Y.

GOUNOD, C. F.
1863. Nov. 18. " Faust " opera. Philadelphia, Pa.
1867. July 1. " La Reine de Saba " ballet music of. New York, N. Y.
1867. Dec. 14. " Roméo et Juliette " opera. New York, N. Y.
1874. May 14. " Le Médecin Malgré Lui " overture. New York, N. Y.
1874. May 20. " Mireille " overture. New York, N. Y.
1882. Dec. 6. " Redemption " oratorio. New York, N. Y.
1884. Dec. 18. " Mireille " opera. New York, N. Y.
1889. Jan. 12. " La Reine de Saba " opera. New Orleans, La.
1893. Nov. 16. " Philemon et Baucis " opera. New York, N. Y.
1902. Feb. 9. " Gallia " oratorio. Boston, Mass.

GRAEDENER, K. G. P.
  1888. Feb. 18. Overture. Boston, Mass.
GRAINGER, P.
  1913. April 17. Folk Tune Settings. Norfolk, Conn.
  1916. June. "In a Nutshell" suite. Norfolk, Conn.
  1917. Jan. 26. "The Warriors." New York, N. Y.
GRANADOS, P.
  1916. Jan. 28. "Goyescas" opera. New York, N. Y.
DE GREEF, A.
  1918. Dec. 8. Four Old Flemish Songs. New York, N. Y.
GRELL, E.
  1889. Mar. 27. "Missa Solemnis." New York, N. Y.
GRÉTRY, A. E. M.
  1790–1800. "Zémire et Azor" opera. New Orleans, La.
  1790–1800. "Fausse Magie" opera. New Orleans, La.
  1790–1800. "Richard Coeur de Lion" opera. New Orleans, La.
  1908. Mar. 14. "Céphalus et Procris" three dances from. Boston, Mass.
GRIEG, E.
  1874. Oct. 28. Pianoforte Concerto (A minor). Boston, Mass.
  1881. Dec. 11. Norwegian Melodies. New York, N. Y.
  1883. Feb. 3. Two Melodies for Strings. Boston, Mass.
  1888. Nov. 24. "In Autumn" overture. Brooklyn, N. Y.
  1889. Jan. 24. "Peer Gynt" suite. New York, N. Y.
  1899. Jan. 17. Symphonic Dances. Chicago, Ill.
  1911. Nov. 18. Old Norwegian Romance. Boston, Mass.
GRIFFES, C. T.
  1919. Mar. 24. Three Songs. Philadelphia, Pa.
  1919. Nov. 16. Poem for flute and orchestra. New York, N. Y.
  1919. Nov. 28. "The Pleasure Dome of Kubla Khan" Boston, Mass.
GRIMM, J. O.
  1866. Dec. 3. Suite in Canon Form. New York, N. Y.

1873. May 22. Second Suite in Canon Form. New York, N. Y.

1884. Feb. 23. Symphony in D minor. Boston, Mass.

GRISAR, A.
1858–9. "Les Amours du Diable" opera. New Orleans, La.

GUILMANT, A.
1879. Dec. 5. First Symphony (1st movement). Boston, Mass.

1882. Nov. 29. First Symphony complete. Boston, Mass.

GRUENBERG, LOUIS
1921. Oct. 23. "The Hill of Dreams" symphonic poem. New York, N. Y.

GUIRARD, E.
1900. Mar. 10. Caprice for violin and orchestra. New York, N. Y.

1906. Jan. 2. Chasse Fantastique. Boston, Mass.

HADLEY, H. K.
1897. Dec. 2. First Symphony, "Youth and Life." New York, N. Y.

1901. Dec. 20. Second Symphony, "The Four Seasons." New York, N. Y.

1902. Mar. 14. Suite Orientale. Pittsburgh, Pa.

1907. April 13. "Salome" tone poem. Boston, Mass.

1908. April 11. Third Symphony (B minor). Boston, Mass.

1909. May 28. "The Culprit Fay" rhapsody. Grand Rapids, Mich.

1910. Jan. 7. Symphonic Fantasia. St. Louis, Mo.

1911. June 6. Fourth Symphony — "North, South, East and West." Norfolk, Conn.

1911. Aug. 10. "The Atonement of Pan" suite. San Francisco, Cal.

1914. June 2. "Lucifer" tone poem. Norfolk, Conn.

1917. Dec. 26. "Azora" opera. Chicago, Ill.

1918. Oct. 18. "Bianca" opera. New York, N. Y.

1920. Jan. 31. "Cleopatra's Night" opera. New York, N. Y.

1921. Nov. 17. "The Ocean" tone poem. New York, N. Y.

HALÉVY, J.
  1843. "L'Eclair" opera. New Orleans, La.
  1858–9. "La Juive" opera. New Orleans, La.
  1858–9. "Jacquarita l'Indienne" opera. New Orleans, La.
  1858–9. "Reine de Chypre" opera. New Orleans, La.

HALM, AUG.
  1910. April 23. Symphony (D minor). Boston, Mass.

HAMERIK, A.
  1873. Sept. 23. "Nordish" suite. New York, N. Y.
  1884. May 1. Christian Trilogy. Baltimore, Md.

HANDEL, G. F.
  1770. Jan. 9. "Messiah" (13 numbers). New York, N. Y.
  1801. "Messiah" (in part). Philadelphia, Pa.
  1818. Dec. 25. "Messiah" (complete). Boston, Mass.
  1842. Oct. 31. "Israel in Egypt" oratorio. New York, N. Y.
  1842. Nov. 22. "Acis and Galatea" oratorio. New York, N. Y.
  1845. Jan. 26. "Samson" oratorio. Boston, Mass.
  1845. Dec. 21. "Moses in Egypt" oratorio. Boston, Mass.
  1847. Dec. 5. "Judas Maccabeus" oratorio. Boston, Mass.
  1850. Mar. 9. "Jephtha" oratorio. Boston, Mass.
  1855. Nov. 18. "Solomon" oratorio. Boston, Mass.
  1868. Oct. 21. Royal Fireworks Music. New York, N. Y.
  1871. Nov. 23. Concerto for Oboe. Boston, Mass.
  1876. April. 16. "Joshua" oratorio. Boston, Mass.
  1881. Feb. 25. "L'Allegro, Il Penseroso, ed Il Moderato." New York, N. Y.
  1891. Sept. 25. "Occasional Oratorio" overture. Worcester, Mass.
  1891. Dec. 26. Concerto for strings and two wind instruments. Boston, Mass.
  1894. Sept. 27. Concerto for organ (B flat). Worcester, Mass.
  1896. April 17. Concerto for strings. Chicago, Ill.

1896. Dec. 26. First Overture (D minor). Boston, Mass.
1900. Oct. 30. Fourth Organ Concerto (D minor). Boston, Mass.
1907. Mar. 31. " Belshazzar " oratorio. Boston, Mass.

d'HARCOURT, E.
1906. Mar. 24. Overture to " Tasso." Boston, Mass.

HARTMANN, E.
1894. Feb. 7. " Nordishe Heerfahrt " overture. Boston, Mass.

HARTMANN, P.
1907. April 3. " St. Peter " oratorio. New York, N. Y.

HAUSEGGER, S. von
1901. Nov. 16. " Barbarossa " symphonic poem. New York, N. Y.

HAYDN, JOSEPH
1796. July. " Stabat Mater." Charleston, S. C.
1810. " The Creation " oratorio (part). Bethlehem, Pa.
1810. " The Seasons " oratorio (part). Bethlehem, Pa.
1816. " The Creation " oratorio (part). Boston, Mass.
1819. Feb. 13. " The Creation " oratorio complete. Boston, Mass.
1843. Jan. 7. Military Symphony (G major). Boston, Mass.
1853. Jan. 1. Eighth Symphony. Boston, Mass.
1855. Feb. 17. Fifth Symphony. Boston, Mass.
1864. " The Seasons " oratorio (complete). Boston, Mass.
1865. Mar. 11. First Symphony (E flat). New York, N. Y.
1867. Nov. 9. Kaiser Fritz Hymn. Brooklyn, N. Y.
1868. Dec. 4. Symphony in B flat. Boston, Mass.
1871. Dec. 7. Third Symphony (E flat). Boston, Mass.
1872. Feb. 1. Oxford Symphony (G). Boston, Mass.
1877. Jan. 22. Ninth Symphony (C). New York, N. Y.
1877. Jan. 30. " The Tempest." New York, N. Y.
1888. April 6. " The Bear " symphony. New York, N. Y.
1890. Nov. 22. Concerto for violoncello. Boston, Mass.
1910. Mar. 6. Concerto for violin. New York, N. Y.

HENBERGER, R.
  1886. Nov. 13. Overture to "Cain." Boston, Mass.

HENSCHEL, G.
  1883. Feb. 17. Serenade for Strings. Boston, Mass.
  1892. April 16. Suite from "Hamlet." Boston, Mass.
  1896. April 24. "Stabat Mater" cantata. New York, N. Y.
  1902. Dec. 2. "Requiem." Boston, Mass.

HERBERT, V.
  1888. Dec. 1. "Serenade." New York, N. Y.
  1891. Sept. 24. "The Captive" oratorio. Worcester, Mass.
  1894. Mar. 10. Second Violoncello Concerto. New York, N. Y.
  1901. Jan. 18. "Hero and Leander" symphonic poem. Pittsburgh, Pa.
  1901. Dec. 6. "Woodland Fancies" suite. Pittsburgh, Pa.
  1902. Jan. 2. "Columbus" suite. Pittsburgh, Pa.
  1911. Feb. 25. "Natoma" opera. New York, N. Y.
  1914. Jan. 24. "Madeline" opera. New York, N. Y.

HÉROLD, L. J. F.
  1840. Mar. 20. "Zampa" opera. New York, N. Y.

HILL, E. B.
  1915. Dec. 31. "The Parting of Lancelot and Guinevere" symphonic poem. St. Louis, Mo.
  1918. Jan. 27. "Stevensoniana" suite. New York, N. Y.
  1920. Oct. 29. "The Fall of the House of Usher" symphonic poem. Boston, Mass.

HILLER, F.
  1858. Mar. 6. Symphony in E. New York, N. Y.
  1860. May 19. "Saul" oratorio. New York, N. Y.
  1863. Nov. 7. Second Concerto (A). New York, N. Y.
  1874. May 21. Dramatic Fantasia. New York, N. Y.

HINTON, A.
  1907. Oct. 4. Pianoforte Concerto (D minor). Worcester, Mass.
  1913. Nov. 21. Second Symphony (C minor). Minneapolis, Minn.

HOFFMAN, H.
  1880. Feb. 22. "Cinderella" cantata. New York, N. Y.
HOFMANN, H.
  1874. May 14. "Hungarian" suite. New York, N. Y.
  1875. Feb. 6. "Frithjof" symphony. New York, N. Y.
  1877. July 11. "Pictures from the North." Chicago, Ill.
  1882. July 12. Overture to a Drama. Chicago, Ill.
HOFMANN, J.
  1908. Feb. 28. Third Pianoforte Concerto. New York, N. Y.
HOHNSTOCK, C.
  1865. Mar. 4. "Hail Columbia" overture. Brooklyn, N. Y.
HOLBROOKE, J.
  1913. Jan. 11. "Queen Mab" symphonic poem. Boston, Mass.
HOLLAENDER, G.
  1884. Dec. 3. Romance for violin and orchestra. New York, N. Y.
HOLMÉS, A.
  1904. Jan. 5. "Irlande" symphonic poem. Boston, Mass.
HOLST, G.
  1920. Dec. 31. "The Planets" symphony. Chicago, Ill.
HOPEKIRK, H.
  1904. April 16. Concert Piece (D minor). Boston, Mass.
HOWE, J. H.
  1916. July 12. Festival Overture. Seattle, Wash.
HUBAY, J.
  1918. Jan. 6. Violin Concerto. New York, N. Y.
HUBER, H.
  1882. Feb. 11. "Tell" symphony. New York, N. Y.
  1887. July 21. "Römische Karneval." Chicago, Ill.
  1902. Oct. 25. Second Symphony (E minor). Boston, Mass.
HÜE, G.
  1905. April 18. "Titania" symphonic suite. Boston, Mass.
  1914. Jan. 25. Fantasia for flute and orchestra. New York, N. Y.

1916. Feb. 17. "Croquois d'Orient" suite. New York, N. Y.

HUGO, J. A.
1919. Mar. 12. "The Temple Dancer" opera. New York, N. Y.

HUMISTON, W. H.
1906. May 3. Southern Fantasy. Orange, N. J.
1919. Jan. 26. Suite (F sharp minor). New York, N. Y.

HUMPERDINCK, E.
1895. Oct. 8. "Hänsel und Gretel" opera. New York, N. Y.
1896. Dec. 26. "Königskinder" selections from. Boston, Mass.
1907. Dec. 21. "The Forced Marriage" ("Die Heirat wider Willen") overture. Boston, Mass.
1910. Dec. 28. "Königskinder" opera. New York, N. Y.

HUSS, H. H.
1887. July. Rhapsody. New York, N. Y.
1894. Dec. 29. Pianoforte Concerto (B major). Boston, Mass.
1896. April 1. "Cleopatra's Death" dramatic poem. New York, N. Y.
1897. June 25. Festival March. New York, N. Y.
1906. April 2. Violin Concerto (D minor). New York, N. Y.

ILYINSKY, A. A.
1907. Dec. 12. "Mir and Antra" suite. New York, N. Y.

d'INDY, V.
1888. Dec. 1. "Wallenstein Trilogy. New York, N. Y.
1898. April 23. "Istar" symphonic variations. Chicago, Ill.
1900. Feb. 10. "Médie" suite. Boston, Mass.
1901. Dec. 16. "La Forêt Enchantée" legende. Chicago, Ill.
1902. Jan. 7. "Fervaal" introduction. Boston, Mass.
1902. April 5. Second Symphony (B flat major) "On a Mountain Air." Boston, Mass.

1903. Jan. 5. Fantasia of French Folk Themes. Boston, Mass.
1903. Oct. 31. " L'Etranger " introduction. Chicago, Ill.
1904. Jan. 5. Choral Varie. Boston, Mass.
1906. Feb. 6. " St. Mary Magdalene " oratorio. Boston, Mass.
1907. Oct. 19. " Jour d'été à la Montagne " symphonic poem. Boston, Mass.
1910. Jan. 26. " Souvenirs " symphonic poem. Boston, Mass.
1916. May 4. " Le Chant de la Cloche " symphonic poem. Boston, Mass.
1919. Oct. 24. Sinfonia Brevis de Bello Gallico. Boston, Mass.
1919. Oct. 31. " La Queste de Dieu." Chicago, Ill.
1919. Nov. 13. Third Symphony. New York, N. Y.

IVANOF, I.
1904. Feb. 11. Caucasian Sketches. New York, N. Y.
1907. Feb. 28. Second Caucasian Suite. New York, N. Y.
1912. Nov. 21. American Rhapsody. New York, N. Y.

JACOBI, F
1917. Dec. 6. " California " suite. San Francisco, Cal.

JÄRNEFELT, A.
1902. Nov. 4. " Korsholm " symphonic poem. Chicago, Ill.
1913. Nov. 14. " Praeludium." New York, N. Y.

JENSEN, A.
1886. Jan. 21. Wedding Music. Jersey City, N. J.

JERAL
1918. Mar. 2. Violoncello Concerto. New York, N. Y.

JOACHIM, J.
1868. Dec. 10. Hungarian Concerto (D minor). Boston, Mass.
1871. June 27. March in C. New York, N. Y.
1871. July 21. March in D. New York, N. Y.
1881. Nov. 26. Violin Concerto (Op. 11). Boston, Mass.

1891. Jan. 10. Violin Concerto in G (Op. 3). New York, N. Y.

1894. Dec. 7. Theme and Variations. New York, N. Y.

JUON, P.

1907. Jan. 25. "Watchman's Song" fantasie. Philadelphia, Pa.

JURASSORSKY

1918. Jan. 19. "The Phantoms" symphonic poem. New York, N. Y

KAHN, R.

1895. Mar. 23. "Elégie" overture, C minor. Boston, Mass.

KALINNIKOF

1905. Feb. 25. Symphony in A. New York, N. Y.

1918. Jan. 6. Second Symphony (G minor). New York, N. Y.

1920. Jan. 23. "The Fir Tree and the Palm" symphonic poem. New York, N. Y.

KALLIWODA, J. W.

1846. Mar. 7. First Symphony (D minor). New York, N. Y.

KAUN, H.

1898. Jan. 7. Festival March and Hymn. Chicago, Ill.

1898. Jan. 14. Symphony (D minor). Chicago, Ill.

1899. Feb. 3. "Der Maler von Antwerpen" overture. Chicago, Ill.

1903. Feb. 7. "Minnehaha" symphonic poem. Chicago, Ill.

1903. Feb. 7. "Hiawatha" symphonic poem. Chicago, Ill.

KELLEY, E. S.

1892. June 9. "Puritania" comic opera. Boston, Mass.

1913. June 3. "New England" second symphony. Norfolk, Conn.

1918. May 10. "The Pilgrim's Progress" cantata. Cincinnati, O.

1918. Nov. 14. "A California Idyll." New York, N. Y.

KERNOCHAN, M.

1914. Feb. 6. "The Foolish Virgins." E. Orange, N. J.

KIEL, F.
 1879. April 15. "Christus" oratorio. New York, N. Y.
KIENZL, W.
 1913. Feb. 24. "Les Ranz des Vaches." Philadelphia, Pa.
KLEIN, B. O.
 1903. Dec. 8. Suite in F for cello and orchestra. New York, N. Y.
KLOSE, F.
 1915. April 3. Prelude and Double Fugue for organ and orchestra. Boston, Mass.
KLUGHARDT, A.
 1891. Mar. 7. Symphony (D major). Boston, Mass.
 1912. Dec. 21. Violoncello Concerto (Op. 59). Boston, Mass.
KNORR, I.
 1895. Mar. 30. Variations on an Ukraine Folk-Song. Boston, Mass.
KOESSLER, H.
 1902. Mar. 15. Symphonic Variations. Boston, Mass.
KOLAR, V.
 1911. Mar. 3. "Hiawatha." New York, N. Y.
 1912. Feb. 16. "A Fairy Tale." New York, N. Y.
 1914. Jan. 25. Suite for Orchestra. New York, N. Y.
KONIUS, G. E.
 1906. Feb. 24. "Childhood" suite. New York, N. Y.
KORNGOLD, E. W.
 1912. Nov. 28. Overture to a Play. New York, N. Y.
 1914. April 3. Sinfonietta (Op. 5). Chicago, Ill.
 1921. Nov. 19. "Die Tote Stadt" opera. New York, N. Y.
de KOVEN, R.
 1920. Jan. 2. "Rip van Winkle" opera. Chicago, Ill.
KRUG, A.
 1887. Jan. 15. Symphonic prologue to "Otello." Boston, Mass.

KURTZ, E. F.
  1920. Dec. 12. Victory March. Cincinnati, O.

LACHAUME, A.
  1897. Dec. 21. "In Old Japan" opera. New York, N. Y.

LACHNER, F.
  1860. Feb. 11. Festival Overture. New York, N. Y.
  1864. Dec. 3. Suite in D minor. New York, N. Y.

LALO, E.
  1884. Dec. 20. Rhapsodie Norvégienne. Boston, Mass.
  1886. Jan. 15. Rhapsodie and Scherzo. New York, N. Y.
  1887. Nov. 12. "Espagnole" symphony. Boston, Mass.
  1890. Jan. 23. "Le Roi d'Ys" opera. New Orleans, La.
  1896. Jan. 4. "Namouna" suite. Boston, Mass.
  1899. Oct. 21. Violoncello Concerto (D minor). Boston, Mass.
  1906. Jan. 2. Valse de Cigarette. Boston, Mass.
  1909. Nov. 28. "Arlequin" symphonic poem. New York, N. Y.

LAMOND, F.
  1893. Dec. 3. "From the Highlands" overture. Chicago, Ill.

LANG, M. R.
  1893. April 8. "Dramatic Overture." Boston, Mass.
  1893. "Witches" overture. Chicago, Ill.
  1895. "Sappho's Prayer." New York, N. Y.

LANGER, F.
  1895. April 13. Introduction to opera "Dornröschen." Boston, Mass.

LAPARRA, R.
  1910. Dec. 4. "Habañera" opera. Boston, Mass.
  1919. April 18. "Un Dimanche Basque." Boston, Mass.

LAUCELLA, N.
  1911. Nov. 26. "Consalvo" symphonic poem. New York, N. Y.
  1915. Jan. 31. Prelude and Temple Dance. New York, N. Y.

1917. June. "Whitehouse" symphonic impressions. Norfolk, Conn.

LAZZARI, S.
1910. April 19. "Effet de Nuit" suite. Boston, Mass.
1911. Jan. 25. Prelude d'Armor. Boston, Mass.
1911. Jan. 25. "Marche pour une Fête Joyeuse." Boston, Mass.
1918. Jan. 19. "Le Sauteriot" opera. Chicago, Ill.
1919. Dec. 19. "Impressions of Night" symphonic picture. New York, N. Y.

LE GRAND, H.
1895. Feb. 21. "The Resurrection" oratorio. New York, N. Y.

LEKEW, G.
1914. Jan. 25. Adagio for Strings. New York, N. Y.
1918. Nov. 30. Symphonic Fantasy on Two Angevin Tunes. New York, N. Y.

LEMARE, E.
1904. Jan. 1. Rhapsody and Caprice Orientale. Pittsburgh, Pa.

LENDVAI, E.
1913. Feb. 15. Symphony (D major). Boston, Mass.

LEONCAVALLO, R.
1894. June 15. "Pagliacci" opera. New York, N. Y.
1913. Mar. 23. "Zingari" opera. Chicago, Ill.
1920. Jan. 17. "Zaza" opera. New York, N. Y.
1920. Dec. 13. "Edipo Rè" opera. Chicago, Ill.

LEONI, F.
1915. Jan. 4. "L'Oracolo" opera. New York, N. Y.

LEPS, W.
1905. Dec. "Andon." Philadelphia, Pa.

LEROUX, X.
1919. Jan. 24. "La Reine Fiamette" opera. New York, N. Y.
1919. Jan. 25. "Le Chemineau" opera. Chicago, Ill.

LIADOF, A. C.
   1905. Oct. 27. "Baba Jaga" symphonic poem. Philadelphia, Pa.
   1910. Nov. 16. "Le Lac Enchanté" legend. New York, N. Y.
   1910. Nov. 16. "Kikimora" folktale. New York, N. Y.

LIAPONOF, S. M.
   1907. Dec. 7. Pianoforte Concerto. New York, N. Y.
   1917. Nov. 17. Second Concerto. New York, N. Y.

LINDNER, A.
   1888. Dec. 29. Violoncello Concerto (Op. 34). Boston, Mass.

LISZT, F.
   1859. April 20. "Les Préludes" symphonic poem, New York, N. Y.
   1860. Mar. 3. "Feste-Klänge" symphonic poem. Boston, Mass.
   1860. Mar. 24. "Tasso" symphonic poem. New York, N. Y.
   1861. Jan. 9. "Ce qu'on entend sur le montagne" symphonic poem. New York, N. Y.
   1862. April 26. "Orpheus" symphonic poem. New York, N. Y.
   1864. Jan 30. "Faust Symphonie." New York, N. Y.
   1865. Nov. 11. "Mazeppa." New York, N. Y.
   1865. Dec. 2. First Pianoforte Concerto (E flat). New York, N. Y.
   1866. Nov. 17. "Nächtliche Zug" from "Faust." New York, N. Y.
   1866. Dec. 8. "Mefisto Waltz." Brooklyn, N. Y.
   1867. July 5. "Vom Fels zum Meer" march. New York, N. Y.
   1868. Jan. 11. "Die Ideale" symphonic poem. New York, N. Y.
   1868. April 18. "Héroïde Funèbre" symphonic poem. New York, N. Y.
   1869. April 3. "Prometheus" symphonic poem. New York, N. Y.

1870. May 9. "Goethe March." New York, N. Y.
1872. Dec. 3. " Hunnenschlacht " symphonic poem. Boston, Mass.
1873. Jan. 18. " Hirtengesang " from " Christus." New York, N. Y.
1875. May 27. First " Rhapsodie Hongroise." New York, N. Y.
1875. June 22. Sixth " Rhapsodie Hongroise " (Pester Carneval). New York, N. Y.
1876. Feb. 28. " Christus " oratorio (1st part). New York, N. Y.
1880. Nov. 19. " Divina Commedia," symphony (1st part). Boston, Mass.
1882. July 18. Second " Mefisto Waltz." Chicago, Ill.
1883. Nov. 3. " Rhapsodie Hongroise " (in D). Boston, Mass.
1884. Feb. 9. Third suite " Roma." Boston, Mass.
1884. Feb. 23. Second Pianoforte Concerto (A). Boston, Mass.
1886. Mar. 16. Pianoforte Concerto " Pathétique." New York, N. Y.
1888. Feb. 24. " O Salutaris " psalm. New York, N. Y.
1888. Nov. 10. " St. Francis Assisi's Sermon to the Birds." New York, N. Y.
1891. Nov. 5. " Hungaria " symphonic poem. Boston, Mass.
1894. Jan. 27. " Espagnole " rhapsodie. Boston, Mass.
1902. Jan. 11. " Tödten-Tanz " pianoforte concerto. Boston, Mass.
1911. Dec. 11. " Legend of St. Elizabeth " oratorio. New York, N. Y.
1917. Dec. 6. Twenty-third Psalm. New York, N. Y.
1918. Jan. 3. " St. Elizabeth " opera. New York, N. Y.

LITOLFF, H. C.
1892. Jan. 6. Overture to " King Lear." Boston, Mass.

LOEFFLER, C. M.
1891. Nov. 21. "Les Veillées de l'Ukraine " suite. Boston, Mass.

1894. Feb. 3. Concerto Fantastique (cello). Boston, Mass.
1895. Jan. 5. Divertissement in A minor. Boston, Mass.
1898. Jan. 8. "Le Mort de Tintagiles" symphonic poem. Boston, Mass.
1901. Jan. 29. "Divertissement Espagnol" for saxophone and orchestra. Boston, Mass.
1902. Feb. 28. "By the Waters of Babylon." Boston, Mass.
1902. April 12. Two Poems for Orchestra. Boston, Mass.
1907. Nov. 23. "A Pagan Poem." Boston, Mass.
1916. June. "Hora Mystica" symphony. Norfolk, Conn.

LONGY, G.
1903. Jan. 7. "Impression." Boston, Mass.

LOOMIS, C.
1915. Nov. 9. Pianoforte Concerto. Chicago, Ill.

LUIGINI.
1901. Jan. 23. "La Voix des Cloches." Boston, Mass.

MacCUNN, H.
1892. Nov. 11. "Land of the Mountain and the Flood." Chicago, Ill.

MacDOWELL, E.
1888. April 3. First Pianoforte Concerto (A minor). Boston, Mass.
1889. Mar. 5. Second Pianoforte Concerto (B minor). New York, N. Y.
1890. Jan 11. "Lancelot and Elaine" symphonic poem. Boston, Mass.
1891. Sept. 24. Suite in A minor (Op. 42). Worcester, Mass.
1896. Jan. 23. "Indian Suite." New York, N. Y.
1908. Oct. 24. "Lamia" symphonic poem. Boston, Mass.

MACKENZIE, A.
1883. Mar. 3. "Bobbie Burns" Scotch rhapsody. Brooklyn, N. Y.
1885. April 16. "The Rose of Sharon" oratorio. New York, N. Y.
1887. Feb. 19. "La Belle Dame sans Merci" ballad. Boston, Mass.

1889. Mar. 9. "Twelfth Night" overture. New York, N. Y.
1889. Mar. 14. "Benedictus." New York, N. Y.
1895. Jan. 25. "Britannia" overture. Chicago, Ill.
1898. Oct. 21. Three Dances from "The Little Minister." Chicago. Ill.
1901. Sept. 27. "Coriolanus" suite. Worcester, Mass.
1903. Jan. 31. "Pibroch" suite. Boston, Mass.

MAGNARD, A.
1905. Dec. 4. "Chant Funèbre." Philadelphia, Pa.
1919. April 11. "Hymne à la Justice." Boston, Mass.

MAHLER, G.
1904. Nov. 6. Fourth Symphony (G). New York, N. Y.
1905. Mar. 25. Fifth Symphony. Cincinnati, O.
1908. Dec. 8. Second Symphony. New York, N. Y.
1909. Dec. 16. First Symphony. New York, N. Y.
1916. Mar. 3. Eighth Symphony. Philadelphia, Pa.
1916. Dec. 14. "Lied von Erde." Philadelphia, Pa.

MALIPIERO, G. F.
1919. April 4. "Pause del Silenzio." Boston, Mass.
1920. Dec. 23. "Impression del Vero." Boston, Mass.
1921. Jan. 10. Grottesco. New York, N. Y.

MANCINELLI, L.
1899. Mar. 10. "Ero e Leandro" opera. New York, N. Y.

MANDL, R.
1911. Mar. 4. Overture to a Gascony Comedy. Boston, Mass.

MAQUARRE, A.
1909. Mar. 27. "On the Sea Cliffs" overture. Boston, Mass.

MARINUZZI, G.
1920. Nov. 17. "Jacquerie" opera. Chicago, Ill.

MARSCHNER, H.
1895. Mar. 23. Overture to "Hans Heiling." Boston, Mass.

MASCAGNI, P.
1891. Sept. 9. "Cavalleria Rusticana" opera. Philadelphia, Pa.

1893. Jan. 31. "L'Amico Fritz" opera. New York, N. Y.
1902. Oct. 8. "Zanetto" opera. New York, N. Y.
1902. Oct. 16. "Iris" opera. New York, N. Y.
1917. Nov. 12. "Isabeau" opera. Chicago, Ill.
1918. Jan. 12. "Lodoletta" opera. New York, N. Y.

MASON, D. G.
1916. Feb. 18. First Symphony (C minor). Philadelphia, Pa.
1914. Nov. 16. Four Songs (baritone and orchestra). Chicago, Ill.
1921. Mar. 4. Prelude and Fugue. Chicago, Ill.

MASSÉ, V.
1861. Oct. 25. "The Marriage of Jeannette" opera. Philadelphia, Pa.
1886. Dec. 30. "Galatea" opera. Brooklyn, N. Y.

MASSENET, J.
1874. July 29. "Scènes Pittoresques." New York, N. Y.
1877. July 20. Variations. Chicago, Ill.
1882. Feb. 18. "Phèdre" overture. Boston, Mass.
1883. Jan. 20. "Scènes Alsaciennes." Boston, Mass.
1884. Mar. 8. "Les Erinnyes" entr'acte and finale. Boston, Mass.
1885. Dec. 23. "Manon" opera. New York, N. Y.
1886. Oct. 26. "Marche Héroique." New York, N. Y.
1886. Oct. 28. "La Vierge" for Strings. New York, N. Y.
1891. Feb. 5. "Eve" cantata. New York, N. Y.
1891. April 15. "Esclarmonde" suite. Chicago, Ill.
1892. Feb. 13. "Hérodiade" opera. New Orleans La.
1894. April 20. "Werther" opera. New York, N. Y.
1895. Nov. 15. "Thaïs" ballet music. Chicago, Ill.
1895. Dec. 11. "La Navarraise" opera. New York, N. Y.
1896. Nov. 7. "Sevigliana" from "Don César de Bazan." Boston, Mass.
1897. Feb. 12. "Le Cid" opera. New York, N. Y.
1897. Dec. 13. "Le Portrait de Manon" opera. New York, N. Y.

1902. April 8. "The Promised Land." Boston, Mass.
1902. Dec. 23. "Cendrillon" opera. New Orleans, La.
1904. Nov. 27. Hungarian Scenes. Boston, Mass.
1906. Jan. 2. "Pastorale Mystique" from "Le Jongleur." Boston, Mass.
1907. Nov. 25. "Thaïs" opera. New York, N. Y.
1908. Nov. 27. "Le Jongleur de Notre Dame" opera. New York, N. Y.
1909. Nov. 15. "Sappho" opera. New York, N Y.
1910. Jan. 10. "Griselidis" opera. New York, N. Y.
1912. Jan. 27. "Don Quichotte" opera. New Orleans, La.
1916. Jan. 10. "Cléopâtre" opera. Chicago, Ill.

MÉHUL, E.
1807. "Une Folie" opera. New Orleans, La.
1877. July 5. "Horatio Cocles" overture. Chicago, Ill.

MENDELSSOHN, F.
1838. "St. Paul" oratorio. New York, N. Y.
1840. "Elijah" oratorio. Boston, Mass.
1844. Nov. 16. "The Hebrides" overture. New York, N. Y.
1845. April 19. "Melusine" overture. New York, N. Y.
1845. Nov. 22. "Scotch Symphony." New York, N. Y.
1846. Jan. 17. Pianoforte Concerto (G minor). New York, N. Y.
1848. April 14. "Midsummer Night's Dream" Music. New York, N. Y.
1849. Nov. 24. Violin Concerto. New York, N. Y.
1850. Jan. 12. "Meerstille" overture. New York, N. Y.
1850. Jan. 12. Capriccio Brillante. New York, N. Y.
1851. Nov. 15. "Italian Symphony." Boston, Mass.
1852. April 17. Pianoforte Concerto (D minor). New York, N. Y.
1860. Mar. 3. "Die Weihe des Hauses" overture. Boston, Mass.
1861. April 20. First Walpurgis Night. New York, N. Y.
1862. Jan. 30. "Hymn of Praise." Boston, Mass.
1867. Nov. 9. "Trumpet Overture." Brooklyn, N. Y.

1869. Feb. 6. "Reformation Symphony." New York, N. Y.
1870. Feb. 22. "Ruy Blas" overture. Boston, Mass.
1875. May 1. "The Wedding of Camacho." Chicago, Ill.
1880. Jan. 27. "Lauda Zion." New York, N. Y.
1887. Jan. 27. "Athalie." Boston, Mass.

MERCADANTE, F. S.
1832. Oct. 19. "Elise e Claudio" opera. New York, N. Y.
1847. Feb. 14. "Il Guiramento" opera. New York, N. Y.

MESSAGER, A.
1920. Jan. 19. "Madame Chrysanthème" opera. Chicago, Ill.

MEYERBEER, G.
1834. April 7. "Roberto" opera. New York, N. Y.
1839. April 29. "Les Huguenots" opera. New Orleans, La.
1850. April 1. "L'Etoile du Nord" opera. New Orleans, La.
1850. April 2. "Il Profeta" opera. New Orleans, La.
1862. Nov. 24. "Dinorah" opera. New York, N. Y.
1865. Dec. 1. "L'Africaine" opera. New York, N. Y.
1874. Jan. 28. Inauguration March. New York, N. Y.
1880. Feb. 28. "Struensee Music." New York, N. Y.

MINETTI, C.
1915. Nov. 9. Prize Aria for tenor and orchestra. Chicago, Ill.

MLYNARSKY, E.
1906. Mar. 17. Violin Concerto. New York, N. Y.

MOLIQUE, B.
1867. April 13. Violoncello Concerto. Brooklyn, N. Y.

MONSIGNY, P. A.
1790-1800. "Le Deserteur" opera. New Orleans, La.

MONTEMEZZI, I.
1914. Jan. 2. "L'Amore dei Tre Rè" opera. New York, N. Y.
1919. Nov. 18. "La Nave" opera. Chicago, Ill.

MONTEVERDE, C.
1912. April 14. "Orfeo" opera in concert form. New York, N. Y.

MOÓR, E.
1908. April 18. Pianoforte Concerto (Op. 57). Boston, Mass.
1921. Mar. 5. Concerto for String Quartet. Chicago, Ill.

MOREAU, L.
1910. April 19. Pastorale. Boston, Mass.

MORRIS, H.
1919. Mar. 6. Tone Poem. New York, N. Y.

MOSZKOWSKI, M.
1887. Mar. 23. First Suite. New York, N. Y.
1890. Nov. 15. Second Suite. New York, N. Y.
1892. Oct. 21. "Boabdil" music of. Chicago, Ill
1893. Jan. 24. "Boabdil" opera. New York, N. Y.
1894. Feb. 23. Torchlight Dance. Chicago, Ill.
1907. Mar. 16. "The Steppe" symphonic poem. Boston, Mass.
1910. Feb. 20. Third Suite. New York, N. Y.

MOZART, W. A.
1823. May 3. "Le Nozze di Figaro" opera in English. New York, N. Y.
1826. May 23. "Don Giovanni" opera. New York, N. Y.
1832. Mar. 7. "Die Zauberflöte" opera. Philadelphia, Pa.
1844. Jan. 15. "Jupiter Symphony." New York, N. Y.
1847. Nov. 14. Third Symphony (E flat major). New York, N. Y.
1850. Dec. 21. Symphony in G minor. Boston, Mass.
1856. Symphony in D major. New York, N. Y.
1857. Jan. 18. Requiem. Boston, Mass
1858. Nov. 23. "Le Nozze di Figaro" (Italian). New York, N. Y.
1859. Feb. 26. Pianoforte Concerto in E flat. Boston, Mass.
1861. Mar. 16. Eighth Pianoforte Concerto (D). New York, N. Y.

1862. Oct. 10. "Die Entführung aus dem Serail" opera. New York, N. Y.
1865. April 8. Symphony Concertante (piano, violin and viola). New York, N. Y.
1866. Feb. 10. Concerto for Two Pianos (E flat). New York, N. Y.
1866. Aug. 29. Andante, Variations, Minuetto. New York, N. Y.
1866. Aug. 29. Turkish March. New York, N. Y.
1868. Dec. 12. First Three Motets. New York, N. Y.
1870. Feb. 17. Second Pianoforte Concerto (D minor). Boston, Mass.
1870. Nov. 12. "Die Schauspieldirektor" opera. New York, N. Y.
1871. May 7. Overture to "Idomeneo." New York, N. Y.
1871. Nov. 23. Symphony in C. Boston, Mass.
1872. Mar. 7. Seventh Pianoforte Concerto (C minor). Boston, Mass.
1873. Mar. 13. Pianoforte Concerto in A. Boston, Mass.
1875. Aug. 5. Intermezzo and Fugue for strings. New York, N. Y.
1878. Dec. 19. Pianoforte Concerto in A major. Boston, Mass.
1881. Mar. 24. Andante and Finale (Serenade No. 12). Boston, Mass.
1881. April 1. Nocturno from Serenade (Op. 8). New York, N. Y.
1884. Jan. 12. Concerto for flute and harp. Boston, Mass.
1885. Nov. 14. "Haffner Serenade." Boston, Mass.
1888. Mar. 17. Violoncello Concerto (Op. 193). New York, N. Y.
1895. Oct. 19. Andante and Variations (D minor). Boston, Mass.
1897. Mar. 24. Symphony in A major. New York, N. Y.
1902. April 1. Adagio and Minuet. New York, N. Y.
1908. Jan. 18. Three German Dances. Boston, Mass.
1909. Nov. 7. "Les Petits Riens" ballet music. New York, N. Y.

1910. Nov. 26. Adagio and Fugue for strings. Boston, Mass.
1917. Oct. 26. "Bastien et Bastienne" operetta. New York, N. Y.

MRACZEK, J. C.
1912. Mar. 15. Symphonic Burlesque. Boston, Mass.

MUÉLLER-BERGHAUS, K.
1883. Dec. 1. Romance for violoncello. Boston, Mass.

MUSSORGSKY, M. P.
1893. June. "Une Nuit sur le Mont Chauvée," Chicago, Ill.
1905. Feb. 25. "Khovanstchina" excerpts from opera. New York, N. Y.
1913. Mar. 8. "Boris Godunof" opera. New York, N. Y.

NESSLER, V. E.
1887. Nov. 23. "Der Trompeter von Säkkingen" opera. New York, N. Y.

NEVIN, A.
1914. Aug. 20. "Love Dreams" suite. Peterboro, N. H.
1918. Jan. 5. "The Daughter of the Forest" opera. Chicago, Ill.

NICODÉ, J. L.
1885. Jan. 10. Symphonic Variations (Op. 27). New York, N. Y.
1886. Oct. 26. Jubilee March. New York, N. Y.

NICOLAI, O.
1858. Jan. 9. "The Merry Wives of Windsor" opera. New York, N. Y.
1909. Jan. 2. Religious Festival Overture. Boston, Mass.

NOREN, H. G.
1908. Dec. 12. "Kaleidoscope" theme and variations. Boston, Mass.
1917. April 20. "Vita" symphony. Boston, Mass.

NOUGUÉ, J.
1911. Mar. 25. "Quo Vadis" opera. Philadelphia, Pa.

NOVAK, V.
  1919. Nov. 13. "In the Tatra Mountains" symphonic poem. New York, N. Y.

OFFENBACH, J.
  1867. April "La Grande Duchesse" opera bouffe. New York, N. Y.
  1882. Oct. 16. "Les Contes d'Hoffman" opera. New York, N. Y.

OLDBERG, A.
  1907. Jan. 17. "Paolo and Francesca" overture. Chicago, Ill.
  1912. May. Symphonic Variations. Evanston, Ill.

PACINI, G.
  1834. July 12. "Gli Arabi nelli Gallie" opera. New York, N. Y.
  1847. June 12. "Saffo" opera. New York, N. Y.
  1860. Sept. 27. "Medea" opera. New York, N. Y.

PADEREWSKI, I. J.
  1891. Mar. 14. Pianoforte Concerto (A minor). Boston, Mass.
  1895. Nov. 4. Polish Fantasia. New York, N. Y.
  1902. Feb. 14. "Manru" opera. New York, N. Y.
  1909. Feb. 13. Symphony (B minor). Boston, Mass.

PAGANINI, N.
  1898. Jan. 15. Caprice in A minor, for violin. Boston, Mass.

PAINE, J. K.
  1873. June. "St. Peter" oratorio. Portland, Me.
  1876. Jan. 26. First Symphony. Boston, Mass.
  1876. May 11. Centennial Hymn. Philadelphia, Pa.
  1880. Mar. 10. "Spring Symphony." Cambridge, Mass.
  1883. Mar. 10. "The Tempest" symphonic poem. Boston, Mass.
  1883. May 2. "The Nativity" oratorio. Boston, Mass.
  1889. April 20. "An Island Fantasy." Boston, Mass.
  1892. Oct. 22. Columbus March and Hymn. Chicago, Ill.
  1900. Mar. 10. "Azara" ballet music. Boston, Mass.
  1907. April 9. "Azara" opera. Boston, Mass.

PAISIELLO, G.
  1794. " Il Barbiere di Seviglia " opera. Baltimore, Md.
PALMGREN, S.
  1917. Nov. 30. Second Symphony. Chicago, Ill.
PARKER, H. W.
  1886. Jan. 30. Scherzo for orchestra. New York, N. Y.
  1890. Dec. 10. " Count de Paris " overture. New York, N. Y.
  1893. May 3. " Hora Novissima " oratorio. New York, N. Y.
  1895. Mar. 30. Rhapsody for baritone and orchestra. Boston, Mass.
  1898. April 15. " St. Christopher " oratorio. New York, N. Y.
  1899. Dec. 30. " Northern Ballad." Boston, Mass.
  1902. Dec. 27. Organ Concerto (E flat). Boston, Mass.
  1908. June. Ballad for chorus and orchestra. Norfolk, Conn.
  1911. Mar. 14. " Mona " opera. New York, N. Y.
  1911. June. " Collegiate " overture. Norfolk, Conn.
  1915. July. 1. " Fairyland." Los Angeles, Cal.
  1918. Jan. 5. " Dream of Mary " cantata. Norfolk, Conn.
PARKER, J. C. D.
  1877. May 17. " Redemption Hymn " oratorio. Boston, Mass.
  1890. April 8. " St. John " oratorio. Boston, Mass.
  1895. April 14. " The Life of Man " oratorio. Boston, Mass.
PAULY, F.
  1914. April 2. Pianoforte Concerto (E flat). Minneapolis, Minn.
PAUR, E.
  1909. Jan. 15. Symphony (A major). Pittsburgh, Pa.
PELLESIER
  1796. Dec. 19. " Edwin and Angelina " ballad opera. New York, N. Y.
  1799. " The Vintage " ballad opera. New York, N. Y.

PERELLI, A.
  1911. Mar. 6. "A Lover's Quarrel" opera. Philadelphia, Pa.
PERI, A.
  1863. Nov. 11. "Judith" opera. New York, N. Y.
PERKINS, C. C.
  1850. Mar. 23. Grand Symphony. Boston, Mass.
  1855. Feb. 17. The Pilgrim's Cantata. Boston, Mass.
PEROSI, L.
  1899. April 24. "The Transfiguration" opera. Boston, Mass.
PESSARD, F.
  1900. Feb. 11. "Danses Espagnoles." Boston, Mass.
PETRELLA, E.
  1863. Mar. 7. "Ione" opera. New York, N. Y.
  1867. April 3. "Il Carnival de Venezia" opera. New York, N. Y.
PFITZNER, H.
  1907. Nov. 15. "Christelflein" overture. Boston, Mass.
PHELPS, E. C.
  1880. May 10. "Hiawatha" symphony. New York, N. Y.
  1885. Mar. 31. "American Legend." New York, N. Y.
  1889. Aug. "Elegy." Brighton Beach, N. Y.
  1890. Dec. 10. "Meditation." New York, N. Y.
PICK–MANGIALLI
  1920. Dec. 2. "Il Carillon Magico." New York, N. Y.
PIERNÉ, G.
  1906. Dec. 4. "La Croisade des Enfants" (The Children's Crusade) oratorio. New York, N. Y.
  1908. Dec. 19. "Les Enfants à Béthléem" ("The Children at Bethlehem) oratorio. New York, N. Y.
  1910. Jan. 26. "Ramuntcho." Boston, Mass.
  1913. Oct. 2. "St. Francis d'Assisi" oratorio. Worcester, Mass.
PIZETTI, I.
  1919. April 9. "Fedra" prelude to Act. I. Philadelphia, Pa.

PONCHIELLI, A.
 1871. Dec. 20. " La Gioconda " opera. New York, N. Y.
POWELL, J.
 1918. Mar. 3. " The Fair " suite. New York, N. Y.
PRAEGER, F. C. W.
 1888. April 14. " Life and Love, Battle and Victory " symphonic poem. New York, N. Y.
PRATT, S.
 1886. Mar. 23. " Court Minuet." New York, N. Y.
PROKOFIEV, S.
 1918. Dec. 6. First Pianoforte Concerto. Chicago, Ill.
 1918. Dec. 6. " Scythian Suite." Chicago, Ill.
 1919. Dec. 11. Classical Symphony. New York, N. Y.
 1921. Dec. 30. " Love for Three Oranges " opera. Chicago, Ill.
PUCCINI, G.
 1894. Aug. 29. " Manon Lescaut " opera. Philadelphia, Pa.
 1898. May 16. " La Bohème " opera. San Francisco, Cal.
 1901. Feb. 4. " La Tosca " opera. New York, N. Y.
 1906. Nov. 12. " Madama Butterfly " opera. Washington, D. C.
 1908. Dec. 17. " Le Villi " opera. New York, N. Y.
 1910. Dec. 10. " La Fanciulla " (The Girl of the Golden West) opera. New York, N. Y.
 1918. Dec. 14. " Il Tabarro " opera. New York, N. Y.
 1918. Dec. 14. " Gianni Schecchi " opera. New York, N. Y.
 1918. Dec. 14. " Suor Angelica " opera. New York, N. Y.
RABAUD, H.
 1900. Nov. 30. " La Procession Nocturne " symphonic poem. Cincinnati, O.
 1902. April 1. Fantasia sur Chansons Russes. Boston, Mass.
 1904. Jan. 5. " Poëme Virgilien." Boston, Mass.
 1908. Jan. 21. Second Symphony. Boston, Mass.
 1917. Dec. 19. " Marouf " opera. New York, N. Y.

RACHMANINOF, S. V.
  1903. "The Cliff" tone poem. New York, N. Y.
  1904. Nov. 19. Dances from "Aleko." New York, N. Y.
  1904. Dec. 17. Pianoforte Concerto (F sharp minor). Boston, Mass.
  1905. Nov. 18. Second Pianoforte Concerto. New York, N. Y.
  1906. Dec. 20. "Tzigane" capriccio. New York, N. Y.
  1909. Jan. 14. Second Symphony (E minor). New York, N. Y.
  1909. Nov. 28. Third Pianoforte Concerto. New York, N. Y.
  1909. Dec. 3. "The Isle of the Dead" tone poem. Chicago, Ill.
  1911. Feb. 16. Fantasia (pianoforte and orchestra). New York, N. Y.
  1918. Jan. 19. "Veralize." New York, N. Y.
  1919. Jan. 28. First Pianoforte Concerto. New York, N. Y.
  1920. Feb. 6. Third Symphony "The Bells." Philadelphia, Pa.

RAFF, J.
  1865. Feb. 18. "An Das Vaterland" symphony. New York, N. Y.
  1867. Jan. 12. Second Suite (C. Op. 101). New York, N. Y.
  1870. Jan. 8. Second Symphony (C). New York, N. Y.
  1871. Dec. 6. Third Symphony (F). Boston, Mass.
  1872. Aug. 1. "Dame Kobold" overture. New York, N. Y.
  1872. Dec. 14. Fourth Symphony (G). New York, N. Y.
  1873. Dec. 5. Fifth Symphony "Lenore" (E). Boston, Mass.
  1874. Nov. 14. Pianoforte Concerto (Op. 185). New York, N. Y.
  1875. Jan. 8. Sixth Symphony (D minor). New York, N. Y.
  1875. June 24. Sinfonietta for wind instruments. New York, N. Y.

1876. Feb. 26. Suite in F. New York, N. Y.
1877. Nov. 20. Suite for pianoforte and orchestra. New York, N. Y.
1882. Jan. 29. " Die Tagenzeiten " (piano, chorus and orchestra). New York, N. Y.
1886. Mar. 20. " Die Jahreszeiten." Brooklyn, N. Y.
1886. Nov. 4. Festival March. New York, N. Y.
1890. Nov. 20. " Romeo and Juliet " overture. Boston, Mass.

RAMEAU, J. P.
1877. July 20. " Romaneska." Chicago, Ill.
1885. Feb. 7. Gavotte, Tambourine, and Minuet from " Castor and Pollux." New York, N. Y.
1895. Nov. 1. Suite de Ballet " Acanthe and Cèphise." New York, N. Y.
1900. April 7. Ballet Suite. Boston, Mass.
1904. April 11. " Les Indes Galantes " ballet. Boston, Mass.

RAVEL, M.
1909. Nov. 12. Rhapsodie Espagnole. Chicago, Ill.
1912. Nov. 8. " Ma Mère l'Oye " suite. New York, N. Y.
1913. Dec. 27. " Juon " fantasy. Boston, Mass.
1913. Dec. 27. " Vaegtervise " (Watchman's Song). Boston, Mass.
1914. Nov. 29. " Daphnis and Chloe " (symphonic fragments). New York, N. Y.
1915. Oct. 22. " Daphnis and Chloe " (more fragments). New York, N. Y.
1916. Oct. 26. " Valses Nobles et Sentimentales." New York, N. Y.
1916. Dec. 3. Intermezzo and Allegro for harp and orchestra. New York, N. Y.
1920. Jan. 5. " L'Heure Espagnol " opera. Chicago, Ill.
1921. Feb. 1. " Alborada del Gracioso." Boston, Mass.
1921. Oct. 28. " La Valse." San Francisco, Cal.

REGER, M.
1907. April 13. Serenade (Op. 95). Boston, Mass.

1907. Dec. 20. Variations and Fugue (Op. 100). Philadelphia, Pa.
1908. April 7. Violin Sonata (unaccompanied). New York, N. Y.
1909. Oct. 16. Prologue to a Tragedy. Boston, Mass.
1911. Sept. 27. "The Nuns." Worcester, Mass.
1911. Oct. 7. A Comedy Overture. Boston, Mass.
1912. April 7. "Romantic Suite." New York, N. Y.
1912. April 7. "Ballet Suite." New York, N. Y.
1912. Nov. 19. Concerto in Ancient Style. New York, N. Y.
1915. Mar. 27. First Tone Poem (Op. 126). Boston, Mass.

REINECKE, C.
1868. May 24. "King Manfred" overture. New York, N. Y.
1871. June 13. Festival Overture. New York, N. Y.
1872. Jan. 6. Pianoforte Concerto (F sharp minor). New York, N. Y.
1874. Aug. 13. "In Memoriam." New York, N. Y.
1887. Nov. 12. "Ein Feste Burg" variations. New York, N. Y.
1895. Mar. 23. "Der Gouverneur von Tours" entr'acte. Boston, Mass.

REINHOLD, H.
1883. Jan. 10. Concert Overture. New York, N. Y.
1886. Jan. 23. Prelude, Minuet and Fugue, for Strings. Boston, Mass.

RESPIGHI, O.
1919. Feb. 13. "Fontana di Roma" symphonic poem. New York, N. Y.
1921. Feb. 3. Four Songs of the Sixteenth Century. New York, N. Y.

REYER, L.
1888. Dec. 8. "The Waking of the Valkyrie." New York, N. Y.
1891. Dec. 25. "Sigurd" opera. New Orleans, La.
1900. Jan. 25. "Salammbo" opera. New Orleans, La.

REZNICEK, E. N. von
  1895. Dec. 7. "Donna Diana" overture. Boston, Mass.
  1907. Nov. 23. Adagio, Scherzo, and Finale from Suite in E minor. Boston, Mass.
  1914. April 25. "Schlemihl" symphonic poem. Boston, Mass.

RHEINBERGER, J.
  1871. Aug. 10. "Wallenstein's Camp." New York, N. Y.
  1881. Mar. 11. "Demetrius" oratorio. New York, N. Y.
  1883. Jan. 31. Symphony in F. Boston, Mass.
  1888. April 14. Passacaglia. New York, N. Y.
  1895. Feb. 22. Organ Concerto in G minor. Chicago, Ill.

RHENÉ-BATON
  1911. Jan. 25. Variations. Boston, Mass.

RIEMENSCHNEIDER, A.
  1893. Mar. 4. "Tödtentanz." Boston, Mass.

RICCI, L.
  1844. Oct. "Chiara de Rosenberg" opera. New York, N. Y.

RIESENFELD, H.
  1920. Feb. 6. Overture in Romantic Style. New York, N. Y.

RIMSKY-KORSAKOF, N. A.
  1891. Dec. 8. Second Symphony "Antar." New York, N. Y.
  1897. Jan. 8. "Mlada" suite. Chicago, Ill.
  1897. April 17. "Scheherazade" suite. Boston, Mass.
  1897. Oct. 23. "La Grande Paque Russe" overture. Boston, Mass.
  1901. Jan. 11. Fantaisie de Concert. New York, N. Y.
  1902. Nov. 15. "To the Betrothed of the Tsar" overture. Boston, Mass.
  1904. Nov. 19. "Mlada" third act from ballet. New York, N. Y.
  1904. Dec. 24. "May Night" overture. New York, N. Y.
  1905. Jan. 21. "Tsar-Saltan" suite. New York, N. Y.

1905. Feb. 3. Pianoforte Concerto (C sharp minor). Philadelphia, Pa.
1905. Mar. 25. "Sadko" musical picture. Boston, Mass.
1905. Nov. 18. "Snow Maiden" suite. New York, N. Y.
1908. Feb. 15. Caprice on Spanish Themes. Boston, Mass.
1909. Nov. 7. Russian Song. New York, N. Y.
1916. Feb. 17. Serbian Fantaisie. New York, N. Y.
1918. Jan. 19. "Le Coq d'Or" four tableaux. New York, N. Y.
1918. Mar. 6. "Le Coq d'Or" opera. New York, N. Y.

RITTER, A.
1903. Jan. 30. "Olaf's Wedding Dance" symphonic waltz. Chicago, Ill.

RITTER, F. L.
1867. Dec. 21. "Othello" overture. New York, N. Y.
1881. Feb. 17. Second Symphony. Boston, Mass.

ROENTGEN, J.
1896. Dec. 11. Ballad on Norwegian Folk Song. Chicago, Ill.

ROGERS, B.
1919. Nov. 13. "To the Fallen" dirge. New York, N. Y.

ROPARTZ, J. G.
1905. April 29. Fantaisia (D major). Boston, Mass.
1914. Feb. 12. "La Chasse du Prince Arthur" symphonic poem. New York, N. Y.
1914. Oct. 24. Fourth Symphony (C major). Boston, Mass.
1920. Oct. 22. "Divertissement." Boston, Mass.

ROSSINI, G. A.
1819. "The Barber of Seville" (English). New York, N. Y.
1825. Nov. 26. "Il Barbiere di Seviglia" (Italian). New York, N. Y.
1825. Dec. 31. "Tancredi" opera. New York, N. Y.
1826. "Il Turco in Italia" opera. New York, N. Y.
1826. "La Cenerentola" opera. New York, N. Y.
1826. April 25. "Semiramide" opera. New York, N. Y.

1832. "L'Inganno Felice" opera. New York, N. Y.
1832. Nov. 5. "L'Italiana in Algieri." opera. New York, N. Y.
1832. Dec. 22. "Mosè in Egitto" opera. New York, N. Y.
1833. Mar. 13–20. "Otello" opera. New York, N. Y.
1833. Nov. 18. "La Gazza Ladra" opera. New York, N. Y.
1834. Mar. 21. "La Donna del Lago" opera. New York, N. Y.
1834. Mar. 24. "Matilda de Shabran" opera. New York, N. Y.
1834. Nov. 25. "Edouardo e Cristina" opera. New York, N. Y.
1835. Feb. 6. "L'Assedio di Corinto" opera. New York, N. Y.
1842. Dec. 13. "Guillaume Tell" opera. New Orleans, La.
1843. Feb. 26. "Stabat Mater." Boston, Mass.
1871. May 3. "Messe Solennelle." Boston, Mass.

ROUSSEL, A.
1912. Mar. 11. "Poëme de la Fôrét." Boston, Mass.
1914. Jan. 2. "La Ville Rose" Evocation. Philadelphia, Pa.
1914. Oct. 23. "La Festin de l'Araignée." New York, N. Y.

ROUSSEAU
1790–1800. "Pygmalion." New Orleans, La.
1790–1800. "Devin du Village." New Orleans, La.

RUBINSTEIN, A.
1869. Jan. 16. "Faust" picture. New York, N. Y.
1871. Jan. 7. "Ocean" symphony (C). New York, N. Y.
1871. July 19. "Demitri Donskoï" overture. New York, N. Y.
1871. Dec. 2. Pianoforte Concerto (D minor). Boston, Mass.
1872. May. 30. "Don Quixote" humoresque. New York, N. Y.

1874. Jan. 24. "Ivan IV" character sketch. New York, N. Y.

1874. Sept. 17. Overture Triomphale. New York, N. Y.

1875. Mar. 4. Fourth Symphony "Dramatic" (D minor). New York, N. Y.

1881. April 2. "The Demon" ballet music. Boston, Mass.

1881. May 1. "The Tower of Babel" opera. New York, N. Y.

1881. July 16. "Nero" ballet music. New York, N. Y.

1881. Dec. 10. Fifth Symphony (G minor). New York, N. Y.

1882. Dec. 15. "La Russie" morceau symphonique. New York, N. Y.

1883. July. 18. "Bal Costumé" first series. Chicago, Ill.

1884. Dec. 20. "La Vigne" ballet music. Boston, Mass.

1885. April 28. "Fantasia Eroica." Brooklyn, N. Y.

1886. July 5. "Bal Costumé" second series. Chicago, Ill.

1887. Mar. 12. "Paradise Lost" sacred opera. Brooklyn, N. Y.

1887. Mar. 14. "Nero" opera. New York, N. Y.

1887. April 23. Sixth Symphony (A minor). New York, N. Y.

1888. Feb. 16. Second Violoncello Concerto. Philadelphia, Pa.

1891. Jan. 17. "Anthony and Cleopatra" overture. Brooklyn, N. Y.

1894. May 25. Second and third tableaux from "Moses." Cincinnati, O.

1905. April 1. Romance and Caprice Russe. New York, N. Y.

1908. Dec. 10. Pianoforte Fantasia in C major. New York, N. Y.

1908. Dec. 19. Fifth Pianoforte Concerto (E flat). Boston, Mass.

RUSSELL, L. A.

1887. Nov. 15. "Pastoral." New York, N. Y.

SAAR, V. L.

1916. April 23. "Suite Rococo." Cincinnati, O.

SABATA, V. di
- 1918. Dec. 8. Symphonic Suite. New York, N. Y.
- 1919. Mar. 23. "Juventus" symphonic poem. New York, N. Y.

SAINT-SAËNS
- 1874. May 21. Marche Héroique. New York, N. Y.
- 1875. June 3. "Le Rouet d'Omphale." New York, N. Y.
- 1876. Jan. 29. "Danse Macabre." New York, N. Y.
- 1876. Feb. 3. Second Pianoforte Concerto (G minor). Boston, Mass.
- 1876. Feb. 17. Violoncello Concerto (A minor). Boston, Mass.
- 1876. Oct. 9. "Phaeton" symphonic poem. New York, N. Y.
- 1877. Mar. 1. Third Pianoforte Concerto (E flat). Boston, Mass.
- 1877. Mar. 15. "Samson et Dalila" ballet music. St. Louis, Mo.
- 1877. July 24. Suite in B major (Op. 49). Chicago, Ill.
- 1877. Nov. 14. "La Jeunesse d'Hercule" symphonic poem. Boston, Mass.
- 1878. Feb. 14. Fourth Pianoforte Concerto (C). Boston, Mass.
- 1880. May 7. "Le Deluge" oratorio. Boston, Mass.
- 1881. Mar. 22. "Suite Algérienne." Boston, Mass.
- 1881. Dec. 1. Pianoforte Concerto. Boston, Mass.
- 1881. Dec. 6. "La Lyre et la Harpe" cantata. Providence, R. I.
- 1883. Dec. 22. "Henry VIII" ballet music. Boston, Mass.
- 1886. Jan. 2. "Rhapsodie d'Auvergne." Boston, Mass.
- 1887. Jan. 19. Third Symphony (C minor). New York, N. Y.
- 1890. Jan. 4. Third Violin Concerto (B minor). Boston, Mass.
- 1892. Oct. 22. Second Symphony (A minor). Boston, Mass.
- 1893. Jan. 4. "Samson et Dalila" opera. New Orleans, La.

1894. Feb. 7. Morceau de Concert. Boston, Mass.
1898. Mar. 7. Fifth Pianoforte Concerto (F). Chicago, Ill.
1900. April 27. "La Princesse Jaune." Boston, Mass.
1902. Oct. 31. "Les Barbares" overture. Chicago, Ill.
1904. Nov. 26. First Symphony (E flat). Boston, Mass.
1906. Nov. 3. "Africa" fantasia. New York, N. Y.
1909. Oct. 9. "La Fiancée du Timbalier" ballad. Boston, Mass.
1910. Oct. 6. "Occident and Orient" march. New York, N. Y.
1911. Jan. 25. Ouverture de Fête. Boston, Mass.
1912. Mar. 3. Hymn to Pallas Athene. New York, N. Y.
1915. Dec. 9. "Déjanire" opera. Chicago, Ill.

SALVIONI
1833. Mar. 22. "La Casa da Vendere" opera. New York, N. Y.

SATIE, E.
1905. Jan. 4. "Gymnopédies" (Nos. 1 and 2). Boston, Mass.

SAUER, E.
1908. Oct. 17. First Pianoforte Concerto. Boston, Mass.

SAXE COBURG GOTHA, DUKE OF
1891. Jan. 9. "Diana von Solange" opera. New York, N. Y.

SCHARWENKA, P.
1887. July 28. "Libesnacht" fantasie. Chicago, Ill.
1888. Jan. 28. "Arkadische" suite. New York, N. Y.
1892. Jan. 29. "Frühlingswagen." Chicago, Ill.

SCHARWENKA, X.
1883. Feb. 1. Pianoforte Concerto. New York, N. Y.
1885. Dec. 12. Symphony (C minor). New York, N. Y.
1896. Feb. 13. "Mataswintha," opera in concert form. New York, N. Y.
1907. April 1. "Mataswintha" opera stage performance. New York, N. Y.

1911. Feb. 11. Fourth Pianoforte Concerto (F minor). Boston, Mass.

SCHEINPFLUG, P.
1909. Jan. 23. Overture to a Comedy of Shakespeare. Boston, Mass.

SCHILLING, E.
1908. Jan. 25. Fantastic Suite for piano and orchestra. Boston, Mass.
1912. Oct. 30. Légende Symphonique. Philadelphia, Pa.
1915. Dec. 31. "Impressions" theme and variations. Boston, Mass.
1916. Oct. 20. Violin Concerto. Boston, Mass.

SCHILLINGS, M.
1902. Mar. 1. Symphonic Prologue to "Oedipus Rex." Boston, Mass.
1904. Nov. 11. "The Witch Song." Philadelphia, Pa.
1906. April 7. "The Piper's Holiday" prelude to Act III. Boston, Mass.
1909. Jan. 16. "The Harvest Festival" from "Moloch." Boston, Mass.
1910. Feb. 15. "Meerguss" symphonic fantasy. St. Paul, Minn.

SCHJELDERUP
1908. Feb. 15. "Sunrise on the Himalayas" symphonic poem. Boston, Mass.
1908. Feb. 15. "Summer Night on the Fjord" symphonic poem. Boston, Mass.

SCHMIDT, F.
1912. Mar. 11. Rhapsodie Viennoise. Boston, Mass.
1913. Nov. 11. Tragedy of Salome. Boston, Mass.
1913. Dec. 18. Psaume XLVI. Boston, Mass.
1916. Jan. 23. "Pupazzi." New York, N. Y.
1921. April 27. "Chant du Guerre." Boston, Mass.

SCHNEIDER, E. F.
1915. Aug. 7. "Apollo" opera. Bohemian Grove, Cal.

SCHNEIDER, F.
1854. April 22. Twentieth Symphony. New York, N. Y.

SCHOENBERG, A.
    1912. Oct. 30. Five Pieces for orchestra. Chicago, Ill.
    1915. Nov. 5. " Kammer Symphony." Philadelphia, Pa.
    1915. Nov. 18. " Pelléas et Mélisande " symphonic poem. New York, N. Y.

SCHOLTZ, B.
    1886. Mar. 13. Symphony in B flat. New York, N. Y.
    1893. Nov. 16 " Wanderings " suite. Chicago, Ill.

SCHUBERT, F.
    1851. Jan. 11. Symphony in C. New York, N. Y.
    1862. Mar. 8. Grand Fantasia. Boston, Mass.
    1866. Mar. 22. " Fierabras " overture. Boston, Mass.
    1866. Oct. 27. Reiter March. Brooklyn, N. Y.
    1867. Mar. 13. " Rosamunde " entr'acte. New York, N. Y.
    1867. July 7. " Rosamunde " overture. New York, N. Y.
    1867. Oct. 26. Unfinished Symphony. New York, N. Y.
    1868. Dec. 12. Twenty-third Psalm. New York, N. Y.
    1869. Feb. 6. Symphony in B minor. New York, N. Y.
    1869. May 12. " Italian Overture." New York, N. Y.
    1871. Aug. 17. March in B minor. New York, N. Y.
    1871. Nov. 9. " Alfonse and Estrella " overture. Boston, Mass.
    1875. May 27. Impromptu in C minor. New York, N. Y.
    1875. May 28. " Teufel's Lustschloss." New York, N. Y.
    1875. Aug. 10. Octet for Strings. New York, N. Y.
    1875. Aug. 20. Tenth Symphony (C). New York, N. Y.
    1875. Dec. 27. Pianoforte Sonata (orchestrated by Joachim). Boston, Mass.
    1876. Jan. 6. " Marche Héroique." Boston, Mass.
    1885. Oct. 31. " Trauermarsch." Boston, Mass.
    1888. Jan. 17. Divertissement à la Hongroise. New York, N. Y.
    1888. Nov. 24. Overture in F minor. Boston, Mass.
    1889. Mar. 30. Overture in B. Boston, Mass.

SCHULTZ, L.
    1904. American Festival Overture. St. Louis, Mo.
    1918. Dec. 3. American Rhapsody. New York, N. Y.

SCHUMANN, G.
1900. Oct. 19. Symphonic Variations. Chicago, Ill.
1903. Dec. 26. Variationen und Doppel Fugue. Chicago, Ill.
1910. Feb. 7. " Ruth " cantata. Chicago, Ill.

SCHUMANN, R.
1841. Mar. 31. First Symphony (B flat). Boston, Mass.
1848. April 11. " Paradise and the Peri." New York, N. Y.
1854. Jan. 14. Second Symphony (C). New York, N. Y.
1857. Feb. 7. Fourth Symphony (D minor). New York, N. Y.
1857. Nov. 21. " Manfred " overture. New York, N. Y.
1858. April 24. Overture, Scherzo and Finale. New York, N. Y.
1859. Mar. 26. Pianoforte Concerto (A minor). New York, N. Y.
1861. Feb. 2. Third Symphony (E flat). New York, N. Y.
1861. Mar. 16. " Genoveva " overture. New York, N. Y.
1865. April 8. " Die Braut von Messina " overture. New York, N. Y.
1866. Aug. 13. " Traumerei." New York, N. Y.
1869. May 8. " Manfred " music of. New York, N. Y.
1875. May 27. " Bilder aus Östen." New York, N. Y.
1875. Dec. 4. Concertstücke (Op. 92). New York, N. Y.
1881. Mar. 28. Scenes from " Faust." Boston, Mass.
1884. Nov. 22. Pictures from the Orient. Boston, Mass.
1886. Nov. 4. " Marche Funèbre." New York, N. Y.
1889. Mar. 28. Fantasia for violin. New York, N. Y.
1899. Mar. 13. " Gypsy Life." New York, N. Y.
1901. Mar. 30. " Julius Caesar " overture. Boston, Mass.
1903. Mar. 14. " The Dawn of Love " overture. Boston, Mass.
1904. Jan. 23. " In Carnival Time " suite. Boston, Mass.
1906. April 17. Two pieces in Canon Form. Boston, Mass.

SCHYTTE, L.
1886. July 21. " Pantomimes." Chicago, Ill.

SCOTT, C.
  1920. Nov. 5. Pianoforte Concerto in C. Philadelphia, Pa.
  1920. Nov. 5. Two Passacaglias. Philadelphia, Pa.

SCRIABIN, A
  1900. Dec. 2. Reverie. Cincinnati, O.
  1906. Dec. 20. Pianoforte Concerto. New York, N. Y.
  1907. Feb. 28. First Symphony. New York, N. Y.
  1907. Mar. 14. Third Symphony "Peace Divine." New York, N. Y.
  1908. Dec. 10. Fourth Symphony "Ecstacy." New York, N. Y.
  1915. Mar. 5. "Prometheus — Poem of Fire." New York, N. Y.

SEIFERT, U.
  1875. Jan. 15. Festival March. New York, N. Y.

SEROF, A. N.
  1906. Mar. 17. Cossack Dances. New York, N. Y.

SEVERN
  1915. Jan. 17. Violin Concerto. New York, N. Y.

SGAMBATI, G.
  1884. Dec. 6. Symphony in D major. New York, N. Y.
  1890. Nov. 1. Pianoforte Concerto (G minor). Boston, Mass.
  1893. Dec. 28. "Te Deum." Chicago, Ill.

SHELLEY, H. R.
  1887. July. Dance of Egyptian Maidens. New York, N. Y.
  1888. Mar. 2. Grand Sonata. New York, N. Y.
  1891. Feb. 23. Violin Concerto. New York, N. Y.
  1893. July 7. Carnival Overture. Chicago, Ill.
  1893. July 19. "The Ruined Castle" suite. Chicago, Ill.
  1897. June 25. Symphony in E flat. New York, N. Y.
  1901. Jan. 27. "Santa Claus" overture. New York, N. Y.

SHEPHERD, A.
  1906. Mar. 10. Overture Joyeuse. New York, N. Y.
  1916. Feb. 11. Overture "The Festival of Youth." St. Louis, Mo.

SIBELIUS, J.
  1901. Dec. 7. Two Legends from "Kalevala." Chicago, Ill.
  1902. Jan. 31. "Journeys Homewards" symphonic poem. New York, N. Y.
  1902. Nov. 14. "King Christian II" suite. Opus 27. Chicago, Ill.
  1903. Feb. 7. "The Swan of Tuonela" symphonic poem. Cincinnati, O.
  1904. Jan. 2. Second Symphony (D major). Chicago, Ill.
  1904. April 30. "Eine Saga" tone poem. Chicago, Ill.
  1905. Dec. 24. "Finlandia" symphonic poem. New York, N. Y.
  1906. Nov. 30. Violin Concerto (D minor). New York, N. Y.
  1907. Jan. 5. First Symphony (E minor). Boston, Mass.
  1907. Jan. 17. "Karelia" overture. New York, N. Y.
  1907. Feb. 7. "Karelia" suite. New York, N. Y.
  1908. Jan. 16. Third Symphony (C major). New York, N. Y.
  1908. Nov. 21. "A Spring Day" symphonic poem. Boston, Mass.
  1913. Mar. 2. Fourth Symphony (A minor). New York, N. Y.
  1914. June. "Aalloteret" tone poem. Norfolk, Conn.
  1917. Jan. 12. "Polyola's Daughter" symphonic fantasy. Boston, Mass.
  1917. Jan. 12. "Night Ride and Sunrise" symphonic poem, Boston, Mass.

SIMANDL, F.
  1905. Jan. 20. Concert Piece for double bass and orchestra. Pittsburgh, Pa.

SINDING, C.
  1893. Dec. 9. First Symphony (D minor). Chicago, Ill.
  1900. Jan. 5. Rondo Infinito. Chicago, Ill.
  1900. Jan. 19. Episodes Chevaleresques. Chicago, Ill.
  1900. Mar. 10. Violin Concerto (A major). New York, N. Y.

SINGER, O.
   1869. April 3. Fantasia for pianoforte and orchestra. New York, N. Y.
   1878. May 14. Festival Ode. Cincinnati, O.

SINIGAGLIA, L.
   1911. Mar. 11. "La Baruffe Chiozzote" overture. Boston, Mass.
   1916. Nov. 26. Étude Caprice. New York, N. Y.

SITT, H.
   1905. Jan. 4. Andante (violin and orchestra). Boston, Mass.

SIX RUSSIAN COMPOSERS
   1903. Oct. 24. Variations on a Russian Theme. Chicago, Ill.

SKILTON, C. S.
   1916. Oct. 29. Two Indian Dances. Minneapolis, Minn.

SLAVINSKY
   1918. Jan. 19. "The Shepherdess and the Faun." New York, N. Y.

SMAREGLIA, A.
   1890. Dec. 12. "Der Vassall von Szigeth" opera. New York, N. Y.

SMETANA, F.
   1887. Nov. 12. "Prodaná nevěsta" overture (The Bartered Bride). New York, N. Y.
   1890. Nov. 22. "Ultava" symphonic poem. Boston, Mass.
   1895. Oct. 25. "Sarka" symphonic poem. Chicago, Ill.
   1896. April 24. "Vysehrad" symphonic poem. Chicago, Ill.
   1896. Nov. 13. "Richard III" symphonic poem. Chicago, Ill.
   1897. Jan. 2. "Wallenstein's Lager" symphonic poem. Boston, Mass.
   1900. Dec. 8. "Mà Vlast" (My Country) symphonic poem. Boston, Mass.
   1905. Oct. 21. "Libussa" overture. Boston, Mass.
   1909. Feb. 19. "Prodaná Nevěsta" opera. New York, N. Y.

SMITH, D. S.
- 1912. Dec. 14. Symphony in F minor. Cincinnati, O.
- 1918. May 30. Rhapsody of St. Bernard. Evanston, Ill.
- 1918. June 4. Second Symphony (D major). Norfolk, Conn.
- 1918. Nov. 17. "Impressions" orchestral suite. Minneapolis, Minn.

SOWERBY, L.
- 1917. Jan. 18. "Comes Autumn Time" overture. Chicago, Ill.
- 1918. Feb. 15. "A Set of Four." Chicago, Ill.
- 1920. Mar. 5. Pianoforte Concerto in F major. Chicago, Ill.

SPARCKS, G.
- 1905. Jan. 4. "Boabdil" symphonic poem. Boston, Mass.
- 1906. Jan. 2. "Legende" symphonic poem. Boston, Mass.

SPENDIAROF, A.
- 1914. Feb. 17. "The Three Palms" symphonic poem. New York, N. Y
- 1918. Jan. 19. "The Sermon of Resia" symphonic poem. New York, N. Y.

SPINELLI, N.
- 1900. Jan. 22. "A Basso Porto" opera. New York, N. Y.

SPOHR, L.
- 1842. Mar. 20. "The Last Judgment" oratorio. Boston, Mass.
- 1844. Mar. 16. Symphony in D minor. New York, N. Y.
- 1845. Jan. 11. "Jessonda" overture. New York, N. Y.
- 1846. Feb. 14. "Faust" overture. Boston, Mass.
- 1848. April 29. Symphony in E flat. New York, N. Y.
- 1853. Nov. 26. Ninth Symphony "The Seasons." New York, N. Y.
- 1860. Jan. 14. Double Symphony. Boston, Mass.
- 1875. Feb. 20. Third Symphony. New York, N. Y.

SPONTINI, G.
- 1881. Jan. 6. "Ferdinand Cortes" opera. New York, N. Y.
- 1884. Jan 26. "Olympia" overture. Boston, Mass.

STAHLBERG, F.

1902. Jan. 3. " Die Brautschau " suite. Pittsburgh, Pa.
1903. Mar. 14. " To the Memory of Abraham Lincoln " tone poem. Pittsburgh, Pa.
1904. Jan. 8. Suite (Op. 10). Pittsburgh, Pa.
1908. Mar. 23. " Ueber's Weltenmeer " suite. New York, N. Y.
1912. Feb. 4. " Im Hochland." New York, N. Y.
1912. Mar. 16. Symphonic Scherzo. New York, N. Y.
1916. Feb. 4. Suite (Op. 33). New York, N. Y.

STANFORD, C. V.

1884. Jan. 19. Serenade in G. New York, N. Y.
1888. Jan. 28. Irish Symphony. New York, N. Y.
1915. June. Pianoforte Concerto. Norfolk, Conn.
1917. June. Irish Rhapsody. Norfolk, Conn.
1918. June 6. " Verdun " tone poem. Norfolk, Conn.

STENHAMMER, W.

1914. Jan. 6. " Midwinter." Minneapolis, Minn.

STOCK, F.

1904. Feb. 26. Symphonic Variations. Chicago, Ill.
1907. Nov. 1. Symphonic Waltz. Chicago, Ill.
1911. Feb. 27. Suite for strings. St. Louis, Mo.
1915. June. Violin Concerto. Norfolk, Conn.
1918. Mar. 15. Overture to a Romantic Comedy. Chicago, Ill.
1919. Feb. 28. March and Hymn to Democracy. Chicago, Ill.
1921. May 26. A Psalmodic Rhapsody. Evanston, Ill.

STOJOWSKI, S.

1915. Feb. 5. Suite for orchestra. New York, N. Y.

STRACKOSCH, M

1851. Jan. 3. " Giovanni di Napoli " opera. New York, N. Y.

STRANSKY, J.

1911. Feb. 27. Symphonic Song. New York, N. Y.
1913. Feb. 27. " Moonrise " and " Requiem " New York, N. Y.

1921. Jan. 13. "Thy Fragrant Hair" song, and "Hymnus." New York, N. Y.

STRAUSS, J.
    1867. July 1. "Blue Danube" waltz. New York, N. Y.
    1867. July 7. "From the Mountains" waltz. New York, N. Y.
    1867. July 14. "Bürgesum" waltz. New York, N. Y.
    1867. July 14. "Lob der Frauen" polka mazurka. New York, N. Y.
    1869. July 20. "Wein, Weib, und Gesang" waltz. New York, N. Y.
    1885. Mar. 16. "Die Fledermaus" opera. New York, N. Y.
    1892. Oct. 21. "Seid Umschlungen Millionen Waltz." Chicago, Ill.
    1895. April 13. "Moto Perpetuo" musical joke. Boston, Mass.

STRAUSS, R.
    1884. Dec. 13. Symphony (F minor). New York, N. Y.
    1888. Mar. 8. "Italy" symphonic fantasia. Philadelphia, Pa.
    1891. Oct. 31. "Don Juan" tone poem. Boston, Mass.
    1892. Jan. 9. "Tod und Verklärung" tone poem. New York, N. Y.
    1892. April 1. "Macbeth" symphonic poem. New York, N. Y.
    1895. Nov. 1. "Guntram" overture. Chicago, Ill.
    1895. Nov. 1. "Guntram" prelude to act III. New York, N. Y.
    1895. Nov. 15. "Til Eulenspiegel" tone poem. Chicago, Ill.
    1897. Feb. 5. "Also sprach Zarathustra" tone poem. Chicago, Ill.
    1899. Jan. 7. "Don Quixote" tone poem. Chicago, Ill.
    1900. Mar. 10. "Ein Heldenleben" tone poem. Chicago, Ill.
    1902. Feb. 14. "Feuernot" love scene. Chicago, Ill.

1903. April 18. Burlesque in D minor, piano and orchestra. Boston, Mass.
1904. Mar. 21. "Sinfonia Domestica." New York, N. Y.
1905. April 14. "Taillefer" choral ballad. New York, N. Y.
1907. Jan. 22. "Salome" opera. New York, N. Y.
1910. Jan. 29. "Elektra" opera. New York, N. Y.
1912. Nov. 13. Festival Prelude. New York, N. Y.
1913. April 17. "Der Abend." New York, N. Y.
1913. Dec. 9. "Der Rosenkavalier" opera. New York, N. Y.
1916. April 25. "Alpine Symphony." Cincinnati, O.
1921. Feb. 12. Suite from "Der Bürger als Edelman." Boston, Mass.

STRAVINSKY, I.
1910. Dec. 1. "Feuerwerk." New York, N. Y.
1916. Jan. 15. First Symphony (E flat). New York, N. Y.

STRONG, T.
1885. Mar. 31. "Undine" symphonic poem. New York, N. Y.
1887. Nov. 24. Symphony (F major). New York, N. Y.

STRUBE, G.
1895. Feb. 16. "The Maid of Orleans" overture. Boston, Mass.
1896. April 4. Symphony (C minor). Boston, Mass.
1897. Sept. 22. Violin Concerto (G major). Worcester, Mass.
1898. Jan. 27. Overture for trumpets, horns, tubas and kettledrums. Boston, Mass.
1901. April 20. Rhapsody (Op. 17). Boston, Mass.
1903. Jan. 25. "Hymn to Eros." Boston, Mass.
1904. Mar. 18. Fantastic Overture. Boston, Mass.
1905. April 22. "Longing" symphonic poem. Boston, Mass.
1905. Dec. 23. Violin Concerto (F sharp minor). Boston, Mass.
1908. Mar. 28. Fantastic Dance. Boston, Mass.

1909. April 3. Symphony (B minor). Boston, Mass.
1910. Mar. 19. " Puck " comedy overture. Boston, Mass.
1913. Jan. 25. " Narcissus " and " Echo " symphonic poems. Boston, Mass.
1913. Nov. 21. " Loreley " symphonic poem. St. Louis, Mo.
1920. Nov. 12. Four Preludes. Boston, Mass.

SUK, J.
1900. Nov. 16. Symphony (E major). New York, N. Y.
1901. Nov. 22. " Pohadka " march. Chicago, Ill.
1902. Nov. 29. " A Fairy Tale " suite. Boston, Mass.
1906. Feb. 11. Scherzo. New York, N. Y.

SULLIVAN, A.
1874. July 16. " The Tempest " overture. New York, N. Y.
1877. June 6. " On Shore and Sea " cantata. Chicago, Ill.
1879. Feb. 23. " The Prodigal Son " oratorio. Boston, Mass.
1886. Nov. 4. " In Memoriam " overture. Chicago, Ill.
1910. Feb. 13. " The Golden Legend " oratorio. Boston, Mass.

SVENDSEN, J.
1873. June 12. First Symphony (D). New York, N. Y.
1873. Sept. 18. " Sigurd Slambe " symphonic overture. New York, N. Y.
1880. April 4. " Zorahayda " legende. Boston, Mass.
1881. Mar. 11. " Romeo and Juliet " fantasia. Boston, Mass.
1884. Jan. 5. Second Symphony (B flat). Boston, Mass.
1886. Jan. 12. Norwegian Artist's Carnival. New York, N. Y.
1887. Mar. 1. Festival Polonaise. New York, N. Y.

SWEET, R.
1921. Mar. 4. " Riders to the Sea " overture. New York, N. Y.

TANAIEF, S.
1900. Dec. 1. Symphony in C. Boston, Mass.
1904. Mar. 3. First Symphony. New York, N. Y.

TAUBERT, K. G. W.
1872. Mar. 7. "Arabian Nights" overture. Boston, Mass.
TAUBMANN, O.
1913. Mar. 28. "A Choral Service." New York, N. Y.
TAVAN, E.
1900. April 27. "Noce Arabe." Boston, Mass.
TAYLOR, COLERIDGE
1900. Mar. 14. "The Song of Hiawatha" overture. Boston, Mass.
1900. Dec. 5. "Hiawatha's Departure. Boston, Mass.
1903. Feb. 13. Ballad in D minor. Chicago, Ill.
1910. June. "Bamboula" dance. Norfolk, Conn.
1912. June. Violin Concerto. Norfolk, Conn.
1912. June. Negro Air. Norfolk, Conn.
1912. June. "A Tale of Old Japan." Norfolk, Conn.
1914. June. "From the Prairie." Norfolk, Conn.
TEN BRINK, J.
1904. April 11. Première Suite d'Orchestre. Boston, Mass.
THOMAS, A.
1859. "Le Caid" opera. New Orleans, La.
1871. Nov. 22. "Mignon" opera. New York, N. Y.
1872. Mar. 22. "Hamlet" opera. New York, N. Y.
THOMAS, G.
1898. Feb. 26. "The Swan and the Skylark" cantata. New York, N. Y.
1900. Nov. 19. "Esmeralda" opera. New York, N. Y.
THUILLE, L.
1911. Nov. 18. "Lobetanz" opera. New York, N. Y.
TIERSOT, J.
1906. Jan. 2. "Danses Populaires Françaises." Boston, Mass.
TINEL, E.
1893. Mar. 17. "St. Francis d'Assisi." New York, N. Y.
1907. Feb. 9. "Polyeucte" three symphonic pictures. Boston, Mass.

TIRINDELLI, P.
  1906. Jan. 26.   " Tragi-comedia " symphonic poem. Cincinnati, O.

TOMMASINI, V.
  1919. Mar. 17.   " Claire de Lune " nocturne. New York, N. Y.

TOWNSEND, M. L.
  1912. Feb. 11. Serenade. New York, N. Y.

TSCHEREPIN, N.
  1918. Mar. 23. " Fire Bird." New York, N. Y.

TURINA, J.
  1919. Nov. 13. " La Procession del Racio." New York, N. Y.

URACK, O.
  1914. Mar. 7. First Symphony (E major). Boston, Mass.

URSPRUCH, A.
  1903. Jan. 2. " Der Sturm " overture. Chicago, Ill.

VAN der PALS
  1911. Dec. 17. " Autumn," " Spring " symphonic pieces. New York, N. Y.

VAN der STUCKEN, F.
  1900. July. " Pax Triumphans " festival prologue. Brooklyn, N. Y.
  1901. Feb. 2. " William Ratcliffe " symphonic prologue. Boston, Mass.

VERDI, G.
  1847. Mar. 3. " I Lombardi " opera. New York, N. Y.
  1847. April 15. " Ernani " opera. New York, N. Y.
  1847. " I due Foscari " opera. New York, N. Y.
  1848. April 4. " Nabucco " opera. New York, N. Y.
  1850. April 16. " Attila " opera. New York, N. Y.
  1850. April 24. " Macbeth " opera. New York, N. Y.
  1852. Oct. 27. " Luisa Miller " opera. Philadelphia, Pa.
  1855. April 30. " Il Trovatore " opera. New York, N. Y.
  1855. Oct. 30. " Semiramide " opera. New York, N. Y.

1856. Dec. 3. "La Traviata" opera. New York, N. Y.
1859. Nov. 7. "I Vespri Sicilienne" opera. New York, N. Y.
1860. Mar. 19. "Rigoletto" opera. New Orleans, La.
1860. May 30. "I Masnadieri" opera. New York, N. Y.
1861. Feb. 11. "Un Ballo in Maschera" opera. New York, N. Y.
1863. April 15. "Aroldo" opera. New York, N. Y.
1865. Feb. 24. "La Forza del Destino" opera. New York, N. Y.
1873. Nov. 26. "Aïda" opera. New York, N. Y.
1875. Nov. 17. "Requiem." Boston, Mass.
1877. April 12. "Don Carlos" opera. New York, N. Y.
1888. April 16. "Otello" opera. New York, N. Y.
1895. Feb. 4. "Falstaff" opera. New York, N. Y.

VIDAL, P.
1918. Nov. 9. "Danses Tanagréennes" New York, N. Y.

VIEUXTEMPS, H.
1867. Dec. 14. Violin Concerto in D. Brooklyn, N. Y.

VIVALDI, A.
1913. Mar. 8. Concerto (G minor). Boston, Mass.

VOLBACH, F.
1903. Jan. 23. "Es Waren Zwei Königskinder." Chicago, Ill.
1910. Jan. 18. Symphony (B minor). Philadelphia, Pa.

VOLKMANN, R.
1842. Jan. 10. Serenade in F. New York, N. Y.
1869. April 3. Festival Overture. New York, N. Y.
1874. Jan. 10. Serenade in D minor. Brooklyn, N. Y.
1883. Dec. 22. Symphony in B flat (Second). Boston, Mass.
1885. Mar. 14. "Richard III" overture. Boston, Mass.
1893. Mar. 7. Violoncello Concerto. Chicago, Ill.

VREUILS, V.
1921. Mar. 4. "Jour de Fête" symphonic poem. Cincinnati, O.

WAGNER, R.
1853. Nov. 19. "Rienzi" overture. Boston, Mass.

ANNALS OF MUSIC IN AMERICA

1857. Jan. 3. " Faust " overture. Boston, Mass.
1857. Nov. 19. " Lohengrin " overture. Boston, Mass.
1859. April 4. " Tannhäuser " opera. New York, N. Y.
1859. Aug. 27 " Lohengrin " opera. New York, N. Y.
1862. May 13. " Die Fliegende Holländer " music. New York, N. Y.
1866. Mar. 10. " Tristan und Isolde " introduction. New York, N. Y.
1866. Oct. 20. " Die Meistersinger " vorspiel. New York, N. Y.
1870. May 7. " Die Meistersinger " selections. New York, N. Y.
1871. June 22. " Kaiser March." New York, N. Y.
1871. Sept. 8. " Huldigung's March." New York, N. Y.
1871. Dec. 6. " Tristan und Isolde " introduction and finale. New York, N. Y.
1872. Sept. 17. " The Ride of the Valkyries." New York, N. Y.
1873. Jan. 8. " Wotan's Departure." Philadelphia, Pa.
1873. Jan. 8. " Magic Fire Music." Philadelphia, Pa.
1873. Sept. 14. " Die Walküre " introduction and love scene. New York, N. Y.
1876. May 11. Centennial March. Philadelphia, Pa.
1877. Nov. 8. " Il Vascella Fantasma," " Die Fliegende Holländer," " The Flying Dutchman " opera. Philadelphia, Pa.
1877. April 2. " Die Walküre " opera. New York, N. Y.
1878. Feb. 28. " Siegfried Idyll." New York, N. Y.
1878. Mar. 5. " Rienzi " opera. New York, N. Y.
1880. " Die Götterdämmerung " (third act). New York, N. Y.
1882. Nov. 3. " Parsifal " finale first act. New York, N. Y.
1882. Nov. 3. " Parsifal " " Procession of knights," New York, N. Y.
1882. Nov. 3. " Parsifal " — " Monologue of Amfortas." New York, N. Y.
1882. Nov. 3. " Parsifal " — " The Lord's Supper." New York, N. Y.

1882. Nov. 3. "Parsifal" — "The Holy Grail." New York, N. Y.
1882. Nov. 11. "Parsifal" vorspiel. New York, N. Y.
1883. Feb. 16. "Parsifal" — "Good Friday Spell." New York, N. Y.
1886. Jan. 4. "Die Meistersinger" opera. New York, N. Y.
1886. Dec. 1. "Tristan und Isolde" opera. New York, N. Y.
1887. Feb. 24. "Parsifal" — "Flowergirl Music." New York, N. Y.
1887. Nov. 9. "Siegfried" opera. New York, N. Y.
1888. Jan. 4. "Das Rheingold" opera. New York, N. Y.
1888. Jan. 15. "Die Götterdämmerung" opera. New York, N. Y.
1888. Feb. 25. Symphony in C. New York, N. Y.
1889. Jan. 17. "Traüme." Chicago, Ill.
1903. Jan. 30. Coronation March. Chicago, Ill.
1903. Dec. 24. "Parsifal" opera. New York, N. Y.
1908. Feb. 14. "Christopher Columbus" overture. Philadelphia, Pa.

WAGNER, S.
1898. Jan. 7. "Sehnsucht" symphonic poem. New York, N. Y.
1899. Nov. 4. "Der Bärenhäuter" overture. Boston, Mass.

WALLACE, W. V.
1848. May 4. "Maritana" opera. Philadelphia, Pa.

WALLACE, W.
1910. Oct. 6. "Villon" symphonic poem. New York, N. Y.

WEBBER, A.
1905. Dec. 30. Symphony (E minor). Boston, Mass.

WEBER, C. M. von
1825. Mar. 12. "Der Freischütz" opera. New York, N. Y.
1827. Oct. 9. "Oberon" opera. Philadelphia, Pa.
1842. Feb. 26. Jubilee Overture. Boston, Mass.
1863. "Euryanthe" opera. New York, N. Y.

1866. Feb. 10. "Invitation to the Dance." New York, N. Y.
1874. May 14. "Abu Hassan" overture. New York, N. Y.
1875. June 17. First Symphony (C). New York, N. Y.
1887. Dec. 23. "Euryanthe" opera (revival). New York, N. Y.
1888. Nov. 10. "The Three Pintos" entr'acte. New York, N. Y.
1914. Dec. 9. "Euryanthe" opera (noted revival). New York, N. Y.

WEIDIG, A.
1900. Jan. 5. Scherzo Capriccioso. Chicago, Ill.
1906. Mar. 2. "Semiramis" symphonic fantaisie. Chicago, Ill.
1919. Feb. 23. Concert Overture. Minneapolis, Minn.

WEINGARTNER, F.
1898. April 7. "The Elysian Fields" symphonic poem. New York, N. Y.
1901. April 13. Symphony (G major). Boston, Mass.
1902. Dec. 5. Second Symphony (E flat). New York, N. Y.
1911. Dec. 28. Third Symphony (F major). New York, N. Y.
1912. Nov. 4. "Lustige" overture. New York, N. Y.

WEISS, K.
1921. Mar. 9. "The Polish Jew" opera. New York, N. Y.

WETZLER, H. H.
1921. Nov. 13. Overture to "As You Like It." San Francisco, Cal.

WHITING, A.
1887. Nov. 17. Pianoforte Concerto (D minor). New York, N. Y.
1897. Mar. 6. Fantasy for piano and orchestra (B flat minor). Boston, Mass.

WIDOR, C. M.
1902. Nov. 28. Chorale and Variations for harp and orchestra. Chicago, Ill.
1904. April 14. "Ouverture Espagnol." Boston, Mass.

1917. Feb. 2. Third Symphony for organ. New York, N. Y.
1917. Dec. 14. Prelude. Chicago, Ill.

WILSON, M.
1920. Oct. "New Orleans" overture. New York, N. Y.

WILLIAMS, R. V.
1920. Dec. 31. "A London Symphony." New York, N. Y.

WITKOWSKI, G. M.
1903. April 4. Symphony (D minor). Boston, Mass.

WOLF–FERRARI, E.
1907. Dec. 4. "Vita Nuova" oratorio. New York, N. Y.
1911. Mar. 24. "The Secret of Suzanne" opera. Philadelphia, Pa.
1912. Jan. 16. "Le Donne Curiose" opera. New York, N. Y.
1912. Jan. 16. "I Giojelli della Madonna" (The Jewels of the Madonna) opera. Chicago, Ill.
1914. Mar. 25. "L'Amore Medico" opera. New York, N. Y.

WOLFF, A.
1919. Dec. 27. "The Blue Bird" opera. New York, N. Y.

WOOLLETT, H.
1911. Jan. 25. "Siberia." Boston, Mass.

WOYRSCH, F.
1911. April 10. Symphony (D minor). Chicago, Ill.

YON, P.
1921. Feb. 6. Concerto Gregoriano. New York, N. Y.

YSAYE, E.
1905. Mar. 30. Poème Elégiaque for violin and orchestra. New York, N. Y.
1918. May 9. "Exil" symphonic poem. Cincinnati, O.

YSAYE, TH.
1915. Jan. 8. Fantasia on Walloon Theme. St. Louis, Mo.

ZANDONAI
1913. Feb. 6. "Conchita." Philadelphia, Pa.
1914. Jan. 20 "O Padre Nostro" from "Purgatory." New York, N. Y.

1916. Dec. 22. "Francesca da Rimini." New York, N. Y.
ZELLNER, H.
    1896. Feb. 22. Orchestral Fantasia. Boston, Mass.
    1896. Dec. 11. "Midnight at Sedan" symphonic poem. Chicago, Ill.
ZELLNER, J.
    1873. June 12. Symphony (Op. 7). New York, N. Y.
    1874. Aug. 21. "Melusine." New York, N. Y.
ZOLOTAREF
    1905. Dec. 30. "Rhapsodie Hebraique." New York, N. Y.

MISCELLANEOUS ITEMS

BALLAD OPERAS, ETC.

1733. "Hob in the Well." Charleston, S. C.
1750. April 30. "The Mock Doctor." New York, N. Y.
1750. Dec. 3. "The Beggar's Opera." New York, N. Y.
1757. "The Masque of Alfred." Philadelphia, Pa.
1770. "The Masque of Comus." Philadelphia, Pa.
1787. "The Duenna." Philadelphia, Pa.
1787. "The Maid of the Mill." Philadelphia, Pa.
1790. June 14. "The Mistress and Maid." Baltimore, Md.
1790. Oct. 7. "Le Tonnelier." New York, N. Y.
1790–1800. Various French Operas. New Orleans, La.
1790–1800. Various French Operas. Norfolk, Conn.
1790–1800. Various French Operas. Charleston, S. C.
1790–1800. Various French Operas. Richmond, Va.
1790–1800. Various French Operas. Boston, Mass.
1790–1800. Various French Operas. Philadelphia, Pa.
1790–1800. Various French Operas. New York, N. Y.
1794. "The Barber of Seville" (Paisiello). New York, N. Y.
1796. April 18. "The Archers of Switzerland." New York N. Y.
1796. Dec. 19. "Edwin and Angelina." New York, N. Y.
1797. Jan. 25. "Richard Coeur de Lion." Boston, Mass.
1798. Jan. 29. "The Purse." New York, N. Y.
1799. "The Vintage." New York, N. Y.
1823. "Clari — The Maid of the Mill." New York, N. Y.

CONCERTS

1731. Mr. Pelham's. Boston, Mass.
1732. Mr. Salter's. Charleston, S. C.

1733. Song Recital. Charleston, S. C.
1736. Mr. Pachelbel's. New York, N. Y.
1761. Mr. Dipper's. Boston, Mass.
1765. Musical Glasses. Philadelphia, Pa.
1765. Ranelagh Gardens. New York, N. Y.
1786. Reformed Church. Philadelphia, Pa.
1789. Mr. Graupner's. Salem, Mass.
1798. Columbia Garden. New York, N. Y.
1798. Albany. Albany, N. Y.
1798. Trenton. Trenton, N. J.
1798. Salem. Salem, Mass.
1800. Philharmonic Society, New York, N. Y.
1801. University of Pennsylvania. Philadelphia, Pa.
1821. Musical Fund. Philadelphia, Pa.
1848. Convention. Chicago, Ill.
1849. Saengerfest. Cincinnati, O.
1850. Philharmonic Orchestra. Chicago, Ill.
1850. Symphony Concert. Chicago, Ill.
1860. Briggs House. Chicago, Ill.
1864. Band Festival. New Orleans, La.
1865. Peabody Institute. Baltimore, Md.
1866. Summer Nights'. New York, N. Y.
1869. First Peace Jubilee. Boston, Mass.
1877. Summer Nights'. Chicago, Ill.
1881. Philharmonic Society. Boston, Mass.

CONDUCTORS (Orchestral)

1855. Carl Zerrahn. Boston, Mass.
1856. Carl Bergmann. New York, N. Y.
1860 and 1880. Hans Balatka. Chicago, Ill.
1868 and 1877. Theodore Thomas. New York, N. Y.
1871. A. Hamerik. Baltimore, Md.
1878. Dr. Leopold Damrosch. New York, N. Y.
1885. Walter Damrosch. New York, N. Y.
1889. Carl Venth. Brooklyn, N. Y.
1891. Theodore Thomas. Chicago, Ill.
1893. Frederic Archer. Pittsburgh, Pa.
1895. F. van der Stucken. Cincinnati, O.

1895. Fritz Scheel. San Francisco, Cal.
1898. Victor Herbert. Pittsburgh, Pa.
1900. Fritz Scheel. Philadelphia, Pa.
1901. L. Stokowski. Cincinnati, O.
1903. Guest Conductors. New York, N. Y.
1904. Guest Conductors. New York, N. Y.
1904. Emil Paur. Pittsburgh, Pa.
1905. Guest Conductors. New York, N. Y.
1905. Fred A. Stock. Chicago, Ill.
1905. Walter Rothwell. Minneapolis, Minn.
1906. E. B. Emanuel. St. Paul, Minn.
1907. Carl Pohlig. Philadelphia, Pa.
1907. Max Zach. St. Louis, Mo.
1908. M. Kregizi. Seattle, Wash.
1908. W. B. Rothwell. St. Paul, Minn.
1909. Henry K. Hadley. Seattle, Wash.
1911. Henry K. Hadley. San Francisco, Cal.
1911. Carl Busch. Kansas City, Mo.
1912. L. Stokowski. Philadelphia, Pa.
1912. Ernest Kunwald. Cincinnati, O.
1914. Glenn Dillard Gunn. Chicago, Ill.
1914. Carl Venth. Dallas, Texas.
1915. Alfred Hertz. San Francisco, Cal.
1915. Gustav Strube. Baltimore, Md.
1917. Nov. 17. P. Monteux. New York, N. Y.
1918. Feb. 21. Henri Verbrugghen. New York, N. Y.
1918. N. Sokolov. Cleveland, O.
1918. Ossip Gabrilowitsch. Detroit, Mich.
1920. Dec. 30. Albert Coates. New York, N. Y.
1921. Nov. 6. Rudolf Ganz. St. Louis, Mo.

Boston Symphony Orchestra, Boston, Mass.

1881–1884. Georg Henschel.
1884–1889. Wilhelm Gericke
1889–1893. Arthur Nikisch
1893–1898. Emil Paur
1898–1906. Wilhelm Gericke
1906–1908. Dr. Karl Muck

1908–1912. Max Fiedler
1912–1917. Dr. Karl Muck
1917–1918. Henri Rabaud
1918–   Pierre Monteux

Philharmonic Society, New York, N. Y.

1849–1855. U. C. Hill ⎫
           H. C. Timms ⎪
           W. Alpers ⎬ alternating
           G. Loder ⎪
           L. Wiegers ⎪
           Th. Eisfeld ⎭
1855–1866. Th. Eisfeld and Carl Bergmann
1866–1876. Carl Bergmann
1876–1877. Dr. Leopold Damrosch
1877–1891. Theodore Thomas
1891–1898. Anton Seidl
1898–1902. Emil Paur
1902–1903. Walter Damrosch
1903–1905. Guest Conductors
1905–1908. Willy Safonof
1908–1911. Gustav Mahler
1911–   Josef Stransky

CONSERVATORIES AND SCHOOLS OF MUSIC

1750. Collegium Musicum. Bethlehem, Pa.
1833. Academy of Music. Boston, Mass.
1834. Miss Wyeth's School. Chicago, Ill.
1851. Tourjée's School. Providence, R. I.
1865. Peabody Conservatory. Baltimore, Md.
1865. Oberlin Conservatory. Oberlin, O.
1867. Boston Conservatory. Boston, Mass.
1867. New England Conservatory. Boston, Mass.
1867. Cincinnati Conservatory. Cincinnati, O.
1867. Academy of Music (became Chicago Musical College). Chicago, Ill.
1871. Illinois College Conservatory. Jacksonville, Ill.
1873. Northwestern University Conservatory. Evanston, Ill.
1877. Syracuse University Conservatory. Syracuse, N. Y.

1878. College of Music. Cincinnati, O.
1884. Chicago Conservatory. Chicago, Ill.
1885. American Institute of Applied Music. New York, N. Y.
1886. American Conservatory. Chicago, Ill.
1905. Institute of Musical Art. New York, N. Y.

DÉBUTS, Pianists

1844. Leopold von Meyer. New York, N. Y.
1845. Henry Herz. New York, N. Y.
1848. Richard Hoffman. New York, N. Y.
1852. Oct. 15. Alfred Jaell. New York, N. Y.
1853. Louis M. Gottschalk. New York, N. Y.
1855. Sigismund Thalberg. New York, N. Y.
1862. Teresa Carreno. New York, N. Y.
1869. Dec. 2. Anna Mehlig. Farmington, Conn.
1870. Marie Krebs. New York, N. Y
1872. Sept. 23. Anton Rubinstein. New York, N. Y.
1873. Julié Rivé-King. Cincinnati, O.
1875. Oct. 4. Arabella Goddard. New York, N. Y.
1875. Oct. 18. Hans von Bülow. Boston, Mass.
1876. Nov. 14. Annette Essipof. New York, N. Y.
1879. Oct. 13. Rafael Joseffy. New York, N. Y.
1883. Jan. 11. Fannie Bloomfield Zeisler. Chicago, Ill.
1883. Dec. 8. Helen Hopekirk. Boston, Mass.
1887. Nov. 27. Josef Hofmann. New York, N. Y.
1888. Nov. 13. Moritz Rosenthal. New York, N. Y.
1890. Leopold Godowski. New York, N. Y.
1891. Jan. 23. Xaver Scharwenka. New York, N. Y.
1891. Nov. 13. Feruccio Busoni. Boston, Mass.
1891. Nov. 18. Ignace Jan Paderewski. New York, N. Y.
1892. Feb. 6. Vladimir de Pachmann. New York, N. Y.
1893. Dec. 2. Richard Burmeister. New York, N. Y.
1893. Dec. 5. Josef Slivinski. New York, N. Y.
1893. Dec. 9. Alberto Jonas. New York, N. Y.
1895. Alfred Reisenaur. New York, N. Y.
1897. Dec. 10. Raoul Pugno. New York, N. Y.
1898. Jan. 25. Alexander Siloti. New York, N. Y.

ANNALS OF MUSIC IN AMERICA

1899. Mar. 22. Ernest Dohnanyi. New York, N. Y.
1899. Nov. 3. Mark Hambourg. New York, N. Y.
1900. Nov. 12. Ossip Gabrilowitch. New York, N. Y.
1900. Dec. 1. Harold Bauer. Boston, Mass.
1906. Jan. 9. Rudolph Ganz. Boston, Mass.
1906. Jan. 27. Josef Lhevinne. New York, N. Y.
1907. Jan. 19. Katherine Goodson. Boston, Mass.
1909. Nov. 4. Serge Rachmaninof. Northampton, Mass.
1911. Dec. 10. Arthur Shattuck. New York, N. Y.
1912. Jan. 7. William Bachaus. New York, N. Y.
1913. Jan. 16. Max Pauer. New York, N. Y.
1918. Oct. 20. Alfred Cortot. New York, N. Y.
1919. Feb. 12. Winifred Christie. New York, N. Y.
1919. Nov. 29. Benno Moseivitch. New York, N. Y.
1920. Jan. 21. C. Valderranea. New York, N. Y.
1920. Nov. 5. Cyril Scott. Philadelphia, Pa.
1920. Nov. 21. E. Nyiregyhasi. New York, N. Y.
1921. Jan. 14. Ignaz Friedman. New York, N. Y.
1921. Oct. 15. Elly Ney. New York, N. Y.
1921. Nov. 28. Alfredo Casella. New York, N. Y.
1921. Dec. 25. Artur Schnabel. New York, N. Y.

DÉBUTS, Singers

1793. Mrs. Broadhurst. Philadelphia, Pa.
1794. Mrs. Oldmixon. Philadelphia, Pa.
1817. Oct. 3. Charles B. Incledon. New York, N. Y.
1825. Nov. 26. Manuel Garcia. New York, N. Y.
1825. Nov. 26. F. Garcia (Malibran). New York, N. Y.
1831. Miss Hughes. New York, N. Y.
1832. Sept. 25. Signora Pedrotti. New York, N. Y.
1832. Sept. 25. Signor Fornisari. New York, N. Y.
1832. Sept. 25. Signor Montresor. New York, N. Y.
1833. Sept. 25. Mr. and Mrs. Wood. New York, N. Y.
1834. Mar. 28. Clementina Fanti. New York, N. Y.
1834. Mar. 28. Clothilde Fanti. New York, N. Y.
1835. April 8. Charlotte Cushman. Boston, Mass.
1837. Oct. 30. Maria Caradori-Allan. New York, N. Y.
1838. Mr. and Mrs. Seguin. New York, N. Y.

1841. John Braham. New York, N. Y.
1841. The Hutchinson Family.
1844. Feb. 2. Signora Borghese. New York, N. Y.
1847. April 15. Fortunata Tedesco. New York, N. Y.
1847. Aug. 4. Madame Anna Bishop. New York, N. Y.
1847. Nov. 22. Teresa Truffi. New York, N. Y.
1847. Dec. 1. Amalia Patti. New York, N. Y.
1847. Dec. 8. Eliza Biscaccianti. New York, N. Y.
1848. Rosina Laborde. New York, N. Y.
1849. Dec. 10. Giuletta Perrini. New York, N. Y.
1850. Mar. 11. Signora Steffanone. New York, N. Y.
1850. Mar. 18. Angiolina Bosio. New York, N. Y.
1850. Sept. 11. Jenny Lind. New York, N. Y.
1850. Nov. 4. Teresa Parodi. New York, N. Y.
1851. Sept. 23. Catherine Hayes. New York, N. Y.
1851. Dec. 7. Marietta Alboni. New York, N. Y.
1853. Jan. 10. Henrietta Sontag. New York, N. Y.
1853. Jan. 12. Signor Rocco. New York, N. Y.
1854. Oct. 2. Grisi and Mario. New York, N. Y.
1854. Oct. 9. Louisa Fanny Pyne. New York, N. Y.
1855. Feb. 13. Felicita Vestvali. New York, N. Y.
1855. Mar. 12. Luigi Brignoli. New York, N. Y.
1855. May 8. Anna de la Grange. New York, N. Y.
1855. Oct. 1. Constance Nantier-Didier. New York, N. Y.
1856. Mar. 17. Adelaide Phillips. New York, N. Y.
1857. Feb. 28. Marietta Gazzaniga. Philadelphia, Pa.
1857. Nov. 2. Madame d'Angri. New York, N. Y.
1857. Nov. 30. Carl Formes. New York, N. Y.
1857. Dec. 30. Anna Caradori. New York, N. Y.
1858. Oct. 20. Maria Piccolomini. New York, N. Y.
1859. Nov. 24. Adelina Patti. New York, N. Y.
1860. Sept. 19. Pauline Colson. Nw York, N. Y.
1861. Jan. 23. Isabella Hinkley. New York, N. Y.
1861. Feb. 27. Clara Louise Kellogg. New York, N. Y.
1862. Sept. 22. Carlotta Patti. New York, N. Y.
1864. Nov. 4. Jennie van Zandt. New York, N. Y.
1865. Sept. 11. Euphrosyne Parepa-Rosa. New York, N. Y.
1866. Oct. Minnie Hauck, New York, N. Y.

1870. Sept. 19. Christine Nilsson. New York, N. Y.
1871. Sept. 18. Theodore Wachtel. New York, N. Y.
1872. Feb. 14. Charles Santley. New York, N. Y.
1872. Sept. 30. Pauline Lucca. New York, N. Y.
1873. Oct. 1. Italo Campanini. New York, N. Y.
1873. Oct. 3. Victor Maurel. New York, N. Y.
1873. Oct. 6. Enrico Tamberlik. New York, N. Y.
1873. Oct. 7. Ilma di Murska. New York, N. Y.
1874. Emy Fursch-Madi. New Orleans, La.
1875. Oct. 18. Eugenie Pappenheim. New York, N. Y.
1875. Oct. 21 Emma Albani (also 1883). New York, N.Y.
1876. Jan. 24. Therese Tietjens. New York, N. Y.
1876. Jan. 25. Teresa Carreno (as singer). New York, N. Y.
1876. April 17. Anna de Belocca. New York, N. Y.
1877. Feb. 23. Emma Abbott. New York, N. Y.
1878. Feb. 11. Hermine Rudersdorff. New York, N. Y.
1878. Nov. 11. Etelka Gerster. New York, N. Y.
1879. Oct. 22. Alwina Valleria. New York, N. Y.
1879. Dec. 3. Marie Marimon. New York, N. Y.
1880. Jan. 19. Castelmary (Count de Castan). New York, N. Y.
1880. Oct. 4. Georg Henschel. New York, N. Y.
1880. Oct. 18. Luigi Ravelli. New York, N. Y.
1882. Dec. 20. Sophia Scalchi. New York, N. Y.
1883. Oct. 24. Marcella Sembrich. New York, N. Y.
1883. Oct. 26. Alberto Stagno. New York, N. Y.
1883. Nov. 26. Lillian Nordica. New York, N. Y.
1884. Jan. 14. Marianne Brandt. New York, N. Y.
1884. Nov. 21. Madame Schroeder-Hanfstaengel. New York, N. Y.
1884. Nov. 24. Emma Nevada. New York, N. Y.
1884. Nov. 27. Augusta Seidl-Krauss. New York, N. Y.
1884. Nov. 27. Anton Schott. New York, N. Y.
1885. Jan. 5. Amalie Materna. New York, N. Y.
1885. Nov. 4. Felia Litvinne. New York, N. Y.
1885. Nov. 25 Lilli Lehmann. New York, N. Y.
1885. Nov. 25. Max Alvary. New York, N. Y.
1886. Jan. 20. William Candidus. New York, N. Y.

1886. Nov. 10. Albert Niemann. New York, N. Y.
1890. Mar. 24. Francesco Tamagno. New York, N. Y.
1891. Nov. 14. Emma Eames. New York, N. Y.
1891. Dec. 14. Jean de Reszke. New York, N. Y.
1891. Dec. 14. Édouard de Reszke. New York, N. Y.
1891. Dec. 21. Marie van Zandt. New York, N. Y.
1892. Jan. 15. Jean Lasalle. New York, N. Y.
1893. Nov. 27. Pol Plançon. New York, N. Y.
1893. Nov. 29. Emma Calvé. New York, N. Y.
1893. Dec. 4. Nellie Melba. New York, N. Y.
1893. Dec. Sigrid Arnoldson. New York, N. Y.
1895. Jan. 15. Sybil Sanderson. New York, N. Y.
1895. Mar. 1. Johanna Gadski. New York, N. Y.
1895. Nov. 29. Guiseppe Cremonini. New York, N. Y.
1895. Dec. 17. Yvette Guilbert. New York, N. Y.
1896. Feb. 4. Milka Ternina. New York, N. Y.
1896. Jacques Bars. New York, N. Y.
1896. Aug. David Bispham. New York, N. Y.
1898. Nov. 7. Ernestine Schumann-Heink. Chicago, Ill.
1898. Nov. 8. Albert Saleza. Chicago, Ill.
1898. Nov. 29. Ernest van Dyck. New York, N. Y.
1898. Dec. 14. Anton van Rooy. New York, N. Y.
1899. Jan. 4. Suzanne Adams. New York, N. Y.
1899. Feb. 7. Albert Alvarez. Boston, Mass.
1899. Dec. 23. Antonio Scotti. New York, N. Y.
1900. Jan. 24. Fritz Friedrichs. New York, N. Y.
1900. Nov. 12. Charles Gilibert. San Francisco, Cal.
1900. Nov. 13. Robert Blass. San Francisco, Cal.
1900. Nov. 14. Louise Homer. San Francisco, Cal.
1900. Nov. 14. Imbart de la Tour. San Francisco, Cal.
1900. Nov. 17. Marcel Journet. San Francisco, Cal.
1900. Nov. 19. Fritzi Scheff. San Francisco, Cal.
1901. Jan. 14. Margaret McIntyre. New York, N. Y.
1901. Jan. 16. Lucienne Breval. New York, N. Y.
1902. Dec. 19. Madame Kirkby Lunn. New York, N. Y.
1903. Nov. 23. Enrico Caruso. New York, N. Y.
1903. Nov. 25. Olive Fremstad. New York, N. Y.
1903. Edythe Walker. New York, N. Y.

1904. Luisa Tetrazzini. San Francisco, Cal.
1905. Nov. 25. Jeanne Jomelli. New York, N. Y.
1906. Nov. 20. Florencio Constantino. New Orleans, La.
1906. Nov. 20. Andrea de Segurola. New Orleans, La.
1906. Nov. 20. Fely Dereyne. New Orleans, La.
1906. Nov. 20. Riccardo Martin. New Orleans, La.
1906. Nov. 26. Geraldine Farrar. New York, N. Y.
1906. Dec. 3. Alessandro Bonci. New York, N. Y.
1906. Dec. 5. Maurice Renaud. New York, N. Y.
1906. Dec. 5. Lina Cavalieri. New York, N. Y.
1906. Dec. 7. Pauline Donalda. New York, N. Y.
1907. Feb. 1. Mario Sammarco. New York, N. Y.
1907. Nov. 4. Jeanne Gerville-Reache. New York, N. Y.
1907. Nov. 20. Feodor Chaliapin. New York, N. Y.
1908. Mar. 4. Berta Morena. New York, N. Y.
1908. Sept. 5. Blanche Arral. New York, N. Y.
1908. Nov. 9. Maria Labia. New York, N. Y.
1908. Nov. 14. Ludwig Wüllner. New York, N. Y.
1908. Nov. 16. Emmy Destinn. New York, N. Y.
1908. Nov. 25. Mary Garden. New York, N. Y.
1909. Jan. 22. Carl Jörn. New York, N. Y.
1909. Oct. 25. Tilly Koenen. New York, N. Y.
1909. Nov. 8. Eric Schmedes. New York, N. Y.
1909. Nov. 10. John McCormack. New York, N. Y.
1909. Nov. 16. Alma Gluck. New York, N. Y.
1909. Nov. 16. Edmond Clement. New York, N. Y.
1909. Nov. 17. Otto Slezak. New York, N. Y.
1909. Dec. 14. Jeanne Maubourg. New York, N. Y.
1910. Jan. 5. Liza Lehmann. Boston, Mass.
1911. Nov. 4. Margarete Matzenauer. New York, N. Y.
1912. Jan. 9. Elena Gerhardt. New York, N. Y.
1912. Jan. 11. Vanni Marcoux. Boston, Mass.
1912. Feb. 14. Lucille Marcel. Boston, Mass.
1912. Nov. 4. Titta Ruffo. Philadelphia, Pa.
1912. Dec. 27. Frieda Hempel. New York, N. Y.
1913. Nov. 28. Sophie Braslau. New York, N. Y.
1916. Nov. 18. Amelita Galli-Curci. Chicago, Ill.
1917. Nov. 19. Anna Fitziu. Chicago, Ill.

1917. Nov. 29. May Peterson. New York, N. Y.
1917. Dec. 1. Genevieve Vix. Chicago, Ill.
1918. Jan. 31. Hipolito Lazaro. New York, N. Y.
1918. Nov. 11. B. Cousinou. New York, N. Y.
1918. Nov. 13. G. Crimi. New York, N. Y.
1918. Nov. 13. Montesanto. New York, N. Y.
1918. Nov. 15. Rosa Ponselle. New York, N. Y.
1918. Dec. 7. A. Dolci. Chicago, Ill.
1919. Jan. 31. Charles Hackett. New York, N. Y.
1919. Dec. 10. Madame Besanzoni. New York, N. Y.
1921. Jan. 9. Selma Kurtz. New York, N. Y.
1921. Nov. 14. B. Gigli. New York, N. Y.
1921. Nov. 15. Tino Pattiera. Chicago, Ill.
1921. Nov. 16. Edith Mason. Chicago, Ill.
1921. Nov. 19. Marie Jeritza. New York, N. Y.
1921. Nov. 29. Claire Dux. Chicago, Ill.

DÉBUTS, Violinists

1843. Nov. 25. Ole Bull. New York, N. Y.
1844. Dec. 15. Henri Vieuxtemps. New York, N. Y.
1844. Alexandre Artot. New York, N. Y.
1846. Oct. 12. Camille Sivori. New York, N. Y.
1848. Édouard Remenyi. New York, N. Y.
1850. Miska Hauser. New York, N. Y.
1850. Pablo Sarasate. New York, N. Y.
1852. Oct. 29. Camilla Urso. New York, N. Y.
1872. Sept. 23. Henri Wieniawski. New York, N. Y.
1872. Emil Sauret, New York, N. Y.
1878. Sept. 26. August Wilhelmj. New York, N. Y.
1883. Nov. 16. Ovide Musin. New York, N. Y.
1885. Dec. 3. Maud Powell. Philadelphia, Pa.
1887. Teresina Tua. New York, N. Y.
1888. Nov. 10. Fritz Kreisler. New York, N. Y.
1893. Henri Marteau. New York, N. Y.
1894. Oct. 30. César Thomson. New York, N. Y.
1894. Nov. 25. Eugene Ysaye. New York, N. Y.
1895. Willy Burmester. New York, N. Y.
1895. Nov. 15. Franz Ondricek. New York, N. Y.

1896. Nov. 8. Carl Halir. New York, N. Y.
1896. Nov. 24. C. Gregorovitch. New York, N. Y.
1896. Martin Marsick. New York, N. Y.
1898. Dec. 28. Maud MacCarthy. New York, N. Y.
1899. Feb. 8. Madame Norman Neruda (Lady Hallé). Boston, Mass.
1899. Nov. 17. A. Petchnikof. New York, N. Y.
1901. Dec. 2. Jan Kubelik. New York, N. Y.
1902. Nov. 19. J. Kocian. New York, N. Y.
1903. Feb. 5. Hugo Heerman. New York, N. Y.
1903. Oct. 30. Jacques Thibaud. New York, N. Y.
1905. Dec. 1. Kathleen Parlow. New York, N. Y.
1908. Nov. 7. Albert Spaulding. New York, N. Y.
1908. Dec. 10. Mischa Elman. New York, N. Y.
1910. Oct. 29. Anton Witek. Boston, Mass.
1911. Oct. 27. Efrem Zimbalist. Boston, Mass.
1917. Oct. 27. Jascha Heifetz. New York, N. Y.
1918. Jan. 12. Max Rosen. New York, N. Y.
1918. Feb. 25. Mayer Wadler. New York, N. Y.
1918. Nov. 3. Thelma Given. New York, N. Y.
1918. Nov. 13. Raoul Vidas. New York, N. Y.
1919. Jan. 28. Leopold Auer. New York, N. Y.
1920. Mar. 3. S. Culbertson. New York, N. Y.
1920. Oct. 3. Michel Piastro. New York, N. Y.
1920. Oct. 16. Josef Stopak. New York, N. Y.
1920. Oct. 25. Michel Gusikov. New York, N. Y.
1920. Nov. 2. D. Karekjarto. New York, N. Y.
1920. Nov. 22. Vasa Prihoda. New York, N. Y.
1920. Nov. 29. Daisy Kennedy. New York, N. Y.
1921. Jan. 14. Alexander Schmuller. New York, N. Y.
1921. Jan. 17. Izzy Mitnisky. New York, N. Y.
1921. Feb. 2. Erika Morini. New York, N. Y.
1921. Feb. 14. Paul Kockanski. New York, N. Y.
1921. Feb. 22. Carlo Sabatini. New York, N. Y.

VIOLONCELLISTS

1902. Nov. 19. Elsa Ruegger. New York, N. Y.
1904. Jan. 12. Pablo Casals. New York, N. Y.

1909. Dec. 5. J. Malkin. New York, N. Y.
1921. Jan. 19. Daisy Jean. New York, N. Y.

FESTIVALS

1847. Mendelssohn Festival. New York, N. Y.
1857. Musical Festivals. Worcester, Mass.
1864. Band Festival. New Orleans, La.
1869. First Peace Jubilee. Boston, Mass.
1873. May Festivals. Cincinnati, O.
1876. Centennial Exposition. Philadelphia, Pa.
1877. Wagner Festival. Boston, Mass.
1884. Wagner Festival. New York, N. Y.
1886. Litchfield County Festivals. Norfolk, Conn.
1900. Bach Festivals. Bethlehem, Pa.
1907. Beethoven Festival. New York, N. Y.
1910. MacDowell Festivals. Peterboro, N. H.
1911. Brahms Festivals. New York, N. Y.
1921. Pilgrim Pageant. Plymouth, Mass.

INSTRUMENTS

1700. Pipe Organ. Fort Royal, Va.
1713. Brattle Organ. Boston, Mass.
1716. Flageolets, Oboes, etc. Boston, Mass.
1728. Organ, Christ Church. Philadelphia, Pa.
1733. Organ, Trinity Church. Newport, R. I.
1737. Organ, Trinity Church. New York, N. Y.
1743. Organ Moravian Church. Philadelphia, Pa.
1743. Violins, Horns, etc. Bethlehem, Pa.
1745. Bromfield Organ. Boston, Mass.
1756. Organ, City Hall. New York, N. Y.
1756. Organ, King's Chapel. Boston, Mass.
1769. Spinet (J. Harris). Boston, Mass.
1770. Organ, Congregational Church. Philadelphia, Pa.
1774. Pianoforte. John Behrent. Philadelphia, Pa.
1787. Pipe Organ, J. Downer. Cookstown, Pa.
1803. Pianoforte, Benj. Crehore. Milton, Mass.
1823. Pianoforte, J. Chickering. Boston, Mass.
1837. Pianoforte, Wm. Knabe. Baltimore, Md.

ANNALS OF MUSIC IN AMERICA

1853. Pianoforte, Steinway & Sons. New York, N. Y.
1863. Organ, Music Hall. Boston, Mass.
1878. Organ, Music Hall. Cincinnati, O.
1914. Organ, Pan American Exposition. San Francisco, Cal.

MUSICIANS

1735–1794. James Lyons.
1737–1791. Francis Hopkinson.
1746–1800. William Billings.
1792–1872. Lowell Mason.
1813–1893. John S. Dwight.
1820–1895. George F. Root.
1826–1864. Stephen Foster.
1829–1869. Louis N. Gottschalk.
1829–1908. William Mason.
1834–1891. Eben Tourjée.
1835–1905. Theodore Thomas.
1839–1905. John K. Paine.
1839–1909. Dudley Buck.
1854–1910. William Sherwood.
1861–1908. Edward MacDowell.
1862–1901. Ethelbert Nevin.

NATIONAL HYMNS

1798. April 25. "Hail Columbia." Philadelphia, Pa.
1814. Sept. 14. "The Star-Spangled Banner." Baltimore, Md.
1832. July 4. "America." Boston, Mass.

OPERA COMPANIES (Managers, etc.)

1790. French Company. New Orleans, La.
1793. French Company. Charleston, S. C.
1825. Garcia's Company. New York, N. Y.
1827. French Company. New York, N. Y.
1832. L. da Ponte's Company. New York, N. Y.
1838. Seguin's Company. New York, N. Y.
1847. Havana Company. New York, N. Y.
1848. Maretzek's Company. New York, N. Y.

1849. Artists' Union Company. New York, N. Y.
1850. First opera in Chicago, Ill.
1853. First opera in San Francisco, Cal.
1855. German Company (J. Ungher's Co.). New York, N. Y.
1857. Strakosch. New York, N. Y.
1867. Opera Bouffe. New York, N. Y.
1869. Russian Opera. New York, N. Y.
1878. Mapleson's Company. New York, N. Y.
1883. Henry E. Abbey's Company. New York, N. Y.
1890. Abbey and Schoeffel. New York, N. Y.
1893. Abbey and Grau. New York, N. Y.
1895. Damrosch's German Company. New York, N. Y.
1897. Damrosch-Ellis Company. New York, N. Y.
1902. H. Conried. New York, N. Y.
1906. Hammerstein. New York, N. Y.
1908. Gatti-Casazza. New York, N. Y.
1909. Boston Opera Company. Boston, Mass.
1910. Philadelphia-Chicago Company. Chicago, Ill.

OPERA HOUSES, ETC.

1722. First Theatre in America. Williamsburg, Pa.
1753. Nassau St. Theatre. New York, N. Y.
1798. Park Theatre. New York, N. Y.
1807. Le Theatre St. Philippe. New Orleans, La.
1813. Theatre d'Orléans. New Orleans, La.
1818. Theatre d'Orléans rebuilt. New Orleans, La.
1833. First Opera House. New York, N. Y.
1847. Palmo's Opera House. New York, N. Y.
1847. Astor Place Opera House. New York, N. Y.
1852. Music Hall. Boston, Mass.
1854. Academy of Music. New York, N. Y.
1856. Academy of Music. Philadelphia, Pa.
1859. New French Opera House. New Orleans, La.
1865. Crosby Opera House. Chicago, Ill.
1877. Tivoli Opera House. San Francisco, Cal.
1879. Central Music Hall. Chicago, Ill.
1883. Metropolitan Opera House. New York, N. Y.

1889. Auditorium. Chicago, Ill.
1893. New Metropolitan Opera House. New York, N. Y.
1904. Orchestral Hall. Chicago, Ill.
1906. Manhattan Opera House. New York, N. Y.
1908. Academy of Music. Brooklyn, N. Y.
1908. Hammerstein Opera House. Philadelphia, Pa.
1909. Opera House. Boston, Mass.
1911. Aeolian Hall. New York, N. Y.

PUBLICATIONS, EARLY

1640. The Bay Psalm Book. Cambridge, Mass.
1712. Instruction book. Newbury, Mass.
1759. "My days have been so wondrous free." Phila., Pa.
1761. "Urania." Philadelphia, Pa.
1770. "The New England Psalm Singer." Boston, Mass.
1788. "Seven Songs." Philadelphia, Pa.
1792. "American Harmony." Charlestown, Mass.
1793. "Rural Harmony." Topsfield, Mass.
1793. "The Union Harmony." Charlestown, Mass.
1852. Dwight's Journal of Music. Boston, Mass.

PUBLIC SCHOOL MUSIC

1838. Lowell Mason. Boston, Mass.

PUBLISHER (MUSIC)

1835. Oliver Ditson. Boston, Mass.

SOCIETIES (Choral and Orchestral)

1720. New England (Sundry)
1742. Singstunde. Bethlehem, Pa.
1759. Orpheus Club. Philadelphia, Pa.
1762. St. Cecilia Society. Charleston, S. C.
1780. Handel Society of Dartmouth College. Hanover, N. H.
1784. Harmonic Society. Fredericksburg, Va.
1786. Stoughton Musical Society. Stoughton, Mass.
1786. Mr. Hulett's Singing Society. New York, N. Y.
1787. Uranian Society, Philadelphia, Pa.

1788. Musical Society of New York. New York, N. Y.
1791. Cecilia Society. New York, N. Y.
1793. Uranian Society. New York, N. Y.
1793. St. Cecilia Society. Newport, R. I.
1797. Musical Society. Concord, N. H.
1799. Musical Society. Baltimore, Md.
1799. Euterpean Society. New York, N. Y.
1800. Philharmonic Society. New York, N. Y.
1802. Harmonic Society. Philadelphia, Pa.
1807. Mass. Musical Society. Boston, Mass.
1808. Pierian Sodality. Cambridge, Mass.
1809. Haydn Society. Philadelphia, Pa.
1815. Handel and Haydn Society. Boston, Mass.
1819. Haydn Society. Cincinnati, O.
1820. Philharmonic Society. Bethlehem, Pa.
1820. Philharmonic Society. New York, N. Y.
1820. Euterpean Society. New York, N. Y.
1820. Musical Fund Society. Philadelphia, Pa.
1821. Beethoven Society. Portland, Me.
1821. Psallion Society. Providence, R. I.
1821. New Hampshire Musical Society. Hanover, N. H.
1823. Sacred Music Society. New York, N. Y.
1824. St. Cecilia Society. Philadelphia, Pa.
1829. Central Musical Society. Concord, N. H.
1834. Old Settlers Harmonic Society. Chicago, Ill.
1835. German Männerchor. Philadelphia, Pa.
1837. Harvard Musical Association. Boston, Mass.
1837. Academy of Music Orchestra. Boston, Mass.
1838. Philharmonic Society. St. Louis, Mo.
1839. Musical Convention. Montpelier, Vt.
1842. Philharmonic Society. New York, N. Y.
1842. Sacred Music Society. Chicago, Ill.
1843. Philharmonic Concerts. Boston, Mass.
1844. Musical Institute. New York, N. Y.
1846. Steyermark's Orchestra. New York, N. Y.
1847. Deutscher Liederkrantz. New York, N. Y.
1847. Mozart Society. Chicago, Ill.
1847. Musical Fund Society. Boston, Mass.

1848. Germania Orchestra. New York, N. Y.
1848. Gungl's Orchestra. New York, N. Y.
1848. Lombardy Orchestra. New York, N. Y.
1848. Musical Convention. Chicago, Ill.
1849. Sacred Harmonic Society. New York, N. Y.
1849. Musikverein. Milwaukee, Wis.
1850. Worcester Festival Association. Worcester, Mass.
1850. Philharmonic Orchestra. Chicago, Ill.
1852. Männergesang Verein. Chicago, Ill.
1853. Julien's Orchestra. New York, N. Y.
1855. Philharmonic Society. Boston, Mass.
1856. Cecilia Society. Cincinnati, O.
1856. Harmonic Society. Cincinnati, O.
1857. Musical Union. Chicago, Ill.
1857. Brooklyn Orchestra. Brooklyn, N. Y.
1858. Mendelssohn Quintet. Boston, Mass.
1859. Gilmore's Band. Boston, Mass.
1860. Philharmonic Society. Chicago, Ill.
1860. Oratorio Society. San Francisco, Cal.
1863. Mendelssohn Society. New York, N. Y.
1864. Th. Thomas Orchestra. New York, N. Y.
1865. German Männerchor. Chicago, Ill.
1868. Salem Oratorio Society. Salem, Mass.
1869. Oratorio Society. Chicago, Ill.
1869. Church Music Association. New York, N. Y.
1870. Russian Male Choir. Boston, Mass.
1871. Apollo Club. Boston, Mass.
1872. Apollo Musical Club. Chicago, Ill.
1873. Germania Orchestra. Pittsburgh, Pa.
1874. Cecilia Society. Boston, Mass.
1875. Cecilia Club. Philadelphia, Pa.
1876. Loring Club. San Francisco, Cal.
1876. Music Teachers' National Association. Delaware, O.
1878. Symphony Society. New York, N. Y.
1879. Philharmonic Society. Boston, Mass.
1881. Manhattan Choral Union. New York, N. Y.
1881. N. Y. Choral Society. New York, N. Y.
1881. Boston Symphony Orchestra. Boston, Mass.

1885. Kneisel Quartet. Boston, Mass.
1886. Norfolk Co. Festival Association. Litchfield, Conn.
1886. Chicago Symphony Society. Chicago, Ill.
1889. Brooklyn Symphony Orchestra. Brooklyn, N. Y.
1892. Peoples' Choral Union. New York, N. Y.
1892. Sousa's Band. Tours.
1893. Pittsburgh Symphony Orchestra. Pittsburgh, Pa.
1895. Cincinnati Symphony Orchestra. Cincinnati, O.
1895. San Francisco Symphony Orchestra. San Francisco, Cal.
1896. Los Angeles Symphony Orchestra. Los Angeles, Cal.
1899. Society of American Musicians and Composers. New York, N. Y.
1900. Vienna Orchestra. Tour.
1901. Leipzig Philharmonic Orchestra. Tour.
1901. Century Club. Atlanta, Ga.
1902. Minneapolis Symphony Orchestra. Minneapolis, Minn.
1903. Symphony Society reorganized. New York, N. Y.
1903. Russian Symphony Orchestra. New York, N. Y.
1904. Volpe's Orchestra. New York, N. Y.
1905. St. Paul Symphony Orchestra. St. Paul, Minn.
1906. Musical Art Society, Chicago, Ill.
1906. "La Scala" Orchestra of Milan. Tour.
1906. Philharmonic Society. New Orleans, La.
1907. Mendelssohn Choir (Toronto). Tour.
1912. London Symphony Orchestra. Tour.
1911. Kansas City Symphony Orchestra. Kansas City, Mo.
1912. London Symphony Orchestra. Tour.
1914. Detroit Symphony Orchestra. Detroit, Mich.
1914. Fort Worth Symphony Orchestra. Fort Worth, Texas.
1914. American Symphony Orchestra. Chicago, Ill.
1915. Baltimore Symphony Orchestra. Baltimore, Md.
1917. New Orleans Symphony Orchestra. New Orleans, La.
1919. Musicians' New Symphony Orchestra. New York, N. Y.
1920. Civic Music Students' Orchestra. Chicago, Ill.
1920. Toscanini's "La Scala" Orchestra. Tour.